ROBOTS HOW BRING

GLOBAL ECONOMIC BENEFITS

JOHN LOK

ISBN 979-888555824-2

Contents

Preface

Introduction

What is future (AI) artificial intelligent products development trend and reasonable development stages? How to predict consumer behaviors to persuade who to feel (AI) products are more satisfactory to their needs? Why do consumers feel them to need to buy any (AI) products to use? Will it have other similar products to replace (AI) any products? How is the reasonable stages to achieve future (AI) development in success? If next ten year, it has not another new technological invention to impact artificial intelligence application, whether which aspects, AI is worth to invest in order to be applied to different market.

In this book, I shall give actual data to predict what the future (AI) products development trend is. Giving my opinions to predict how (AI) consumers' choices are more absolutely. In the (AI) past first stage, I shall concern travel, education, transportation, financial , hospital, administrative service etc. different job natures to indicate how to apply (AI) products to assist these industries more beneficial. In the (AI) nowadays second stage, I shall concentrate on how (AI) developing on education aspect. In the (AI) future third stage, I shall explain why (AI) will have possible to invent (AI) brain technology, even it will bring (AI) war occurence in possible.

How does (AI) bring micro and macro economy benefits to our future society, when it is continued to develop? Predicting AI future 10 years three stage.In the first (AI) stage, it concerns to be given my opinions to explain how artificial intelligent technology will impact our life and will influence economic development in the future as well as how to influence human job market change. In (AI) labor market stage, I shall indicate how artificial intelligence technology influences future macro global economy change. In part two, explaining how (AI) can be applied to predict travellers' entertainment choice behaviors. In third part aims to let readers to analyse whether future (AI) artificial intelligent machine can assist humans to learn how to reduce food waste or food loss to consumers' food habits or manufacturers' manufacturing processed in order to avoid the actual food or energy shortage challenges are caused from human's food or energy consumption negligent behaviours. Consequently, I hope my readers can make judgement whether future (AI) artificial intelligence can help human to reduce or avoid environmental pollution or food/ energy waste challenges to cause social cost to be raised to influence human future living quality to be poor.

Advances in artificial intelligence (AI) technology is for the progress in critical areas, such as health, education, energy, economy inclusion, social welfare and the environment. Thus, it brings this question: Which (AI) workers be instead of traditional human workers in these different new markets? In recent years, machines had been used to be human's tasks in the performance of certain tasks related to intelligence , such as aspects of image recognition. Experts also forecast that rapid progress in the field of specialized artificial intelligence will continue. Then, it also brings this question: Does (AI) exceed that of human performance on more and more tasks? If it is truth, will some of human jobs to be disappeared? (AI) will be instead of human some simple jobs, then unemployment rate to the low skillful and low educated workers will be increased. Whether (AI) will be raised either production or performance or unemployment to bring human job market more advantages or more disadvantages? In my this book, I shall explain whether (AI) will bring benefits or disadvantages to human job market. I shall give example to let my readers to think how to support my final view point. What is future (AI) artificial intelligent products development trend? How to predict consumer behaviors to persuade who to feel (AI) products are more satisfactory to their needs? Why do consumers feel them to need to buy any (AI) products to use? Will it have other similar products to replace (AI) any products?

In (AI) second stage, I shall indicate how (AI) is developed on education aspect, artificial intelligent technology and online technology and online book stores are high technological intelligent product. Hence, human ourselves will have possible to cause artificial intelligent machine men to own human's mind to learn how to read books and/or write books abilities. When artificial intelligent machine men can learn how to read books and/or write books. Consequently, it means that artificial intelligent machine men can own human mind to do any jobs.

In (AI) second stage, I shall assume when artificial intelligent machine men can learn how to write books and/or read books. Then, they will have human's mind ability in possible. Can future artificial intelligent machine men be invented to learn how to write books and/or read books ability? In my this book, I shall attempt to answer this question. Finally, I hope my readers can attempt to make judgement whether artificial intelligent machine men can really learn how to write and/or books. I shall apply online technology to answer this answer. Finally, I shall give my opinions what are the influences when AI machine men had invented to achieve owning human's mind and judgement ability to our future society.

In (AI) third stage development, artificial intelligence (AI) technology is popular to be applied to different industry aspects, such as medical, construction, transportation, hospital, education etc. Although, (AI) is a human invention new development. IN fact, it seems only beneficial to human's daily life. But, it will also have threats to influence human's safety in possible , if some scientists or self-interest mind people who aim to apply (AI) to earn more profit or apply (AI) tools to be weapon to attack other countries to achieve to dominate all human's ambitious intention. Thus, (AI) will bring negative influences to our society, instead of positive influences if we can not apply this kind of new technological tools immorally.

In this stage, I shall give my opinions to indicate what reasons will cause (AI) artificial intelligent tools to be applied to social military defense weapon by human's intention. In my this books, I hope my readers can know what will cause human's immoral behaviors to bring our societies to bring more dangerous or risks or threats if human applied (AI) technology to achieve whose immoral or ambitious intention. Finally, I hope that human ought not apply (AI) technology to do any behavioral attack to satisfy ourselves interest or dominate global world ambition to avoid (AI) technological war occurrence in the future one day.

In (AI) final stage, I shall give some university lecturers' personal analytical mind to judge whether what will be occurred if artificial intelligence could be invented to match to own human brain's mind ability? What will be the advantages and/or disadvantages if (AI) robots would be invented to match to own human brain's mind ability? I shall follow current (AI) technological development to judge whether what the potential abilities are that (AI) will achieve to satisfy human's life needs when (AI) is invented to own human brain in future one day. The main central point is discussed that whether what effects that it will bring to influence our lives when (AI) is invented to match human brain. In this book final chapter, I shall indicate how (AI) can bring positive benefits to our society in micro and macro view point.

Acknowledgements

Table of contents

● Why does human need artificial intelligence machines?
● How does artificial intelligence influence future working changing in automation employment and productivity aspects?
● Is artificial intelligence possible to replace labor ?
● Can (AI) technology replace human labour nature of work?
● Why can artificial intelligence satisfy human needs?
● Is artificial intelligence one good choice for human future technological benefit?

Chapter 2 How can artificial intelligence technology influence economy

2.1 What is relationship between (AI) and economy growth? p.80-91
● How can artificial intelligence technology influence economy?
● Can (AI) influence global economy growth?
● How can artificial intelligence impact global economy growth?
● What is the relationship between (AI) and (CRM)?
● What is the relationship between (AI) and global digital economy development ?
● How can (AI) technology influence digital economy?
● Could work activities in China be automated making in the nation with the world's largest automation potential?
● Will (AI) technology influence digital economy change to manufacturing industry ?
● What is artificial intelligence potential benefits and ethical considerations?
● Can (AI) technology impact on customer relationship management (CRM) ?
● How can (AI) technology influence to global health care economy development?

human needs?

Is artificial intelligence one good choice for human future technological benefit?

Chapter 8
What is relationship between
(AI) productivity and economy growth
How can artificial intelligence technology
influence economy? p.270-288
Can (AI) influence gloabl economy
growth?
How can artificial intelligence
impact global economy growth?
How can (AI) influence GDP of high income
countries in the next ten years? p.289-299
How can artificial intelligence
impact on workplace?
What is the relationship
between (AI) and (CRM)?
Can (AI) technology
impact on customer relationship
management (CRM) ?

What is relationship between
(AI) and digital economy

How can (AI) technology influence digital
economy? p.300-315
What is the relationship between
(AI) and global digital economy development?

Could work activities in China be automated making in the nation with the world's largest automation potential?

How does (AI) technology influence the future of employment change?

CHAPTER ONE

Artificial intelligent development changes human job nature

Although, (AI) technology will be popular to applied to different jobs, but it still needs social acceptance to replace some human jobs. Today, it is increasingly common for people to use robots in various situations at home and in retail stores, hotels and hospitals. Robots are classified into several types based on their functionality (service and utility robots or those designed to communicate with humans) and appearance (humanoid robots or mechanical robots). The types of robot to which every country attaches particular important in the advance of robotics, reflects the sense of values and preferences of its population . Thus, (AI) will be applied to replace human to do these above different kinds of job nature. For example, U.S. has the highest level of robot utilization at home and an retail stores with its people being the most enthusiastic about the future use of robots. Otherwise, Germany shows a strong tendency to consider robots for industrial purposes, and its people feel strong to the presence of robots in their households. Japanese accepts to apply" human aid robot" that can communicate with humans and they have a high level of familiarity with robots.

Hence, it implied those three countries have accept (AI) to replace human to do any these kinds of job duty and it will influence these three countries‘ workers lose their old occupations and who will unemployed absolutely, due to many (AI) robots replace them to do their job duties in the future. Also, US will have many retail service workers or retail warehouse workers are unemployed. Germany will have many manufacturing industry's workers are unemployed. Japanese will have many communication industry workers are unemployed, such as telephone service, shopping center services etc. different kind of service industry's service staffs . It will cause these kind of workers' competitive abilities are lost in themselves countries‘ jobs that require such skills include software developers, court judges, nurses, high school teachers, dentists and university lecturers, these occupations are still difficult to be replaced by (AI) robots.

Are robots taking our jobs or making them? In fact, our societies will have unemployment challenges, even (AI) technology has not created before. However, after (AI) robots invention, some of human jobs will be replaced and it can raise many low skillful and low knowledge level worker unemployment number. However, I think that high productivity driven by increasingly powerful IT -enabled machines is the causes of global labor market problems and accelerating technological change will only make those problems worse.

IT technology brings this question: Are robots killing human's jobs or benefiting human's jobs? I suppose that there is a limited amount of labor to be done. The implication is that technology can create unemployment by displacing workers, such as (AI) invention, because the more efficiently worker work (using machines or (AI) robots), the loss work there is for workers to do. Even, any new jobs will be better done by machines or (AI) robots, and unemployment will still skyrocket. How do we know that humans will always be better at some work, or more importantly, enough work, than machines or (AI) robots, e.g. human drivers drive more safe or careful to compare (AI) robot drivers. But, the challenge is that it is not ensure that (AI) robots drivers must not drive careless to cause the chance of accident occurrences more than human drivers. However, technological change can be beneficial to innovation, automation and increasing productivity for businesses.

Consequently , it may seem machines can hurt wages and job for low skillful, less educated workers. Also, high educated workers are likely as less educated workers to find themselves displaced and devalued, and more education may create as many problems as it solves. Thus, in negative influence, automation effects on particular jobs shift workers to other jobs that are equally or more desirable. Workers may be highly compensated for possessing human capital that is specialized to a labor market. If technological advance is very rapid, such as (AI) invention, causing a large and very rapid drop in demand in a large labor market, the economy may not be able to absorb the sudden surplus of labor in a short period of timer when (AI) robots are popular to replace some workers to do some occupations in global societies.

For example, self-driving vehicles threaten to send truck drivers to the unemployment office. Computer programs can now write journalistic accounts of sporting events and stock price movement. There are even computers that can grade essay revolutionize some part of teaching jobs. Hence, (AI) robots will have possible to replace human brain to do any judgement, argument, and mind job duties. It implies some occupations which need human' mind will be threaten by (AI) robots, e.g. author, accountant, nurse, engineer. Thus, (AI) robots will have possible to replace some professional and high educated workers' jobs in the future.

But, technology can create new nature of jobs in possible. For example, a 60 minutes program indicated technology is putting new categories of jobs in the sites (sic) of automation, the 60% of the workforce that makes its living gathering and analyzing information. Also, recession: technology kills middle -class jobs that overall technology is eliminating for more jobs than it is creating by (AI) technology. Hence, human's brain work may be assisted by 60% of (AI) gathering and analyzing information for some occupation , e.g. space scientists, ocean scientists, earth scientists etc.

However, I believe the (AI) invention and human job competition may influence global productivity change. Productivity is economic output per unit of input, the unit of on input can be labor hours(labor productivity), but if (AI) robots replace human job, then the unit of input may be (AI) machine hours (AI) robot productivity or all production factors including labors, machines and energy (total factor of productivity). Producing more output with less input can take several forms.

The traditional notion of productivity is a form reorganizing production and/or using better or more technology to produce more output per worker hour. But when (AI) robots invention, the form can be reorganizing production and/or using better or more (AI) robots to produce more output per (AI) robot hour. Hence, if the firm apply (AI) robots to produce its products. Then , productivity improvements in the firm may result in less workers employment, due to (AI) robots replace more worker number to achieve more productivity improvement, it has economic benefits (less factor of production) , but more production in long term.

Thus, (AI) robots can help any firm to achieve productivity improvement in long term, for example, if unproductve farmers move to the city and start working for high-tech. manufacturers. The shift effect can be more dynamic and disruptive as low-productivity industries lose out in the marketplace to high -productivity industries and the compositional mix of the economy changes. Thus, in the long term (AI) robots can also be beneficial to high productivity industries to bring the mix of economy positive changes.

Moreover, automation will also produce some new jobs in firms that sell the new robot or other labor-saving technology. This means that, in general, there will be shift in the economy in the direction of higher-skill and higher wage jobs. Even if the (AI) robot invention country, US becomes a leader in (AI) robots producing productivity-enhancing technology, it will experience a growth in jobs serving foreign (AI) robots product buyers. Hence, (AI) robots can also create (AI) salespeople, (AI) manufacturing workers , (AI) inventors, scientists, (AI) software designer etc. occupations, when if all society does is move workers from insurance firms, restaurants and car factories to robot factories, productivity will have remained the same to create job needs for insurance, restaurant and car manufacturing worker service occupations for (AI) software designer, (AI) service robots manufacturer, (AI) service robot seller etc. related (AI) service robot product occupation created in (AI) robot technology job market. Hence, (AI) invention also create new (AI) technology job chance. (AI) impacts management job market.

In future, organization management will be changed from (AI) introduction. Division of labor will change and collaboration among humans and machines will increase. Companies will have to adapt their training, performance and talent acquisition strategies to account for a new found emphasis on work that hinges on human judgement and skills, including experimentation and colloboration.

How (AI) impacts any organizational administrative management work? (AI) 's greatest impact will be on administrative coordination and control tasks, such as scheduling, resource allocation and reporting, (AI)-driven will place a higher premium on what we call " judgement work", the application of human experience and expertise to critical business decisions and practices when information available is insufficient to suggest a successful course of action. This kind of work will require new skills and mindsets; replacing people with machines is not goal in itself. When, artificial intelligence enables cost-cutting automation of routine work, it also empowers value -adding augmentation of human capabilities.

Thus, administrative and routine tasks, such as scheduling, allocation of resources, and reporting, will within intelligent machines, responsibilities that have long been reserved for humans. For instance, a typical store manager or a lead nurse at a nursing home must constantly juggle shift schedules, accounting for staff members' absense owing to illness, vaction, time or sudden departures. Many of these tasks will be automated by (AI). Imagine (AI) writing management monthly reports, it is not a distant dream. Leading news providers and Wall street banks are now using (AI) report generators to write news and analytical reports by drawing on quantitative data. The associated press, for example, expanded its quarterly earnings reporting from approximately 300 companies to nearly 3,000 with the help of (AI) powered software robots, freeing up journalists to conduct more investigative and interpretive reporting. For another example, Jobalime, a job-placement site, uses intelligent voile analysis algorithms to evaluate job applicants. The algorithm assesses paralinguistic elements of speech, such as tone and inflection, products which emotions a specific voice will elicit, and identifies the type of work at which an applicant will likely excel. In the future , (AI) machines can be applied to assist some kind of office administrative jobs duties. It's attractive to office managers to achieve more accurate judgment to do any administrative matters when who can be assisted from (AI) machines. Thus, managers need to spend time to learn how to apply (AI) machine to assist them to do more accurate judgement, and better informed choices. (AI) robots can be applied to improve the speed quality and cost of available products and services, instead of applying on productivity improvement and administrative improvement aspects. Thus, they may also displace large numbers of workers. This, possibility challenges the traditional benefits model of trying health care and retirement savings to jobs.

In an economy that employs dramatically fewer workers to deliver benefits to displaced workers. For example, the worldwide number of industrial robots has increased rapidly over the past few years. The fall prices of robots, which can operate all day without interruption, make them cost- competitive with human workers. In special consideration, in the service sector, computer algorithums can execute stock trades in a fraction of a second, much faster than any human. As those technologies become cheaper, more capable, and more widespread, they will find even more applicants in an economy.

Consequently, (AI) technology brings unemployed number increasing many businesses continued automating their operations rather than hiring additional workers. A trend among technology companies that receive massive valuations with relatively few workers. For example, in 2014 year Google was valued at $370 billion with only 55,000 employees, a tenth the size of AT & T's workforce in the 1960 year. Hence, if automation technologies like robots and artificial intelligence make jobs less secure in the future, there needs to be a way to deliver benefits outside of employment " flexi security" or flexible security is one idea for providing healthcare, education and housing assistance whether or not someone is formally employed.

In conclusion, (AI) and robots technology will raise unemployment to some occupations when (AI) replaces same industries' workers job duties in our societies in the future, but it also create new jobs to raise employment in any related (AI) robots and automated machine products in (AI) manufacturing. (AI) design, (AI) sale self-related industry, when (AI) replaces same industries' workers' job duties.

1.1 (AI) journalism, media publishing, digital communication technology trend

How to apply (AI) technology in digital communication journalism media, publishing industry? Some scientists indicate future (AI) and digital technology may consist such as: voice driven assistants, emerge. For example, Amazon e book publish applying digital technology and (AI) auto printing technology to sell e books to let readers to listen any e book content by (AI) voice driven speaker when they turn on computer to read e book contents; capable phones start to unlock the possibilities of 3D image of mobile story telling. New smart wearables include ear buds that handle instant translation and glasses that talk and hear. China and India will become a key focus for digital growth with innovations around payment online identity, and artificial intelligence. Thus, future (AI) technology can be applied to 3D image mobile story telling, online payment method to dealt online transaction publishing industry.

Thus, future (AI) technology can be applied to online e book publishing industry to make sound books to let readers feel more attractive . Such as Amazon publish has published sound e books to attract readers to choose to read any its books from online. Also, (AI) technology can also be applied to communication industry. For example, some online pure-play news, opinion and entertainment websites. It is a digital communication media, e.g. online journalism blog (AI) technology can be applied to visual storytellers to let online book readers to enjoy to listen to watch and send any online electronic book contents more attractive. Thus, future (AI) technology will be popular to assist any electronic book publishers to publish visual and sound talking storybook to let readers who can watch motive image and listen and read words from e books more attractive.

Thus, (AI) technology can be applied to internet ecommerce publishing or media industry to help any electronic book publishers to publish sound, image motion electronic book to attract global readers to read, even (AI) technology can be applied to digital entertainment industry, e.g. electronic 3D image virtual video games, computer games. It can be also applied to education industry, e.g. the first true digital native generation and are the native speakers of the digital language of computers to let student to learn different languages or translate words to compare to classroom learning more easily. It can be also applied to communication industry, e.g. (AI) mobile phone. Hence, it seems (AI) technology can be applied to publishing, communication, education , entertainment etc. different industries in the future. (AI) technology will be one kind of tool to satisfy human's daily life needs in the future and these industries has one characteristics is that they need to apply internet to operate to operate to do online business.

Thus, it has three trends of (AI) technology and internet technology need to be linked to achieve one kind of attractive technological business to satisfy client's needs. These three trends as below: All consumer trends involve the internet. It will be many consumer's online habits, shopping, working, socializing, watching TV, studying, travelling, listening. Thus, (AI) music, eating and exercising are just a few examples. This is happening because human usually use mobile broadband or Wi-Fi, rather than cables. Thus, (AI) technology will be applied to mobile to satisfy client's need absolutely.

The mobile phone can be more popular to be used more than computer or laptop tools. The reasons are because women dive the smartphone market by defining mass-market use. But as the speed of technology adoption increases mass market use becomes much quicker then before. Successful new technological products and services , such a (AI) mobile phone products now reach the mass market in popular use. It means that the time period when early adopters influence others is shorter than before. Also, since new products and services increasingly use the internet mass markets are not only faster , but are also more important than ever to consumer themselves. Most internet services become more valuable to individuals when many use them. Thus, it causes why (AI) mobile phone will be popular to be used.

Since, new products and services increasingly use the internet, in the future several trends focus on (AI) smart phone users. Consumers' familiarity with using smartphone apps. Essentially, the technologies will bring other related (AI) and internet service needs, e.g. sound and image emotion e book needs, (AI) mobile communication needs, e-virtual games or e-3D image virtual games etc. entertainment activities needs with such a large part of the world's population now online, it is clear that there is strength in numbers.

Thus, (AI) imagines , if future any (AI) and internet related services or products new technology is easy to use and inexpensive, when the latest products reach the mass market almost as quickly as they reach the early adopters and industry experts. I believe that any (AI) and internet related products or services must be popular to accept to consume for entertainment or useful aim. For example, with major players including Apply, Facebook and Google had invested (AI) technology to develop their businesses. (AI) technology has the potential to disrupt everything in the coming years, from the lives of connected consumers to every industry (AI) will be an alternative route for brands to reach consumers with convincing and relevant messages. Digital technology will assist of the future, then it can improve technology to bring this effect, such as sophisticated software machine learning and speech recognition effective. Hence, Google, Facebook , Yahoo web site service companies can apply (AI) technology to help other companies to advertise their businesses, such as travel, retail, and education etc. industries more attractive. (AI) technology can be applied to internet company to be aware and familiar enough to drive among mainstream consumers, it can create online experience to travel, retail , education and other entertainment needs to online consumers to seek their entertainment needs more easily. Hence, in the future (AI) technology and internet related entertainment service needs will be raised in this (AI) and online consumption market.

1.2 (AI) healthcare service industry development

In the future, (AI) medical internet technology tool can be applied to assist individual's health at the center of their focus, e.g. smartwatch compatible mobile app. patients can let personalized reminders for taking their medication snap pictures of their prescriptions to expedite refills, and scan their insurance card. So that, store clerks are prepared with up-to-date patients' information . (AI) owned health operated technological clinics can help patients to receive treatment for minor illnesses, flu shots, cholesterol screenings and more than a dozen other medical services, all of which can be patients who can't make it to a physical location. (AI) healthcare services organizations can provide various telemedicine services. So, patients can receive care via phone or video chat.

For example, one London-based intelligent Brewing company has developed an (AI) system to continuously collect and incorporate customer feedback, which the system itself uses to brew ne various of the company's beers. Thus, the beer clients can give feedback to talk to the algorithm (AI) machine, whenever or anywhere who're drinking the beer. It is such any healthcare services organizations can apply (AI) machine to collect patient's feedback to talk to the algorithum (AI) machine whenever or anywhere who're eating any medicines. So doctors can know every patient's health conditions any time. If the patients feel uncomfortable, the doctor can know from (AI) machine notification to decide whether the patient needs to eat another new medicine or keep to eat same medicine is better. Hence, (AI) medial internet technological body check report machine will be proper to be needed to serve any hospitals' patients in the future.

However , it brings this question. How can (AI) medical internet technological body check report machine apply to hospital more efficient? The essential new medicine co-workers for the health service digital age health service leaders need apply (AI) medical report machines and artificial intelligence to the newest recruits to the workforce bringing new skills to help health service staffs do new jobs and reinventing what's possible, building the health service workforce for today's digital health service demands for patients. Thus, technology-driven health service model innovation from the health service organization outside in and providing digital health service ecosystems for patients to use the (AI) health service equipment will be popular to be accepted to be used.

1.3 Robot and internet things future machine men invention

Nowadays, there are some company, which apply internet and (AI) I Robot technology to do any similar human job nature. For fishing industry example, one company, known for creating the Roomba, I Robot is now working with marine conservationists to launch an ocean-patrolling intelligent robot to hunt and manage invasive species, protecting native populations. And evolved industries like precision agriculture are ramping of our increasing population. Area of practice that once seemed impossible to digitize are fundamentally changing because of the impacts of (AI), internet of things capabilities and big data analytics, which have many potentially positive impactions for society.

For textile industry example, automation is nothing new, it has shaped the workplace to replace human jobs to boost productivity in the textile industry. Textile machines have had a generally positive impact over gears, creating value and allowing textile workers to take up more rewarding age will likely continue to create opportunities and lead to new textile industries, companies and textile occupations. It may also compensate for a demographically driven slowdown in the growth of the textile workforce. The future impact of textile (AI) and automatic and internet link is somewhat uncertain. It seems textile industry will be trend to accept (AI) textile workers and internet of thing to replace traditional manual textile workers to produce any shirts, cloths etc. wearing products in factories popularly, during the (AI) textile machine and internet thing technology can be invented to reach the mature stage in the future.

For factory worker transportation job example, they have also expanded their influence, migrating from the factory floor to the service sector and taking the place of humans in a range of activities from financial transactions to transport route optimization. Further (AI) machines and robots are increasingly programmed to learn, meaning they improve with time and undertake cognitive activities. Hence, (AI) machines and internet technology enable automation of work activities to raise factory workers' efficient and performances, also factories can reduce manual worker numbers, due to (AI) machine workers' assistance.

Future, (AI) robotics technologies and internet technique have these different kinds of characteristics: For soft robotics example, it is non-rigid robots construct with soft and deformable materials that can manipulate items of varying size, shape and weight with a single device. For swarm robotics, it coordinated multi-robot systems often involving large numbers of mostly physical robots. For touch/factile robotic example, it robotic body pails (often biologically inspired hands) with capability to sense, touch , dexterity robots example, serpentine robots with many internal degrees of freedom to threat through tightly packed spaces for humanoid robots example, robots physical is similar to human being often bi-pedal that investigate variety capable of performing human tasks , including movement across terrains, object recognition, speech sensing etc. For autonomous cars and trucks example, it is capable of operating with a human pilot, e.g. the unarmed general atomics Predator XPUAV with roughly half the wingspan of a Boeing 737 can fly autonomously for up to 35 hours from take-off to landing, for unmanned aerial vehicles example, flying vehicles capable of operating without a human pilot, the unarmed general atomics predator -XPUAV , with roughly half the wingspan of a Boing 737, and fly autonomously for up to 35 hours from take off to landing, for (AI) chat bots example, (AI) systems designed to simulate conversation with human users, particularly those integrated into massaging apps.

In Dec. 2015. the general service administration of the US Govt. described how it used a chat bot named Mrs. Landingham (a character from the television show the west wing) to help onboard new employees. Finally, for robotic process automation example, class of software robots that replicates the actions of a human being interacting with the user interfaces of both software systems. Enables the automation of many back-office work flows without requiring expensive IT integration . Hence, future (AI) robot machine men will have different functions to be applied to different industries to use in possible.

Statistics Denmark shows that (AI) automation potential robots will influence few jobs are completely automatable , but close to half consists of 40% automatable tasks: It showed example occupations include share of automated, such as brewing machine operators are more than 80%, logging equipment operators are more than 50%, roofers , stock tasks clerks, travel agent are more than 50%, farmers , nursing assistants are more than 30%, physicians, teachers , managers are more than 10%.

For example, humans perform a wide variety of tasks from planting corn to examine spreadsheets, meeting clients and lifting crates in a store. Each of these actions requires a combination of innate or acquired capabilities, internet technique assistance, ranging from social perceptiveness to fine motor skills and natural language understanding. To understand and map automation feasibility by existing technology. Mc Kinsey has developed a framework of 18 technical capabilities that can substitute tasks performed by humans. The capabilities are grouped in five categories: sensory, cognitive, language, social and emotional and physical. So, it seems (AI) robot machine men and internet technique will have possible combination to invent to own human's emotion , language, learning, task skill abilities.

Mckinsey global institute analysis also showed current technologies have achieved different levels of human performance across 18 capabilities include: sensory perception, autonomously infer and integrate complex input using sensors, cognitive capabilities reorganizing known patterns/categories supervised learnings, generating novel, logical reasoning/problem solving, optimization and planning, creative, information retrieval, coordination with multiple agents, output articulation/presentation, national language processing, social and emotional capabilities-natural language understanding, social and emotion sense, reasoning output, physical capabilities-fine motor skills, navigation mobility. Hence, it seems (AI) robots and internet technological will combine to invent to own human' some skills to replace human to do some kind of tasks in possible.

In conclusion, future (AI) robot and internet will be needed to link to cooperate together to raise human's work efficiency in popular.

1.4 How artificial intelligence replaces human job possibility

What is the risk of automation for jobs to replace human job? In recent years, there has been a revival of concerns that automation and digitalization night after all result in jobless future. As I argue, this might lead to an overestimation of job (AI) automate , as occupations labelled as high-risk occupations often still contain a substantial share of tasks that are hard to automate.

For example, when the share of (AI) automatable jobs is 6% in Korea, the corresponding share is 12% in Australia. Differences between countries may reflect general differences in workplace organization, differences in previous investments into (AI) automation technologies as well as differences in the education of workers across countries. I also discover that (AI) automation and digitalization are unlikely to destroy large numbers of jobs. But, however, low qualified labors are likely to raise costs as the (AI) automate of their jobs is higher compared to highly qualified workers.

In fact, (AI) technology will influence some new technology to replace some human's job, such as driverless car, the largely autonomous smart factory , service robots or 3D printing. These technologies are driven by advances in computing power, robotics and artificial intelligence and ultimately redefine what type of human capabilities machines are able to do.

Hence, question brings whether (AI) invention will influence general human jobs to be replaced by (AI) autonomous jobs? Whether will the potential foe automation with actual employment loss? In particular, the technical possibility to use (AI) machines rather tasks need not mean that the substitution of humans by machines actually takes place.

Whether (AI) technology replaces human's some job, it is beneficial to our society or not. Instead, machines are increasingly capable of performing non-routine cognitive tasks, such as driving or legal writing . In particular, advances in the field of machine learning (ML), e.g. computational statistics and visions, data mining, artificial intelligences allow for automating cognitive task, when the use of (ML) in mobile robotics (MR) also allows for automating certain manual tasks. So, it seems, (AI) technology can replace some labor job, e.g. warehouse transportation, even mind's job, e.g. legal writing, driving in possible.

For example, if (AI) automatic non-manual driving can reduce hurt or death risk, it is beneficial to our society, or (AI) automatic robots can more any heavy things (products) in warehouse safely. Then, it can reduce the warehouse labor's bodies hour risk, it is beneficial to the workers. Even, if (AI) robot can write any legal documents, no any word errors in short time. It is beneficial to the law companies , but it also bring unemployment chance, due to these jobs can be replaced by (AI) robots to do in the future. Hence, it will cause some occupation to be disappeared, due to (AI) robots can do our these kinds of jobs in the future.

Frey & Osborne (2013) reported these kinds of occupations will be replaced by (AI) robots in possible. They include computer, engineering, financial, management, legal , art and medium, community service, education, healthcare practitioners and technical service, sales and related, office and administrative support, farming, fishing and forestry, construction and extraction, installation, maintenance, and repair , production, transportation and material moving. It seems our future some professional occupations will have possible to the replaced by (AI) robots to replace, instead of labor jobs. Hence, (AI) robots technology will have much trend to replace high knowledge or low knowledge skillful labors in the future.

In conclusion, it implies that only using information on task-usage at the individual level leads to significantly lower estimates of jobs " at risk", some workers in occupations with according to high automate nevertheless often perform tasks with are hard to automate. Why can (AI) replace human to do some kinds of jobs? (AI) artificial intelligence refers to the ability of a computer or a computer enable robotic system to process information and produce outcomes in a manner similar to the thought process of humans in learning, decision making and solving problem. By extension, the goal of (AI) systems is to develop systems to capable of tasking complex problems in ways similar to human's logic and reasons who feel in our future. Hence, it means future (AI) robots has effort to replace human to do any jobs in possible.

1.5 (AI) directions for future non-manual control road vehicles market

Future road vehicle products and technologies must meet social, economic and environmental protection and driving safety goals , and satisfying market requirements for mobility, accident reducing, performance, cost desirability. Thus, (AI) auto-non manual control vehicles need to be followed this direction to invent. To satisfy future driver's safety of needs, enhanced vehicle speed desired functional performance of road transportation system, required and desired technological response, including research needs. It is long term up to 20 years vision, for (AI) auto non-manual research. Thus, (AI) auto non manual vehicle manufacturers need often to revise their (AI) vehicles functions to raise to improve their system performance and driving industry driver's needs, e.g. private drivers need or public transportation driver's need or business client's need. Hence, future (AI) transportation will need have individual driving consumer and business driving consumer both targets.

Thus, future (AI) automation manual control vehicles need to deliver high impact technology solutions to meet social , economic and environmental and safe goals. Engine needs to be improved efficiency , performance, drivability, reliability, durability and speed-to-market together with reduced emissions and cost; hybrid, electric and alternatively fuel (AI) non manual control vehicle technology development, leading to new fuel and power systems, such as hydrogen, fuel cells and batteries, which satisfy future social, economic and environmental and safe goals. Software, sensors, electronics and telematics technology development are needed to be lead to improve vehicle performance, control and adaptability, intelligent , mobility and security, structure and materials technology development, leading to improved safety, performance and leading to flexibility with reduced cost and environmental pollution to achieve the (AI) non manual drivers to feel (AI) vehicle performance, auto control and adaptability is better to compare traditional manual driving vehicles.

In fact, in traditional manual driving market, Japan and USA had had over 80% of world car production by six major global groups. In the future, it is possible only USA can dominate (AI) non manual auto driving vehicle manufacturing market if Japan had no effort to manufacture any (AI) auto non manual control vehicles. So, it means that it is only Japan is USA potential (AI) auto non manual control vehicle manufacturing competitors. Also, it means that it is only USA has effort to export (AI) auto non manual control vehicles to global (AI) auto non manual control vehicle market.

Thus, in long term, (AI) non manual control vehicle product market development, USA (AI) vehicle manufacturers will have these requirement to win new technological competition to traditional manual control vehicle. The requirements include: low cost fuel, low carbon, fuel cell and telematics technologies, the technological roadmap function, such as detailed consideration clear provision of other important areas to the drivers. When the (AI) non manual auto drivers are sitting in the non manual control auto vehicle. Although, who does not need to drive, but who need to know how to go to anywhere by electric road map show clearly. So, the driver won't lose direction and he/she can know the (AI) non manual control vehicles is driving to anywhere in any time, even when who is sleeping.

In the future, the (AI) non manual control vehicles need to be invented to satisfy any business , transportation clients' needs, instead of individual clients needs, e.g. cans, trucks, buses, emergency and utility vehicles, trains, trams etc. Hence, technological road mapping is one important tool to help any business, transportation (AI) non manual control vehicle clients. Technological roadmap is a technique that is used in industry to support strategic planning for (AI) non manual driving vehicles in the future. Electronic road maps generally take the form of multi-layered time based charts, linking technology developments to future (AI) non manual control vehicle market requirements.

Technology road mapping is a flexible technique and the roadmap architecture and process for developing the roadmap most generally be customized to meeting the particular aims. Why technology roadmap will be popular to (AI_ non manual control vehicles. It's advantages include: It is a technology solutions and options that can enable the performance targets to be achieved engine hybrid, electric and alternatively fueled vehicles, software, sensors electronics and telematics, structures and materials design and manufacturing process. It is road transport system performance measures and targets tool, in response to the trends and get (AI) non manual control vehicle drivers to get society, economy, environment protection, low cost driving benefits, also it can help any transportation clients to know how to go to anywhere clearly. Hence, technological road map will be one good tool to assist (AI) non manual control auto vehicle to develop future road driving market.

Reference(source)

Frey & Osborne (2013), The future of employment: How susceptible are jobs to computerization? University of Oxford.

Mckinsey Global Institute Analysis

Statistics Denmark, Global automation impact model, Makinsey analysis

1.6 (AI) -driven automation industry development

(AI) -driven automation industry will create wealth and expand economy growth to any countries, but it will be accompanied by changed in the skills that workers need to learn. One of main ways that technology increases productivity is by decreasing the number of labor hours needed to create a unit of output. It implies (AI) technology will influence low educated and low skillful labor number to be decreased (reduction employment number).

In contrast, technological change tended to work in a different direction throughout the nowadays. The advance of computer and the internet raised the relative productivity of higher skilled workers. So, routine-intensive occupations that focused on predictable tasks disappearance, such as switch board, operators, filming checkers, travel agents and assembling line workers etc. were particularly replaced by new technologies.

However, today, it may be challenging to predict exactly which jobs will be most immediately affected by (AI) driven-automation. The reason is because (AI) is not a single technology, but rather a collection of technologies that are felt unevenly through the economy to influence job changing both negatively and positively. In positively view point, (AI) driven-automation will make many workers more productive and increase demand for certain skills. Consequently, new jobs are likely to be directly create in areas , such as the development and supervision of (AI) as well as indirectly created in a range of areas throughout the economy as higher incomes lead to expanded demand. Otherwise, in negatively view point, many traditional human needed (demand) skillful jobs will be threatened by automation are highly concentrated among lower-paid, lower-skilled and less -educated workers. It means automation will cause pressure on demand for this group, pressure and employment, if (AI) can replace the low skilled and less educated workers' jobs. Thus, (AI) will have negative influence to impact on the labor market.

(AI) capabilities will enable automation of some tasks that have long required human labor. Why can (AI) replace some simple human jobs? For example, advances in robotics are expanding machines' abilities to interact with and sharp the physical world. Combined , (AI) and robotics will give rise to smarter machines that can perform more sophisticated functions than ever before and brings more advantages that humans have exercised. This will permit automation of many tasks now performed by human workers and could change the shape of the labor market and human activity.

1.7 How (AI) influences labor market

Today, it may be challenging to predict exactly which jobs will be most immediately affected by (AI)-driven automation. Because (AI) is not a single technology, but rather a collection of technologies that are applied to specific tasks. Some specific predictions are possible based on the current (AI) technology. For example, driving jobs and house cleaning jobs, bank counter service jobs, telephone enquiry service operators. Restaurant cooking jobs, simple accounting record service jobs etc. that require relatively less education to perform. Advancements in computer vision and related technologies have made the feasibility of fully appear more likely, potentially displacing some workers in driving-dominant professions. Seemingly similar robot, for which the operational tasks is less specific of navigating to a specific destination when following a set of given rules and preserving safety.

In the future, the effects of (AI) on the labor market in the decade ahead will continue the trend toward skill-biased change that computerization and communication innovations have driven in recent decades. Thus, some human driving occupation will be disappeared or replaced by (AI) automation driven. For example, bus drivers, light truck or delivery services drivers, heavy and tractor-trailer truck drivers, school drivers, tax drivers, travel bus drivers.

However, (AI) technology could enable some workers to focus time on other job responsibilities, boosting their productivity, and actually raised wage growth among those still holding the reshaped jobs. For example, salespeople, who currently spend a considerable amount of time driving could find themselves able to do other work when a car drives them from place to place, or inspectors and appraisers could fill out paperwork, when their car drives itself. This (AI) -driven technology should make these workers more productive, with (AI) -driven technology serving as a complement, not a substitute. New jobs will also likely be created, both in existing occupations cheaper transportation costs with lower prices and increase demand for products and all the related occupations, such as service and fulfillment, and in new occupations not currently foreseeable.

What kind of jobs will be created by (AI) technology? Predicting future job growth is extremely difficult, due to it depends on technologies or substitute for existing today as well as they may complement or substitute for existing human skills and jobs. However, (AI) will also lead to substantial indirect job creation to the degree it raises productivity and wages, it may also lead to higher consumption that would support additional jobs from high-end draft production to restaurant and retail. The future(AI) " augmented intelligence", the technology's role is as assisting and expanding the productivity of individuals rather than replacing human work. Thus, based on the biased-technical change framework, demand for labor will likely increase the most in the areas where humans complement (AI) automation technologies. For example, (AI) technology , such as IBM's Watson may improve early detection of some cancers or other illnesses, but a human healthcare professional is needed to work with patients to understand and translate patients' symptoms, inform patients of treatment options, and guide patients through treatment plans. Shipping companies may also partner workers who pick up and deliver products over the last feet with (AI) enabled autonomous vehicles that move workers efficiently from site to site. In such cases, (AI) augments what a human is able to do and allows individuals to either be move effective in their specially task or to operate on a larger scale. Thus, it seems (AI) technology will also create new jobs, raise productivities and workers' efficiencies.

1.8 Redefining management in the workforce of artificial intelligence

In the future, due to artificial intelligence influences to some kind of human jobs nature. So, the kind of human jobs of management methods will also need to change to adapt the artificial intelligence technology input to their organizations. It will cause challenges for every executive and manager if who won't have effort to manage their teams how to apply artificial intelligence technology to work efficiently and easily. For example, division of labor will change among humans and machines will increase. Thus, companies will have to adapt their training performance and talent strategies how to emphasize on work that how to make human judgment and skills and experimentation. Thus, (IA)'s greatest impact will be on administrative coordination and control tasks, such as scheduling , resource allocation.

In fact, mangers will encounter this challenges: How to apply human experience and expertise to judge critical business decisions and practices when the information available is insufficient to suggest a successful course of action? Due to this kind of work will require new skills and mindsets. I shall indicate these change management methods to adapt (AI) technology. Such as: administration and routine tasks, scheduling , allocation of resources and reporting will fall within the intelligence machines, responsibilities that have long been reserved for humans. For example, a typical store manager or a lead nurse at a nursing home most constantly arrange shift schedules, accounting for staff members' absences owing to illness, vacation time or sudden departures.

Thus, the managers need to learn how to arrange new division of labor within the organizations after (AI) technology had been implemented to the organization. Artificial intelligence is currently influencing into once considered exclusive to humans: assessing and acting on human emotions and personality traits. The influences to managers need to change their strategies to adapt (AI) technology implements include such as below:

Firstly, managers need to spend the bulk of their time on coordination and control tasks from intelligent system implements. Their time spending on these major three aspects from impact of intelligent system: coordinate and control, solve problems and collaborate and people and community , strategy and innovation three aspects. Thus (AI) will influence managers need to change their judgment method to teach whose teams how to adapt the (AI) system operations in any organizations.

Secondly, (AI) will influence top, middle and low level management needs to change to adapt the (AI) technology operations to any owned (AI) technology organizations in the future. Intelligent machines must be trained in context. Just like humans , on-the-job training is a requirement for such machines because they typically arrive with only very general capabilities. To get the most from (AI), managers at all levels must participate in the instructional experience and in the learning process and provides managers' familiarity with such systems on these aspects, e.g. How the system works and generate advice, how the system has a proven track record , how the system provides convincing explanations , how the system can make simple rule- based decisions.

Thirdly, managers need to learn how to make judgment more accurate (AI) systems assistance. Although (AI) will invariably take on more routine work and even augment human decision-making, it won't judgment work, the application of human experience and expertise to critical business decisions when the information available is insufficient to suggest a successful course of action or reliable enough to suggest an obvious course of action. For a sense of the nature of judgment work, consider big data marketing and sales analytics. Such analytics often provide insights that can inform promotional campaigns, including predicting which promotions will generate desired sales brand further into the future, marketing executives need use judgment, combining analytics with their own and others' insight and experience.

The application of experience and expertise to critical business decisions and practice represents the real value of human judgment. But, when artificial intelligent machines are implemented to any organizations to assist the low, middle and top level management to make any business judgment. These forms of judgment work that managers can gather data interpretation, idea development more absolute from (AI) machine assistance. Thus, why these level management executives need to learn how to apply (AI) machines to help them to make any business judgment more accurate.

1.9 How (AI) influences organizational change

Consequently creative and social intelligence will be in even greater demand as (AI) makes in management and the workforce. This development will represent a long term trend in labor markets , one characterized by intensifying demand and reward for social skills with a growing desire for creative capabilities, managers will seek to fashion of ideas and hypotheses from inside and outside of the enterprise to shape solutions to their most pressing business problems. Thus, (AI) will influence overall organizational team members who have chance to participate any decision to make more accurate business judgment.

Many managers mistakenly view judgment work as only an individual discipline, failing to appreciate that it can also involve decide interpersonal and organizational practices. In more complex settings, judgment is typically a collective outcome of individuals' and teams' diverse perspectives, insights and experiences. And often , the resulting choices are better informed than decisions that an individual would have arrived at on his or her own.

Thus, when any organizations apply (AI) technology to assist managers to gather data and ideas to make any judgment. In these cases, organizations can create the conditions for effective collective judgment by establishing structures , such as " shadow advisory boards" that prompt managers and employees to source and synthesize multiple perspectives. Thus, a traditional organization (firm) might freshen its thinking is t put together a shadow advisory board, comprised of young, digital people who can apply (AI) machine assistance to make judgment work more accurate whether related to people development, problem-solving or strategizing and innovating for considerable degrees of creative and social intelligence.

Thus, on the one hand, (AI) technology machine augmentation and automation can give these advantages to human (organization managers) , e.g. developing people and community, solving problems and collaborating, coordinating and controlling work, shaping strategy and leading innovation. Besides, on the other hand, the next generation managers need have these individual attitude to treat intelligent machines to be as colleagues.

When, judgment is a human skill, intelligent machines can accelerate human learning that supports it, assisting in data -driven simulations, scenarios and search and discovery activities. Focuses on judgment work, some decisions require insight beyond what data can tell them. This is the sweet sport for human judgment, the application of experience and expertise to critical business decisions and practices. Thus, managers will also need to find ways to learn how to use digital (AI) technologies to tap into the knowledge and judgment of partners, customer external stakeholders and role models in other industries after the (AI) machine had been implemented to the organization.

1.10 Future works change:
Automation, employment
and productivity

Human future " micro to macro" industry trends will be affected business strategy and public policy by (AI) technology. In the future (AI) technology will influence those six themes: productivity and growth, natural resources, labor markets, the evolution of global financial markets, the economic impact of technology and innovation and urbanization. However, (AI) technology will bring economic benefits of tackling gender inequality, a new global competition, Chinese innovation and digital globalization.

Nowadays, advances in robotics artificial intelligence, and machine learning are in a new age of automation, as machines match or outperform human performance in a development to any countries. For example, automation of activities can enable businesses to improve performance by reducing errors and improving quality and speed, and in some cases achieving outcomes that go beyond human capabilities. For example, some research indicated automation could raise productivity growth globally by 0.8 to 1.4 % annually; more than 2,000 work activities across 800 occupations. When less than 5% of all occupations can be automated using demonstrated technologies about 60% of all occupations have at least 30% of constituent activities that could be automated. Many occupations will change that will be automated away: Activities most susceptible to automation involve physical activities, in highly structured and predictable environments, as well as the collection and processing of data. They are most prevalent in manufacturing , accommodation and food service and retail trade and include some middle-skill jobs. For example, such as natural language processing is a key factor. Beyond technical feasibility, the cost of technology competition with labor including skills and supply and demand dynamics, performance benefits including and beyond labor cost savings, and social and regulatory acceptance will be affected by (AI) automation technology. Thus, (AI) automation will impact to influence global employment in those aspects as below:

Firstly, assuming that people are displaced by automation will find other employment. The anticipated shift in the activities in the labor force is of a similar order as the long-term shift away from agriculture and decreases in manufacturing share of employment. Both of manufacturing and agriculture industries which would be accompanied by the creation of new types of work not foreseen at the time.

Secondly, for business, the performance benefits of automation are relatively clear. Thus, the businessmen have opportunities for their micro economies to benefits from the productivity growth potential and macro economies to benefit to encourage continued progress and innovation , investment and market incentives. At the same time, employers must innovate policies to help workers and institutions adapt to the impact on employment.

This will likely include rethinking education and training, income support and safety nets , as well as support for those dislocated, when employees need to leave themselves homes to move to other cities to learn new (AI) automation works. Thus, individuals in the workplace will need to engage move comprehensively with machines as part of their everyday activities, and acquire new skills that will be in demand in the new automation age. Consequently , the scale of shifts in the labor force over many decades that automation technologies can be a similar order to the long -term technology -enables shifts in the developed countries‘ workforces away from agriculture in the 21 th century. Those shifts did not result in long-term mass unemployment because they were accompanied by the creation of new types of work not foreseen at the time. However, human will still be needed in the workforce when the total productivity gains are caused by (AI) technology.

1.11 What occupations will be influenced by (AI) technology.

In the future, scientists predict that these occupations will be influenced by (AI) technology mostly. They include : retail salespeople, food and beverage service workers, language or translation teachers, health practitioners. Since these work activities have a more relevant occupations are made up of a range of activities with different potential for (AI) automation . For example, a retail salesperson will spend more time interacting with customers, stocking shelves , or ringing up sales. Each of these activities is distinct and requires different capabilities to perform successfully.

Thus, these job activities have similar simple control characteristics. Simple activities include greet customers, answer questions about products and services, clean and maintain work areas, demonstrate product feature process sales and transactions. All these activities can have similar simple activities in order to (AI) machines can be learn how to do these activities from (AI) technology . For example, the capability perception includes sensory perception, cognitive capabilities, such as retrieving automation, recognizing known patterns(supervised learning), logical reasoning problem solving.

Thus, (AI) machine is such human, which has feeling and emotion, such as social and emotional sensing, judgement reasoning methods, natural language understanding and physical capabilities, such as mobility , navigation, gross motor skill, fine motor skills. It seems that the future, (AI) human invents machines which will have these human characteristics to do human similar behavioral job duties more easily and efficiently. It implies these above human occupations will be replaced by (AI) human invention machines in the future. Due to (AI) creation, it is possible to cause unemployment number of these above workers will increase because (AI) machines can do their similar job behavioral activities.

Consequently, employers won't need to employ many of these skillful labor. Otherwise, they can buy less number (AI) machines to attempt to do whose job activities more easily and efficiently. So, it seems (AI) machines will have more high work performance to replace these occupation workers' work performance. Finally, these occupation worker unemployment number will only increase when the (AI) machines had been invented to achieve to do their work behavioral activities absolutely success in the future.

1.12Whether (A) technology machine labor
will replace human worker more or assist
human worker more

There is no single agreed definition of a robot how outcome of a task that is completed without human intervention. When some definitions require the task to be completed by a physical machine moves and respond to its environment, other definitions use the term robot in connection with tasks completed by software , without physical embodiment.

However, to answer the question : Whether (AI) technology machine labor will replace human worker more or assist human worker more. I shall indicate some examples to let readers to judge whether (AI) technology can create new jobs or reduce old jobs.

Firstly, I shall explain what (AI) function is. (AI) is a service robot that performs useful tasks for humans or equipment excluding industrial automation application . Thus, the classification of a robot into industrial robot or service robot is done according to its intended application. It is also a personal service robot or a service robot for personal used for a non commercial task, usually by lay persons . Examples are domestic servant robot, and pet exercising robot. It is also a professional service robot or a service robot for professional used for a commercial task, usually operated by a properly trained operator. Examples, are cleaning robot for public places, delivery robot in offices or hospitals, fire-fighting robot, rehabilitation robot and surgery robot in hospitals. Thus, these functions will be future (AI) application to our daily life necessaries or business necessaries.

However, some authors agree (AI) will bring negative outcomes of automation, due to raise competiveness, reduce human job nature. Otherwise, other authors argue (AI) will bring positive outcomes of automation, due to raise productivities, job creation, assist humans work.

On the positive outcome hand, robots can increase productivity . This is particularly important for small-to medium sized businesses both are in developed and developing countries economies. It also enables large companies to increase their competitiveness through faster product development and delivery. Increased use of robot is also enabling companies in high cost countries to re shore, or bring back to their domestic base parts of the supply chain that will have previously outsourced to sources of cheaper labor. Currently , the greater threat to employment is not a automation, but an inability to remain competitive. Automation has led overall to an increase in labor demand and positive impact on wages. The reason is that the middle-income/middle-skilled jobs have reduced as a proportion of overall contribution to employment and earnings leading to fears of increasing income inequality, the skills range within the middle income bracket is large. Thus, robots are driving an increase in demand for workers at the higher -skilled and with a positive impact on wages. This issue is how to enable middle-income earners in the lower-income range to unskilled or retain. Finally, the (AI) positive impact supporter who argue the future will be robots and humans can work together.

However, on the negative outcome hand, robots can substitute labor activities, but don't replace jobs. They believe that less than 10% of jobs are fully automatable. Increasingly , robots are used to complement and augment labor activities, the net impact on jobs and the quality of work is positive. Automation can provide the opportunity for humans to focus on higher-skilled, higher-quality and higher-paid tasks. Robots can improve productivity when they are applied to tasks that which perform more efficiently and to a higher and more consistent level of quality than humans. For example, increased productivity is enabling some firms, such as Whirlpool, Caterpillar and Ford Motors company in the US restructure their supply chains, bringing back parts of the manufacturing process to the country of origin. Thus, productivity gains due to robotics and automation are important not just at the company level, but also for build industry and nation competitiveness.

I suppose that productivity can be raised. What are the impacts of robots on employment? Firstly, the main focus of development has been on personal entertainment, which does not drive worker productivity (manufacturing production). When the internet (information and communication technology (ICT)) innovation. This is borne and by findings that manufacturing productivity, which has been driven by innovations in automation rather than consumer technologies, has government strongly than productivity in the services sectors of the economy in most nature economies. It seems (AI) automation will create many jobs in internet communication entertainment game industry. For example, many young people like to use internet to play any electronic games from computer or mobile at home or outside home conveniently. Thus, (AI) automation will increase demand to be invented to any new entertainment game from internet channel. It will need to employ many (AI) entertainment game inventors to create many automation entertainment games. Thus, (AI) automation in internet entertainment game industry will need human (AI) entertainment game inventors to invent the knowledge-based capital of (AI) automation entertainment games. The (AI) entertainment game inventors will need own research and development skills, form specific skills, organizational know-how skills, databased knowledge, design and various forms of intellectual property to do these (AI) automation entertainment game invention occupations in the future.

International Federation Of Robotics(2016) indicated that China will be as a major robotics manufacturer and user of robots, benefiting from jobs created by robot manufacturing and productivity gains from robot use. Chins had sold of robots to any one single market every year since 2017 year. The Chinese government has included a focus on robotics in its 10 year strategy. In order to achieve its target of a robot density of 150 units per 10, 000 workers by 2020 year. Thus, Chinese companies will have to install around 650,000 new industrial robots between 2016 to 2020 year, 2.5 times more than installed globally in 2015 year.

Hence, China (AI) manufacturing industry will need to employ many workers . It implies (AI) manufacturing industry will create many new occupations in China. Also, ministry of economy, trade and industry (2015) also showed that Japan currently has the largest stock of industrial robots in operations, primarily in the automation industry. Driven by a rapidly aging population and low productivity rates, the Japanese government has sights on a 20-fold increase in the use of robots in the non-manufacturing sector and a three-fold growth rate of labor productivity in the service sector both by 2020 year. Thus, it also implies Japan will need many robots to be provide to service industry. Due to robots will provide to serve any businessmen's clients. Thus, it is possible that the service workers won't be dismissed as well as it is depended on the serving job nature to decide whether Japan's service workers can still serve to their employer when the service (AI) robots are applied to whose employers.

Consequently, it seems that (AI) can create employment, Ministry of economy, trade and industry (2015) showed that such as China will develop the major (AI) automation manufacturing industry. The (AI) employers will need to employ many workers to manufacture any these different kinds of (AI) robots to satisfy China or overseas individual or business buyers needs. But, (AI) can also cause unemployment to the low skillful service workers. Such as if Japan some service businesses choose to buy any (AI) service robots to replace their service staffs to serve their clients. It is possible that the service staffs will be dismissed, due to (AI) robots can do such as their same service job duties to achieve better service performance.

Thus, today, it is increasingly common for people to use robots in various situations at home and in retail stores, hotels and hospitals these service industries. Robots are classified into server types based on their functionality (service and utility robots or those designed to communicate with humans) and appearance (humanoid robots or mechanical robots). The type of robot, to which each country allocated particular importance in the advance of robotics, reflects the sense of values and preferences of its population. Thus, if the country has high population needs to use robots, then they will influence either more new jobs creation or more old job loss in the country's (AI) manufacturing or (AI) service industries both. For example, Japan respondents often associate the term " robot " with humanoid robots that can communicate with human and they have a high level of familiarity with robot. The US has the highest level of robot utilization at home and in retail stores with its people being the most enthusiastic about the future use of robots. Germany shows a strong tendency to consider robots for industrial purposes and its people feel strong effort to the presence of robots in their households.

In conclusion, to judge whether how (AI) will influence the country's employment to be better or worse. It will depend on the country home buyers (users) or business buyers (users) how to use (AI) for their daily needs. If the country , such as US retail stores need to use (AI) , it will have possible to reduce some or many retail service workers. Even, if the country , such as Japan has many home users need to use (AI) , it will not influence the employment market. Otherwise, it will raise (AI) salespeople numbers. Even, if the country, such as Germany and China will have many (AI) manufacturers, then it will create many (AI) manufacturing occupations for these (AI) manufactory workers.

Consequently, (AI) robots manufacturing and service needs will have positive or negative impact to any country's employment. It will depend on the (AI) service provision and service workers' job nature as well as the manufacturing workers of (AI) knowledge level to decide their employment chance in their country's employment market.

What does artificial intelligence(AI) mean?

● What (AI) function is?

Some scientists explain that artificial intelligence means which is an expert system, computer software that embodies a portion of the specialized knowledge of a human portion in a specific, narrow domain, owns decision making ability of human expert. The (AI)technology is based on the premise that what makes a person an expert is years of experience that enables who recognizes certain patterns in a problem as being similar to pattern. For example, in the future artificial intelligence system can be applied to control air traffic, design to computer configuration, medical diagnosis, instruction/training, speech/interpretation, monitoring to (nuclear plant), planning to mission, factory scheduling, prediction weather, repairing telephone, automatic driving etc. different industries.

Artificial intelligence characteristics include: creative, adaptive , common sense, fact processing, quick replication, broad focus permanent and consistent skill. Otherwise, traditional computer expert system disadvantage includes perishable, unpredictable, slow reproduction, expensive, slow reproduction, slow processing lacks inspiration, needs instruction, narrow focus only machine knowledge. So, artificial intelligence is a branch of computer science devoted to creating computer to influence software and hardware to attempt to create human intelligence or human intelligent behavior. It is learning from experience, responds flexibility in situation that are, new or not anticipated.

Thus, (AI) can be learnt programmed knowledge to solve problems, using reasoning in solving problem, understanding and inferring facts and rules, recognizing the relative importance of different elements in a situation.

In summary, artificial intelligence is concerned with two basic ideas mainly: The first idea, it involves studying the thought processes of humans to understand what intelligence is; the second idea, it deals with representing thought processes using companies to create artificially intelligent entities for testing the theories of intelligence.

- Can (AI) impact human job nature?

Human need concern this question: Will artificial intelligence (AI) reduce some human jobs in order to instead of replacing machines to do? Due to artificial intelligence is the ability of machines to do thing, that people would require intelligence. For example, artificial intelligence machine man driving(self-driver), it (AI) machine man driving research is an attempt to discover and describe aspects of human intelligence that can be simulated by driving machine functions. Alternatively, (AI) mathematical research may be another viewed as an attempt to develop a mathematical theory function to describe the abilities and actions of things (natural or man-made) exhibiting intelligent behavior and server as a design of intelligent calculation machine function.

Why do humans need artificial intelligence machines to instead of traditional human service job? For example, can artificial intelligence machine man (self-driving) driver drive to replace human driver? I shall compare the differences between humans and computers : The characteristics of humans are good at recognizing various things, either seen before or not, recognizing the relationship patterns between things. Human thinking is common sense reasoning, combining all types of sensory input, acting appropriately in novel situations, learning new things and changing behavior patterns, making decisions , even when given incomplete information, working with noisy, incomplete information gathering behaviors . However, characteristics of computers are good at: The tasks humans do naturally are extremely difficult for a computer program as intelligent, which must be able to do the same kind of tack as humans do naturally.

Hence, (AI) is an combination of many different success and technologies: Linguistics - computational and socio, philosophy-logic, philosophy of mind and of language, electronical engineering -image and speech processing, pattern recognition, robotics, machine learning, neural networks, optimization scheduling, management information system and decision making. So, it is possible that (AI) can impact human job nature to instead of human working behavior in the future.

- How can human society job nature
to be changed to artificial intelligent society?

From the first intelligent perspective reason view point, artificial intelligence is making machines " intelligent" acting as humans expect people to act. Artificial intelligence has ability to distinguish computer responses from human responses, it owns knowledge to solve expert problem. From another research perspective reason view point, artificial intelligence is the study of how to make computers do things which, at the moment, people do better (Rich & Knight, 1991, p.3).

(AI) researchers are native in a variety of domains, e.g. formal tasks (mathematics, games), tasks (perception, robotics, natural language, common sense reasoning), expert tasks (financial analysis, medical diagnostics, engineering, scientific analysis and other areas).

From the second business perspective reason view point, (AI) is a set of many powerful tools, and methodologies for using those tools to solve business problems. From a programming perspective reason view point, (AI) includes the study of symbolic programming problem solving and search .

From the third human technological perspective reason view point, today's computer can do many well-defined tasks, for example, arithmetic operations, are much faster and more accurate than human beings. However, the computers' interaction with their environment is not very sophisticated yet. How can human test whether a computer has reached the general intelligence level of a human being? Can a computer convince a human interrogator that it is a human? But before thinking of such advanced kinds of machines, human will start developing our own extremely simple " intelligent" machines. So, it is possible that human society job nature will to be changed to artificial intelligent society when (AI) technology is developed to the mature stage in the future.

- Why does human need artificial intelligence machines?

One of major division in (AI) is between humans who think (AI) is the only serious way of finding out how we (human) work and human who want companies to do very smart things, independently of how we (human) work. This is the important distinction between cognitive scientists vs engineers. One of another major division in (AI) is between symbolic (AI), which represents information through symbols and their relationships. Specific Algorithms are used to process these symbols to solve problems or deduce new knowledge and connectionist. So (AI) , which represents information in network. Biological processes underlying learning, task performance and problem solving are imitated from human mind behaviors. Thus, it is possible that artificial intelligence machines can do the better judgicious behavior to compare human.

- How does artificial intelligence influence future working changing in automation employment and productivity aspects?

In the automation changing influence aspect, as companies increasingly use robots on production lines or algorithms to optimize their logistics manage inventory, any carry out other core business functions. Technological advances are creating a new automation age in which ever-smarter and more flexible machines will be deployed on an ever larger scale in the marketplace. However, researching artificial intelligence with how influences human working nature. We need to answer these questions: How will automation transform the workplace? What will the implications for employment? And what is likely to be its impact both on productivity in the global economy and on employment?

Advances in robotics, artificial intelligence, and machine learning are growing in a new age of automation as machines match or outperform human performance in a range of work activities, including ones requiring cognitive capabilities. What factors are determined the changing in workplace adoption by artificial intelligence innovation? What advantages are automation? Automation of activities can be enabled businesses to improve performance by reducing errors and improving quality and speed, and achieving outcomes that go beyond human capabilities.

Some scientists indicated based on their scenario modeling. They estimated automation could raise producing growth globally by 0.8 to 1.4 percent annually. Almost, the activities people are paid almost $16 trillion in wages to do in global economy have the potential to be automated by adopting currently demonstrated technology. According to their analysis of more than 2,000 work activities across 800 occupations. When less than 5% of all occupations have of least 30% of activities that could be automated. They also indicated that technical economic and social factors will determine automation. Continued technical progress, for example, in areas such as natural language processing is a key factor beyond technical feasibility , the cost of technology, competition with labor including skills, and supply and demand dynamics, performance benefits including and beyond labor cost savings and social and regulatory acceptance will affect (alter) the scope of automation.

Other some scientists also indicate U.S. country for example, the anticipate shift in the activities in labor force of a similar order of magnitude as the long term sight away from agriculture and decreases in manufacturing. Share of employment in the United States both which were achieved. So, those factors can influence why artificial intelligence technology needs. So, it is possible that future agriculture and manufacturing both industries will apply (AI) technology manufacturer-kind of job nature to raise productivity instead of farmers, fruit picking workers, farming transportation labours as well as factory manufacturing workers and supervisors etc. human-kind of job nature.

- Is artificial intelligence possible to replace labor ?

Not just intelligence, but also debating, if machines are capable of having a conscious minds. Artificial intelligence has those characteristics as below:

On functionalism aspect, artificial intelligence inputs mental states, sensory inputs, (beliefs, desires being in pain feeling) and behavioral outputs. Since mental states are identified by a functional role, which are thoughts to be manifested in various systems. Even, perhaps computers which are physical devices with electronic substrate that inform computations on inputs to give outputs similar to brains which are artificial intelligence composed of part any intrinsic relationship to each other. Thus, artificial intelligence activities is not the whole itself, but into parts or on external influence on the parts.

On dualism aspect, artificial intelligence is a set of views about the relationship between mind are matter. On materialism aspect, it builds the only thing that exists is matter, including consciousness.

On biological naturalism aspect, it is similar a human brain than feels pains makes mental situation. So, artificial intelligence is similar biologist which might to be excited to human labor work. Hence, it seems artificial intelligence can change (alter) or replace human labor work of nature in possible in the future.

- Can (AI) technology replace human labour nature of work?

On technological innovation reason view point, the history development of artificial intelligence studying the intelligence is one of most ancient scientific discipline. The history development of artificial intelligence what aims to achieve human use to sense, learn remember and think, logic probability, decision making and calculation develop from mathematics, instead of replacement human labor functions.

Artificial intelligence history development aim is the scientific analysis of skills in connection and practice with the appearance of computers from 1950 year beginning. The artificial intelligence (AI) can deal with the ultimate challenges. How can (either biological or electronic) mind sense, understand and manipulate a world that is much simple and more complex than itself? And what if would human like to construct something with such capabilities?

The general-purpose software of the early period of (AI) were only able to solve simple tasks effectively and failed when which should be used in a wider range or an more difficult tasks. One of the sources of difficulty was that early software had very few or mix knowledge about the problems which handled, and activities successes by simply syntactic manipulation. Moreover, the other difficulty was that many problems that were tried to solve by the (AI) were untreatable.

The early (AI) software whether trying step sequences based on the basic facts about the problem that should be solved, experimented with different combinations till which found a solution. From the end the 1960 year, developing the so-called expert systems were emphasized. These systems had (sue-based) knowledge base about the field which handled. Till to the beginning of the 1970 year, (Prolog) the logical programming language was born, which was built in the computation realization of a version of the resolution calculus. (Prolog) is a remarkably prevalent tool in developing expert systems (on medical, judiciary and other scopes), but natural language parsers were implemented in this language. Then, in 1981 s, the Japanese announced the fifth generation computer system project, a 10 years plan to build an intelligent computer system that use the (Prolog) language as a machine code. Nowadays, (AI) can be applied any industries, such as car manufacturing industry can use (AI) technological machine-men manufacture car, instead of replacing human labors in factory. Even, in the future, using (AI) machine-men drivers can drive any private cars or public transportation tools, instead of replacing human drivers, e.g. bus, train, tram, ferry etc. Also in the future, machine-men can replace housewives to serve families to do housekeeping clean job , e.g. cleaning toilets, bathrooms, kitchens, even cooking functions at home. So (AI) machine-man can reduce housewives works at home. Moreover, (AI) machine man can take care old people , when who are living at homes or elder care centers.

So, it seems artificial intelligence (AI) will be possible developed to manufacture a new generation machine-man to assist (serve) families to do any simply cleaning or cooking jobs at homes. Moreover, the overall demand of (AI) general social needs will also rise, such as security, driving transportation tools, restaurant cleaning, elder centers care service etc. So, it seems that individual or families or social needs of (AI) will be increase in the future. Thus, it will influence macro economy growth (GDP) if there are large house family consumer group and hotel or bus or taxis or ferry etc. different business consumer group demand any artificial intelligence machine numbers increasing. Then, the artificial intelligence products and material manufacturers must need to buy many artificaial intelligence materials to produce any kinds of artificial intelligence machines to prepare to satisfy consumer individual needs. Consequently, macro economy will grow to the owned artificial intelligence development countries, e.g. US, China, UK.

- Why can artificial intelligence satisfy human needs?

First, On machine-man satisfactory demand aspect view point, it makes computers that think, it is the automation of activities. We associate with human thinking: like decision making, learning. It is the act of creating machine that perform function that require intelligence when performed by people. It is the study of mental faculties through the use of computational models. It is the study of computations that make it possible to perceive, reason and act. It is a branch of computer science that is concerned with the automation of intelligent behavior. It is anything in computing service that human don't yet know how to do property.

Second, on thought aspect artificial intelligence means systems thank think like humans, systems that think rationally.

Third, on behavioral aspect, artificial intelligence systems that act like human and that systems act rationally. However, the basic objective of (AI) is to represent human's thought processes in computation . These machines are supposed to exhibit behavior that. It is performed by a human being, would be considered intelligent. However, some authors feel (AI) has disadvantages, such as it is not creative, it is excited in the use of sensory devices, it can't make use of a very wide context of experiences and it does not use common sense.

For speech recognition and understanding function needs example, (AI) can be applied in speech recognition and understanding function, which (AI) speech or voice recognition is a data input method. For example, the computer recognizes and understands one (or a few) word commands. Speech understanding on the other hand is the computer's ability to understanding a spoken language. That is , the computer understands the meaning of sentences, an paragraphs through (AI).

So, (AI) can be attempted to learn human language how to speak. It is similar to translate human language skill, instead of actual human speaking skill. Also, (AI) can assist handicap learning or language student how to listen different languages by machine-man sounds from computers more accurately. So, it seems that it (AI) can replace human language teachers speaking function and can change teaching language nature of job in language speaking and listening education industry.

- Is artificial intelligence one good choice for human future technological benefit?

Nowadays, new technology development is popular. However, artificial intelligence is one kind of new technology choice among different technologies innovation. So it brings this question: Is artificial intelligence technology value to invest? To answer this question. I shall indicate some other new technology developments to compare (AI)

technology development to judge which has urgent needs to achieve human expectation nowadays.
For example, why is green peace interested in new technologies? New technologies features prominently in our ongoing campaigns against genetic modified crops and number power. However, which are also an integral part of our solutions to environmental challenges, including renewable energy technologies, such as solar, wind and wave (water) power energy as well as waste treatment technologies, such as mechanical, biological treatment. It seems humans need concern how to apply (AI) technology to solve environment pollution challenges in our future. So, environment protective, agriculture, natural energy technology will be popular demand to attempt to apply (AI) technology to solve their challenges or apply (AI) to assist to develop their industry.

CHAPTER TWO

How can artificial intelligence technology influence economy

Advances in artificial intelligence (AI) technology and related fields have opened up new markets and new opportunities progress in critical areas, such as health, education, energy, economic development, social welfare and the environment pollution.

(AI) automation will continue to create wealth and expand the global economy development in the future. However, when many will benefits that growth won't be costless and will be accompanied by changes in the skills, that workers need to increase productivity in the economy and structural changes in the economy. So, in the skills that workers need to succeed in the economy and structural changes.

I shall indicate why aggressive policy action will be needed to help Americans who are disadvantaged by these changes , due to (AI) technology is caused. For automation industry change example, artificial intelligence (AI) capabilities will enable automation of some tasks that have long required human labor. These artificial intelligence technology introduction can increase new opportunities for individuals. The economy and society, but (AI) has also the potential to disrupt be current livelihoods of many Americans. However, (AI) leads to unemployment and increase in inequality over the long run depends not only on the (AI) technology itself, but also on the institutions and policies that are changed. Thus, it is possible that (AI) technology will raise some countries unemployment number if the employer apply (AI) technology workers to work instead of human labor in their factories, but it can also raise productivities for these employers.

- Can (AI) influence global economy growth?

Technological progress is main driver of growth of GDP per capita, allowing output to increase faster than labor and capital . However, technology can increase productivity, but also decrease the number of labor hours needed to create a unit of output. So (AI) causes unequal to labor wage decreases, even reduces the number of labor to manufacture, e.g. artificial intelligence technology of automation car manufacturing industry; clothing manufacturing industry; plane manufacturing etc. high technology of artificial intelligence manufacturing method. But (AI) should be potential environment benefit, although it raises unemployment ratio. Moreover, it can rise production , due to many skilled craft were replaced by the combination of machines and lower-skilled labor. The result of (AI) technology introduction , it causes output per hour risen when inequality declined, driving up average living standards, but the labor of some high-skill workers was no longer as valuable in the market. Otherwise, if (AI) technology is continue developed to be success. Some routine intensive occupations will be loss, which focused on predictable, e.g. easily programmable tasks, such as switchboard operators, filing clerks, travel agents, and assembly line workers would be particularly replaced by new (AI) technology. However, at the same time, (AI) technology development will bring these benefits: improvement in education (training (AI) technology scientists) , due to (AI) manufacturing technology needs are raising to businesses and institutional changes, such as the reduction in unionization and raising in the minimum wage to the (AI) manufacturing technology skilled labor in factories.

Because (AI) technology is not a single technology, but rather a collection of technologies that are applied to specific tasks, the effects of (AI) will be felt unevenly though the economy. It will bring some tasks will be most easily automated than others , and some jobs will be affected more than others, both negatively and positively. Finally, new jobs are likely to be directly created in areas , such as the development and supervision of (AI) as well as indirectly created in a range areas though out the economy as higher incomes lead to expanded demand.

However, if (AI) technology could dominate global labor markets. If labor productivity increases, do not influence into wage increases, then the large economic gains brought about by (AI) technology could be increased wealth inequality, due to employers can reduce production cost, but workers (labors) wages will not be increased, even will be decreased. Hence, it seems the (AI) technology will bring disadvantages to labor market to cause unemployment or reduce wages in possible, although it can reduce employer individual salary (wage) expenditure and it can raise productivity.

- How can artificial intelligence impact global economy growth?

Artificial intelligence (AI) technology is a branch of computer science that aims to create intelligent machines that work and react like humans. So, (AI) is a technology that appears to impact (influence) human preference by learning, understanding complex contents, enhancing humans in executing both routine and non-routine tasks. In the future, (AI) technology that can be virtual personal assistant, as well as it may exist, such as robots with human-like processing capabilities.

How can (AI) technology impact global economy growth over the next 10 years? During this time period, (AI) technology is predicted to have wide-ranging applications including: Machine learning that automates analytical model building by using algorithms that allow machines to operate without human assistance.

In global education aspect, potential applications include predicting cause-and-effect relationships from biological data, identifying new drugs, self-driving cars, and protecting against fraud, improved natural language processing that allows computers to continue to better analysis, understand and generate language to interface with humans using natural human languages. For example, transcribing notes dictated by physicians, automatically drafting articles and translating text and speech. So (AI) technology can be applied to education aspect to improve humans‘ knowledge level.

In visual art aspect, (AI) machine vision that allows computers to identify objects, scenes and activities in images. Current applications of (AI) machine vision include providing objective descriptions for the blind seeing(visual) needs.

We except the economic effects of (AI) technology to include both direct GDP growth from sectors that develop or manufacture. (AI) technology and indirect GDP growth through increased productivity in existing sectors that employ some form of (AI). If (AI) technology is an increasingly critical component of more products, it will become an integral part of many people's lives. Thus, (AI)'s ability to influence economic activity, rather than the economic or development status of the region. (AI) has the potential to impact income classes and to bring significant gains to both developed and developing countries. For example, (AI) has the potential to optimize good production around the world by analyzing agricultural regions and identifying what is necessary to improve crop yields.

In estimating the future economic effects by (AI) technology innovation, it is important to note that it is challenging to accurately predict which applications of (AI) will ultimately be commercially successful. In micro level economic influence, we need to apply methodologies to estimate the economic effects of investment in firms developing (AI) technology since investment levels in a technology are a telling sign of the future potential of that (AI) technology.

- How can (AI) influence GDP of high income countries in the next ten years?

How (AI)'s development may affect the global economy over the next ten years. In fact, (AI) technology has the potential to affect business across the global in a wide range of industries in ways only a number of technologies have done in the parts. For example, (AI) technology's expected to be a useful tool for enhancing human capabilities and in some instances replacing functions, such as driving a car, adoption of broadband internet, mobile telephone, industrial robotic automation have served to enhance human capabilities.

However, significant public debate has focused on projections of (AI) technology's effect on the labor force. However, large companies prefer to invest in (AI) technological industry. For example, face book's (AI) research lab., google machine intelligence lab. and micro soft machine learning and artificial intelligence research division are all making advances in (AI) technology and investing in the industry's top talent. Additionally, between 2010 year and 2015 year, nearly $5 billion in venture capital funding invested in firms across the global developing and employing (AI) technology (Facebook (AI) Research).

- How can artificial intelligence impact on workplace?

Modern information technologies and the labor economy growth of machines is powered by artificial intelligence have already strongly influenced the world of work in the 21 ST century. Computers, algorithms and software simplify every tasks and it is impossible to image how most of our life could be managed without them. How can be the information economy characterized by exponential growth replaces the most production industry based on economy of scales? What will the future world of work look like and how long will it take to get? Will the future world of work be a world where humans spend less time earning their livelihood? Alternatively, are mass unemployment, mass poverty and social distortions also possible scenario for the future, where robots, artificial intelligence systems play an increasingly central role? These questions concern how artificial intelligence further development . Can influence labor economy growth on workplace ? When the labor market has widespread impact on intelligence property, information technology, product liability, competition and labor and employment laws.

How (AI) technology impacts on labor workplace.

The future influence any organizations how labor economies use of (AI) can be analyzed, such as deep machine learning is based on a set of model high level data. Unlike human workers, the machines are connected the whole time in workplace. If one machine makes a mistake, all autonomous systems will keep this in mind and will avoid the same mistake the next time.

Over the long run intelligent machines will win against every human expert. Production robots have been replacing employees because of the (AI) technology. They work more precisely than humans and cost loss. Creative solutions like 3D printers and the self learning ability of these production robots will replace human workers, the automatic data recording and data processing, traditional back office activities are no longer in demand. Autonomous software will collect necessary information and will send it to the employee who needs it. Additionally, dematerialization leads to the phenomenon that traditional physical products are becoming software. For example, CD or DVDs are being replaced by streaming services. The replacement of traditional event ticket, e-travel ticket service products or hard cash will be the next step, due to the possibility of payment by smartphone. So, (AI) technology will impact human's daily life consumption behaviors in the future. For another example, transportation tools, such as boats and ferries and private vehicles will use sensors and navigating without human input. Taxi and truck drivers will become obsolete, the stock store applies to stock managers and postal carriers of the delivery is distributed by (AI) machine delivery method,

2.1`What is the relationship between (AI) and (CRM)?

● Can (AI) technology impact on customer relationship management (CRM) ?

Nowadays , (AI) is a technology almost as old as the computer industry itself, it is similar with the advent of personal assistants function to businesses and personal promotion channel, such as (Amazon's Alexa, Apple's Siri, Google's Assistant) image recognition (face book), personalized recommendations (Netflix , Amazon). Those innovations have been driven by a increase in processing power, lower cost hardware, and the exploding creation and availability of data. It seems, (AI) technology can impact global customer service management method.

How to forecast economic impact modeling to (AI) will affect global economy? Can human forecast business revenue growth and job creation (or destruction) based on (AI) applied to customer relationship management (CRM) activities? In addition to the economic impact on (AI) or (CRM) which can include an estimate of the economic impact attributable to sales forces customer base. What can economic benefits be brought to (CRM) from (AI) technology?

Artificial intelligence(AI) comprises a set of technologies that use natural language processing, machine learning, knowledge graphs, and other tools to answer questions, discover insights and provide recommendations. Computer systems can use (AI) hypothesize and formulate possible answers based on available evidence can be trained through the ingestion of vast amounts of content, and automatically adapt and learn from (AI) self mistakes and failures.

So, any business organizations (customer service departments) can provide efficient and effective customer relationship management of excellent customer service quality if which applied (AI) technology system. The different type of (AI) systems include: (AI) system platforms, machine learning (AI) based data preparation and enrichment tools, machine vision/image recognition, voice speech recognition, text analysis and natural language processing, bots , e.g. face book website and virtual digital assistance solutions, social media pattern analysis , sentiment analysis, advanced numerical analysis (e.g. IOT streaming , machine logs), supporting technologies, knowledge base dialog management, Q&A processing etc. different (AI) technology system customer relationship management (CRM) tools.

(AI) (CRM) of activity can include these categories, such as: corporate marketing, marketing operation, field marketing, customer support, digital commerce, customer analytics, customer influenced product or service design, product or service pricing, finance information, presentation, customer billing, inventory , logistics and fulfilment support, partner management etc. different CRM tools.

(AI) technology of CRM has been carrying on plan different stages to achieve CRM personal assistant tool for businesses. The stages are such as, in the beginning stage of (AI) projects in place, implement now, pilot phase next year in the final stage of (AI) customer relationship management tools are foreseeable future. So, this CRM technology has been improved to plan in different stages every year to prepare to achieve full capacity of CRM service quality for businesses to use in the future.

Hence, how to develop an estimate prediction of the economic impact (AI) technologies could have CRM activities, which depends on gathering macroeconomic information on business revenue and the basic marketing of business revenue and the basic markup of business expenses by major functions (customer support, marketing and sales , production etc.)

An economic impact model that can gather data together and forecast the results how (AI) artificial intelligence technology brings (CRM) customer relationship management benefits to businesses, e.g. surveys investigation includes IT spending by sample countries, GDP and population estimates and forecasts, revenue per employee and ratios of IT spend to GDP. Surveys (questionnaire questions) of forecast results are influenced by (AI) impact can include: results are projected from surveys and rely on estimates are made by respondents on the expected financial improvements in categories of (AI) –assisted customer relationship management activities. The forecast assumes that these estimates are correct; financial estimates are based on estimates of “first year” improvement from full (AI) implementation; forecasts are from planning to implement any artificial intelligence of customer relationship management (CRM) projects, the improvement forecast is of categories of activity , e.g. corporate marketing , digital commerce, and customer analytics. They are not estimates of ROI for the (AI) software. They rely on conservative estimates to which each of these entities might affect company revenue, expenses or productivity. They also rely on estimates of the penetration of software in customer relationship management activities . Net new jobs created are based on the ratio of new revenue to jobs required to support that revenue . They can assume that 50% of the net new revenue will support increases in labor and the rest will go for capital and other operating expenses that may replace jobs lost to automation.

In the future, some of the ways in micro economic benefits to any organizations. (AI) technology is expected to impact CRM activities include: Spending up sales cycles, improving lead generation and qualification solving customer support problems faster (raising service quality), helping companies improve brand campaigns and recognition, lowering costs of support calls when increasing resolution rates, lowering the cost of recruiting employees and partners, increasing revenue from optimized product marketing, optimizing price, distribution logistics and preventing loss through fraud detection. So, micro economic benefits view point, it seems that (AI) CRM technology can raise any companies economic benefits for care term.

Artificial intelligence enables machines or the in-build software to behave like human beings which allows these decisions and act. The advent of (AI) is leading , talking, making decisions and act. The advent of (AI) is leading to new technologies advances and transforming the economic and employment opportunities for humans in a positive way. (AI) related technologies can facilitate our live. For example, industrial robotics, robotic medical assistants, smart games, financial forecasting software, big data analysis, algorithms in health and bioinformatics, pilotless cargo places, drone ambulances and general purpose and workplace robots and others. (Disruptors technologies: Advances that will transform life, business and the global economy).

Artificial intelligence also known as computational intelligence is defined as " the human –like intelligence exhibited by machines or software. It is theorized that intelligence of humans can be described and intelligence machines or software can simulate it. These machines software can be reasonable , learn, perceive and process information, like human mind and thus facilitate human life. They can think and act for us. So, artificial intelligence is an interdisciplinary field of study including computer science, neuroscience, psychology, linguistics and philosophy.

However, (AI) research and developments have economically impacted many industries, such as robotics, telecommunications, computer applications , health, finance, heavy manufacturing, transportation, aviation, e-service and e-commerce, military , music and movie, toys and games entertainment etc. industries.

In fact, many ideas, systems and technologies have been developing in the world of (AI) technology. However, which are net called or considered (AI) products, rather which are mentioned with their specific names, such as smart graphics, machine learning, e-commerce etc. (i.e. this is called (AI) effect).

- How can (AI) technology influence digital economy?

Nowadays, (AI) related industrial applications will replace most human power in fields, including call centers, customer services and air cargo transportation. (AI) technologies also help weather forecasting based on repeated rainfall pattern (data) recognition, through robotics (i.e. floor cleaning, moving lawns etc.) transporting people and products with unmanned vehicles, sending space unmanned smart shuttles, developing robotic arms, predicting market values in stock exchanges by internet, making homes safer, helping elderly and disabled using robotic servants etc.

Among the (AI) related technologies , there are a few that significance for the impact on society and especially on digital economy . (AI) is particularly influential in machine learning. Such as robotics, transportation, finance, health and bioinformatics, e-commerce , e-games, big online data gathering and internet-of-things. For example, machine e-learning is based in bioinformatics and robots that can learn new skills for better caregiving in healthcare. What is machine e-learning? Machines can e-learn from e-data gathering, coming up generalizations and making decisions to act in certain ways from internet.

There are important applications , such as e-machine perception, electronic online natural language learning processing, online search engines, online bioinformatics, online brain –computer interface, online game playing, online robot locomotion, online advertising, online computations finances, online health monitoring, online DNA classification and decision making, online in chemistry –cheminformatics . So, online machine learning can positively impact productivity and it can enhance information and analytical system from (AI) online channel.

What is robotics? Robotics is one of the most strongly influenced fields in (AI). For example, heavy manufacturing industries, robots and used and man power is replaced for effectiveness, precision, and accuracy, especially in respective or dangerous tasks, including welding, assembling , picking and placing .

So, robots can acquire new skills or adapt the changing dynamic environment. Also, artificial intelligence can be applied in developing transportation. For example, automated vehicles, driver assistance systems , safety systems, collision avoidance systems and public transportation. Moreover, (AI) technology has proven to produce some of the best tools to predict stock market fluctuations from internet data gathering method. It's predictions are based on ever-evolving predictions algorithms and systems learn new models and make connections between historical data and new data to measure stock market trading more accurate from internet data gathering channel.

In health field, especially in health data processing , analysis, decision making support and medical diagnosis. So, online data can show which patients will need what treatment and what alternative drugs could be used more accurate from (AI) online data gathering method. Bioinformatics is an interdisciplinary field combining statistics, (AI) online technology can help in discovering data patterns and modeling through the application of machine learning, artificial neural networks and genetic algorithms. For example, further (AI) technology development of human genome project of online data sequences.

Online shopping can be facilitated by virtual assistants developed through (AI) technology and these assistants can offer the best advice. (AI) online purchase coming after every product image recommendations and personalization bring important revenue to shopping online sites, like Amazon . Smart computer graphics and games, artificial intelligence is useful in smarter computer, graphics, scene modeling , scene rendering processes in order to create, for example, effective human –robot interactions , online machine learning, online strategic games techniques etc. online computer related (AI) software.

So, online big data analysis and big data does have a critical need in the world of online intelligence machines and software in our future. In other words, (AI) offers online technology to enable online big data analysis to provide industrial organizations with valuable information for effective decision making in short time. For example, what IBM's Watson achieved: this machine used 200 million of structured and unstructured content with a special technology of hypothesis generation, massive evidence gathering, analysis and scoring from internet channel.

Finally, (AI) online technology another related internet invention (internet of things) (IOT) is the network of machines or objects connected through internet. These connected objects can sense their internal and external environment, communicate with each other, can send critical data and finally can make decisions to act or correct their environment from (AI) online technology. For example, factories can monitor and automatically change production processes, hospitals can monitor and regulate the health conditions of their patients , schools can collect data from facilities and cars can send data to car makers from (AI) online technology.
Partner predicts that (IOT) market will create about trillion amount value by 2020 year. Although machines collect big data from their environment, whether which gain an insight or learn from these online data largely depends on the (AI) online machine learning principals and (AI) online technology. In 2013, Mckinsey estimated that disruptive technologies closely related with potential economic impact in 2025 year between $7.1 to $13.1 trillion amount (automation of knowledge work, advanced robotics, autonomous or near-autonomous vehicles).

What is the relationship between
(AI) and global digital economy development ?

● Could work activities in China be automated
making in the nation with the world's largest automation potential?

Can (AI) technology influence China economy? Could China workers be affected and jobs made up of routine work activities and predictable? Will programmable tasks be particularly impact to China employment market ? When impact on labor market is likely to be gradual at the aggregate level, it can be sudden and dramatic at the level of specific work activities, rending some job obsolete fairly. Overall (AI) technology will raise digital skills when reducing demand for medium incomer inequality for China workers. It seems (AI) technology's effect on productivity could be crucial to China's future economic growth as the population ages are increasing.
In China, some biggest technological companies driving significant investments in research and development. Moreover, China is one of the leading global (AI) technology development county. However, China will need to focus on building its innovation capacity. For example, United States and United Kingdom are currently producing more influential (AI) technological research. However, if China planed to achieve (AI) technology success, it's traditional industries will need to develop technical know-how –to and overcoming implementation costs prepare to develop (AI) . When (AI) technology is introduced into China society, China government needs to raise concerning ethical, legal, technological security etc. business questions. Also, surrounding issues include privacy, discrimination, legal liability and regulation. It aims to encourage overseas investors to choose to invest (AI) technological industry to raise GDP growth and manufacturing industries income growth for long term in China.
If China encouraged overseas (AI) technology investment in its country. It is possible to influence China employment market to be changed. Because (AI) technology will impact to influence China people daily life. Due to (AI) technology is introduced to China society, many rich people will prefer to spend to buy any high (AI) technological products for entertainment or learning or machine man driving etc. daily necessity activities. Then

it will raise GDP growth and will raise (AI) manufacturers or related-(AI) technological manufacturers profit. It is beneficial to China because it can become one high knowledgeable and (AI) technological economical society.
But it will bring bad influences to raise unemployment chance for the low skillful labor. In labor economy aspect influence , how (AI) technology can influence China low skillful labor unemployment ratio raising. The raising low skill labor unemployment reason is because China low skillful human labors are argued or are replaced by (AI) technology creating new challenges to introduce to influence China society of simply human manufacturing job nature to be changed to be high (AI) technology manufacturing job nature in any China factories. Moreover, when (AI) technology introduction to China, it will cause other related social challenges in China. The varied (AI) related challenges, including the difficulty of creating safe and reliable hardware for sensing and affecting (transportation and education), the challenges of gaining public trust, a low resource comities and public safety and security, the challenges of overcoming fears or marginalizing humans in China employment and workplace and the risk of diminishing interpersonal trust because the low skillful labors won't believe any China employers will give chance to employ them , due to (AI) technology will replace their skills and man manufacturing of productivity is much less to compare to (AI) technology manufacturing method.

- How does (AI) technology influence

the future of employment change?
Are future nature of jobs changed to computerization from (AI) technology? Where are the probability of computing occupations from (AI) technology influence? What is expected impacts of future computing on labor market from (AI) technology influence? John Maynard Keynes's frequently cited prediction of widespread technological unemployment " du to our discovery of means of economic the use of labor outrunning the pace of which we can find new used of labor" (Keynes, 1933, p.3).
In the future, (AI) technology will impact some nature of occupations to change computing. This chance will also influence some countries' economic change. For example, some factory human labors hand routine manufacturing tasks will be changed to computerization of routine manufacturing tasks by (AI) technological machine men hand manufacturing method. it will cause a structured shift in the labor market, with workers reallocating their labor supply from middle-income manufacturing to low-income service occupations.
Arguably, this is because the manual tasks of service occupations are less computerization, as who require a higher degree of flexibility and physical adaptability. So, (AI) technology will influence the human hand labor skillful occupation nature of task cheaper , such as vehicle manufacturing , ship manufacturing, computer manufacturing, steel manufacturing, television, radio etc. home electronic products of heavy machine industry change. Due to (AI) technology machine man will be proper to be used to manufacturing these electronic products when the (AI) technology innovation can develop to the mature stage. Then, any countries manufacturers will choose to use (AI) technology machine man, instead of human hand production.
Supposing the future prices of computing are fallen, seriously, problem solving skills are becoming relatively productive, explaining the substantial employment growth in manufacturing occupations, involving cognitive tasks

where skilled labor has a comparative advantage, as well as the increase education needs for (AI) technology computing of machine man subject study.

Prediction of education needs for (AI) technology student numbers will increase, due to manufacturing industry needs many (AI) technology students in future employment market. Another (AI) technology influence if the future (AI) technological innovation, e.g. machine man manufacturing or machine man service industries will both increase demand, then with more sophistic software technologies will be disrupted labor markets by marketing workers redundant.

For publishing industry, what is striking about the case in paper book publishing industry will be unpopular? Due to the electronic book publishing industry will be popular, e.g. Amazon publish . (AI) technology can influence paper book manufacturing method which is replaced by machine man electronic book manufacturing method as well as it will cause the computerization is no longer confined to routine manufacturing tasks. Due to (AI) machine man manufacturing technology will be proper to be used to manufacture any products in short time efficiently and effectively , e.g. electronic book products. In the future, if it is fact to occur this case, such as (AI) technological machine man manufacturing method will be adopted (applied) to manufacture electronic books or any products in possible. (AI) technology will cause many manufacturing workers are unemployed. It is beneficial to employers, who can reduce to spend much wages expenditure to employ manufacturing workers, but it will cause many manufacturing workers loss jobs and reduce income to support whose families lives. It will cause social challenges, e.g. increasing stealing crimes if the manufacturing workers had not other skills to find other jobs to do easily. So, manufacturers need to concern over technological unemployment which will be hardly future phenomenon if who decided to dismiss all manufacturing workers, due to (AI) technology machine men replace to them.

If (AI) technology can be innovated to produce any kinds of machine man to serve any service or manufacturing industries successfully. Then, it will bring these questions: Can future that workers be influenced to be automation employment and productivity by (AI) technology influence? Does it impact to influence the (AI) technology countries' productivity and growth and natural resources development and labor markets and evolution of global financial markets and economic impact of technology and innovation and urbanization etc. issues? How will automation transform the workplace? What will be the implication for employment? What is likely to be its impact both on productivity in the global economy and on employment?

In fact, automatic of activities can enable businesses to improve performance by reducing errors chance and improving quality and speed, and same cases achieving outcomes that go beyond human capabilities. Some economists indicate (AI) technology would give a needed boost to economic growth and prosperity have of the working age population in many countries. Based on the scenario modeling, they estimate automation could raise productivity growth globally by 0.8 to 1.4 % annually. They also indicated that almost half the activities people are almost $1.6 trillion in wages to do in the global economy have the potential to be automated adapting current demonstrates technology, according to their analysis of more than 2,000 work activities across 800 occupations. When less than 5% of all occupations can be automated entirely using demonstrated technology, about 60% of all occupations have at least 30% of worker made activities, that would be automated. More occupation will change to be automated. They also indicated for business performance benefits of automation are relatively clear, but the issues are more complicated by policy making to attract foreign investors. Beyond technical feasibility, the cost of technology, competition labor will include skills and supply and demand dynamics, performance benefits and beyond labor cost savings and social and regulatory acceptance will affect the automation. Their predictions suggest that half of today work activities could be automated by 2055 year, but this could happen 10 to 20 years earlier or latter depending on the various factors in addition to their wider economic condition.

Some scientists suggest (AI) technology is finally starting to deliver real-life business benefits. Computer power is growing significantly , algorithms are becoming more sophisticated and perhaps most important of all, the world is generating vast quantities of the fuel that powers (AI) technology data billions of gigabytes of it every day. Also, online firms are digital natives, such as Google online search service company is investing on (AI) technology. For new though most of the news if coming from the suppliers of (AI) technologies. And many new users are only in the experimental phase. Few products are on the market or are likely to arrive these soon to drive immediate and widespread adoption. As a result, analysts believe (AI) technology's potential will give true economic benefit in the future. (AI) industry will introduce to suppliers and users to raise economic potential of (AI) technology.

In the future, (AI) technology systems can solve business problems. Some scientists categorized those into five technology systems that are key areas of (AI) technology development: robotics and autonomous vehicles, computer vision language virtual agents and machine learning , which is based on algorithms that learn from data without replying on rules-based programming in order to draw conclusions or direct an action.

Such as computer vision and language includes natural language processing, analytics, speech recognition technology, some are about learning from information, such as about machine learning and others are related to acting on information, such as robotics, autonomous vehicles and virtual agents, which are computer programs that can converse with humans. Machine learning and a subfield called deep learning are artificial intelligence applications.

● Can artificial intelligence impact
global economy growth?

Artificial intelligence (AI) is a term first defined in 1956 year. It is a branch of computer science that aims to create intelligent machines that work and react like humans. In contrast today, 60 years later, (AI) is characterized by a number of applications, including computers playing games against humans and understanding human languages, virtual personal assistants, and robotics which involve computers seeing , hearing and reacting to sensory stimuli. In the future, technologists predict for (AI) technology ranging from (AI) being used as a tool to aid relatively simple processes for robots with human like mental capabilities, who expect (AI) technology can emulate human performance by learning, coming to mind its own conclusions, understanding complex content, engaging in dialog with people, enhancing human cognitive performance or replacing humans in executing both routine and non-routine tasks. In existing industry, (AI) technology is used , such as targeted advertising and virtual used personal assistant as well as the (AI) technology that my exist in the future, such as robots with human vehicle processing capabilities.

The range of (AI) technology's progress in the future will determine the economic impact future of (AI) technology on the global economy with more limited advances and applications (i.e. weak (AI) only) corresponding to more limited economic impacts and more substantial progress, i.e. strong (AI) technology is corresponding to more significant economic impact.

(AI) technology learning that automates analytical model, including predicting cause-and-effect relationship from biological data, identifying new drugs, self-driving cars and protecting against fraud etc. functions. Also (AI) learning can improve natural language processing that allows computers to continue to better analyze, understand and generate language to interface with human using the natural human language, virtual personal assistant, helps users by providing scheduling appointment, reminds organizing personal finance and finding providers of various services, machine vision allows (AI) machine man to identify object, scenes and activities in detect pedestrians and bicyclists.

We expect the economic effects of (AI) technology to include both direct GDP growth from sectors that develop or manufacture (AI) technology and indirect GDP growth through increased productivity in existing sectors that employ some from of (AI) technology. If (AI) producing sectors could grow, then it could lead to increase revenues and employment of (AI) technological professionals within these existing firms as well as the potential creation of entirely new economic activities to any countries' societies productivity improvement in existing sectors could be realized through faster and move efficient processes and decision making as well as increased (AI) technological knowledge and access to information available in societies easily.

In the future, if (AI) technology is an increasingly critical component of more products, it will become an integral part of necessary products of many people's lives. The extent of (AI)'s economy effort is also likely to vary from region to region, thought variation may be more dependent on the predominate economic activity of a region and the (AI) ability can influence economic activity, rather then the economic or developmental status of the regions. (AI) technology can move accessibility and can use source development to do international business between one country and another country.

So (AI) technology has the potential to give benefits to different income chooses and to bring significant gains to both developed and developing countries. For agricultural technology, (AI) has the potential to optimize food production around the world by analyzing agricultural regions and identifying what is necessary to improve crop yield. In total, (AI) technology gives greater economic impact to any countries agricultural regions if which implemented (AI) technology to grow crop , fruit etc. food production in the farms.

Investment in (AI) technology is such as capital investment to any countries' public or private enterprises. So, it will have large economic impact to the future . If the (AI) technology is reasonable invested to the different needs aspect by the public or private enterprises in the country. Then, it will have good economic impact to the country in the future. However, when (AI) technology is likely to affect both the productivity and employment components of economic growth in many sectors. Significant public debate has focused on projections of (AI)'s effect on the labor force. However, for instance, some researchers have argued that the rise of (AI) technology and automation will led to significant unemployment as capital is substituted for the low skillful labor. So, they point to the concern that the increasing sophistication of (AI) technology may balance skilled and semi-skilled workers and the reduce the size of the middle class. However, this is not a new argument, due to (AI) technology negatively affecting the labor force and leading to mass unemployment. Because the (AI) technology is the substitution of machinery for human labor. Although, employment in certain industries, has been reduced in the past due to technological advancement. For long term, the labor market has adapted to the introduction of new technology, giving rise to new jobs in new areas. (AI) technology may also be accomplished without a reduction to total employment in the long-term to some Asia countries, such as Hong Kong and Japan. Because Hong Kong and Japan many low skilled labor, e.g. security, cleaner who complaint that employers need them to work long time hours. (abnormal working hours) e.g. one day 12 to 15 working hour per day. Hence, if (AI) machine means invention technology success. Security or cleaning job can be worked from (AI) machine man in some hours every day in order to reduce the long time working hours cleaners or security workers, e.g. one (AI) machine man works 4 hours for cleaning or security job, one day as well as another cleaner or security labor only needs to work 8 hours one day. So total security or cleaning employers can employ 12 hours machine cleaners or security workers and human cleaners or security workers in one day. For long term benefit, Hong Kong or Japan every security or cleaning worker does not need to work 12 hours minimum working hours one day. They won't feel tried and bore and without private with whose families, so who will accept to do these cleaning or security jobs, even they can raise work efficient and performance when who feel happy and health.

So, (AI) technology of machine man invention can raise low skillful labor efficiency and it can help them to avoid abnormal working hours demand in some busy work life countries, such as Hong Kong and Japan. Before, one Japan female labor feel unhappy to work, due to who often needs to work abnormal working hours for her employer and who has less sleeping and without any private time to enjoy her life with her families every day. So this abnormal working hours factor causes her to do commit suicide behavior, then she is die unlucky. So (AI) technology of machine man invention ought avoid abnormal working hours demand for employer in any countries in the future.

The most important occurrence to any employers, some researchers had attempted to do one experiment to find that private research and development , venture capital and public research and development investment all have strong net effect or economic growth with venture capital funding further having the strongest such effect from (AI) technology. The researchers hypothesize the venture capital investment contributes to economic growth through (AI) technology innovation and by the capacity of an economy to use existing (AI) technology knowledge to increase productivity. They predict the impacts of venture capital, business-research and development and public research and development can raise multi factor productivity from (AI) technology introduction.

Can (AI) technology influence the economic development to developing countries? The developing regions of the world contain most of natural resources. If one day, (AI) technology has invent one kind of machine man which can assist any gas or oil workers to seek any new oil/gas natural resource locations easily. I believe that (AI) technology can help these natural resource exploitation countries will gain economic benefit more easily. So, (AI) driven technology can be used to change to create any new opportunities to address poor management or resources and improve human well being, such as Africa Latin America and India can use (AI) technology machine man to seek any oil/gas natural resource countries exploitation activities to attempt to gain much economic benefits.

● Why will (AI) technology grow economic development ?

Nowadays, increases in capital and labor are no longer driving the levels of economic growth, such as (AI) technology. The ability of increase in capital investment and in labor of traditional drivers of production, have no longer to be enjoyed in most developed economies ,e.g. developed country, US, UK . However, artificial intelligence has the potential to overcome the physical limitation of capital and labor to avoid missing out on this opportunity. So, policy makers and business leaders must prepare for and work toward a future with artificial intelligence. They must do with the idea that (AI) is another simply method to enhance productivity method . Rather they must see (AI) as the tool that can transform thinking about how growth is created.

Economists have always thought of new technologies are as driving growth their ability to enhancing. It can replace labor and capital factor of production. So, it brings this question: What is the factor of production (AI) technology characteristics. They key factor is to see (AI) technology as a capital-labor .

(AI) can replicate labor activities at much greater scale and speed, and to even perform some tasks began the capabilities of human. For example, by using virtual assistants , 1000 legal documents can be reviewed in a matter of days instead of taking three people six moths to complete. Some (AI) technology may be one kind of factor of production in the future. For another example, people will work in workplace digitalization environment. So, in the future, working environment and information management are automated. Such as Konica camera sale company will use workplace digitalization. So , (AI) technology can provide workplace digitalization in order to raise productivity efficiency. (AI) technology will be one kind of production which is replaced by workplace digitalization and it will grow any organization productivity efficiently. Then, (AI) technology will assist overall social economy growth , due to productivity is raised and products can be produced in short time to prepare to sell in consumption market. So, time will be shortened to increase GDP growth fast for the development of (AI) technology countries.

● How can (AI) technology impact to global economic and social and psychological changes?

What will be the development of (AI) technology and predictions concerning the future evolution? The computers and robots will develop conscious, intelligent and minds into humans, enhancing psychological and behavioral abilities and allowing for direct communication with (AI) minds. (AI) technology will be impacted human life by (AI) technology information communicative and environmental influence. A " world brain" and " world mind", this psychological system will be enhanced and enriched the capacities of both individual and collective cognition by (AI) technology of service industries.

(AI) technology with influence these human needs of service industries changes, such as , biological science, finance, entertainment, business, biological science, transportation, communication military etc. The personal computer evolution, the internet and the world wide web which exploded on the scene, linking business, homes, schools, social organizations which were a completely unpredicted phenomenon to influence human life. Kurzweil (1999) predicts that by 2029 year, most human communication will be with machines. According to Person, by 2100 year, there will be human machine convergence.

How can (AI) technology influence environmental protection to make benefits to farming economic growth? (AI) technology can be applied to predict how to solve environmental pollution challenge to avoid to damage any crop or vegetable or rice or fruit etc. food growth. Because environmental experts can gather global environmental pollution data from an environmental database to build a perform a systematic analysis from (AI) technology. The first step is this broad analysis can include understanding, statistical and data gathering techniques to obtain the relevant data, the correlation among the variables involved, and a list of possible models. The next step is to select a set of methods and models that cover all kinds of knowledge and functionalities needed for the decision making process. Once the models are selected, they must be fully implemented by means of machine learning , data mining, statistical or numerical technique. After that, those models must be integrated to build the whole EDSS. The EDSS must be tested to check its performance, accuracy, usefulness and reliability, both from the user's and (AI) technology/computer scientist's point of view. If these is any wrong feature in any development stage, such as model's integration, models' implementation, selection of models, database, problem analysis etc. the developers must come back in the update th required components. When the evaluation phase is all right, the EDSS is ready to be applied to the environment. The great contribution of artificial intelligence to EDSS the integration of several methods complementing the classical statistical models/simulation , statistical analysis, linear models, etc. and numerical models (control algorithms, optimization techniques etc.) .

This cooperation makes the resulting systems more reliable and powerful in coping with real world environment systems. Date interpretation has been a principal area of research in (AI) technology since the very beginning. The most demanding problem in the environmental assessment context. Knowledge representation permits the definition of the different types of data that the existing methods adapt to the process. There is also a lot of work to clean, repair and transform the huge available quantities of raw data. Apart from this, the availability of meta-information or background knowledge is required to guide the process. Data mining is multi-disciplinary: It covers expert systems, data based technology, statistics, data visualization and unsupervised machine learning. These techniques operate at the level of data and background information, where numerous and often incompatible new commensurate pieces of information from disparate sources have to be brought together (K, Fedra, 1994). So, it seems that in the future, (AI) technology with the increasing maturity in particular those related to knowledge and engineering, new dimensions can be assisted to users in environmental decision making are available. For example, many environmental systems are characterized both by incomplete models and by limited data. Hence, in the future, (AI) technology will be applied to predict climate change to reduce crop or fruit etc. food agriculture challenge by climate change bad influence.

● Will (AI) technology influence digital economy change to manufacturing industry ?

To understand how the manufacturing business must adapt to prosper in the technology, we need to understand how (AI) technology will change us to shape our daily habits to satisfy our expectation of products to how we shop and even the immediate of the entire process. For example, taxi services are in the crosshairs as on demand transportation services like, available of the touch of a smart phone button expand. In fact, Yellow lab, US country , san Francisco city's largest taxi company is filing for bankruptcy as the industry starts to change faster than almost anyone expected. However, at this point, its more than an app that is changing, some our taxi passengers renting taxi transportation to catch consumption behavior.

(AI) technology will influence digital economy for taxi passenger's individual customer experience, offering a growing renting taxi to catch of service and feedback opportunities when any one taxi passenger who chooses to use mobile phone app online tool to prepaid to rent any taxi more easily.

Also in the long term, (AI) technology can influence vehicles drive themselves of behavior. Already, companies like Google and GM are working on projects to bring fleets of autonomous vehicles to cities at the path of a button. Moreover, this on-demand service model is beginning to appear across a much broader range of markets. For example , Amazon company is investing in its own fleet of trucks, planes and even drone at the same time as it pushes for same-day delivery of products. As some point, vehicles will be autonomous too. So, it seems that (AI) technique will influence any transportations choose to use digital autonomous driving technology in the future . For Amazon company case, it is not stopping of logistics. It is also aiming to automatically manage the supply of consumer home products with its recently launched Amazon replenishment service, Dash. Dash is a digital service that enables that connected derive to automatically order physical products from Amazon when supplies are running low. So, it seems (AI) technology will be applied to logistic function by digital technology method introduction in the future.

Hence autonomous vehicles will optimize industry supply chains and logistics operations through increased efficiency and flexibility. In fact, fully automated and lean supply chains will keep reduce load sizes and inventory by leveraging smart distribution technologies and smaller autonomous vehicles by machine man assistance. If Amazon continues to grow market share for online sales by reducing effort required by the consumer to place an order, when also contributing the almost immediate delivery of products to the doorstep. So, it will further fuel the trend toward on-demand derive. As Amazon company fuels the on-demand economy, consumers will expect immediacy in more parts of the digital economy. On top of speed, consumers increasing expect more personalization options.

So, (AI) technology will influence digital manufacturing, such as Amazon publishing to monitor every aspect of every process in real -time and communicating to self-optimized deep learning robotics, new methods of high volume and high customization will become possible. Then, as products merge into product platforms and even services, manufacturers have the opportunity to provide components and platforms used by smaller players. So, (AI) technology will influence manufacturing industry to choose automated SMI lines, robots installed, automation engineers.

Another future (AI) technology development can be applied to space science aspect, such as Automation engineering space in manufacturing process to achieve digital manufacturing benefits to any businesses in the future. Such as reducing cost, shortening manufacturing time, raising efficiency, shortening delivery products to client individual time. How can artificial intelligence give the need and advanced fast and evaluation methods benefits for space exploration? When US NASA (space exploration organization) achieves any space exploration missions, it will answer this question:

When is it useful to have a machine use (AI) technology to achieve a decision? After all, after millions of years of space exploration and rough 10,000 years of civilization, humans are usually quite good at making decisions in complex uncertain environments. Through, Johns Hoplains University's Applied Physical Lab. Research in (AI) technology enabled systems, which has identified three general use cases for (AI) technology to explore space mission:

First, for some tasks (AI) technology is more cost effectiveness than human. Second, (AI) technology is better suited than humans at solving some, but not all problems. Third, (AI) technology allows NASA organization's space exploration mission to develop machines that ate capable of responding faster than when a human is in the decision loop (D. Scheidt, 2012, A. Castano et. al. 2008).

So, the use of (AI) technology to enable science by observing the pace of rapidly evolving phenomena was demonstrated. It is more effectively coordinating and (AI) technology utilizing to earn economic benefits to use for space exploration mission.

However, (AI) technology also have current risk for space exploration. Today (AI) technology is immature and requires further development to reach its potential. For instance, the (AI) technology algorithms that detected the dust derive could not have identified whether the Martain weather represented a threat to the cover. Also it can not yet use instrument input to determine what, where and how to autonomously make the next space science measurement. An equally important factor limiting (AI)'s deployment is that lacks the methodology and technology to effectively test (AI) technology. So, the challenge will testing (AI) enabled system is how (AI) performance can be measured. It would be NASA organization's difficulty to find (AI) technology to develop to carry on researching any space exploration missions in the future. However, (AI) technology will be a good economic benefit choice for space exploration mission in the future.

2.1 What is artificial intelligence potential
benefits and ethical considerations?

The ability of (AI) technology systems to transform vast amounts of complex information into insight has the potential to help solve manufacturing or service challenges for human needs. However, to reap the societal benefits of (AI) systems, humans will need to trust then and make sure that which follow the same ethical principles, moral values, professional codes and social norms that we humans would follow in the same scenario, research and educational efforts as well as carefully designed regulation in order to achieve the most effort of economic benefits goals. For example, international business machines corporation (IBM) is actively engaged both competitors , in global discussions about how to make (AI) ethical and as beneficial as possible for people as social economic benefits. (AI) is usually defined as the " capability of a computer program to perform tasks or reasoning processes " that human usually associate to intelligence in a human being. Often, it has to do with the ability to make a good decision, even when there is uncertainty, too much information to handle. As an example, play chess or complex card games of entertainment activities is believed to need some form of intelligence in a human being, as well as choosing the best medical facilities in a difficult medical case, or creating something new, such as mathematical theorem or even some form of act, or even driving automatic machine man (self driving vehicle) replacing human driving in the middle of a crowded city.

(AI) needs depends on what we consider being intelligence in the behavior of a human being act a certain point in time. If human belief about human intelligence changes and we don't believe any longer that a certain task requires intelligence, then a computer program performing that task is no longer part of (AI), it becomes just another boring computer program. So, it means that (AI) technology will replace some old computer programs, if human can invent new generation of (AI) software for any functions or activities to satisfy human needs.

As IBM, it argues intelligence. This means that we aim to build systems that enhance and scale human expertise and skills rather than replacing them. We therefore focus on practical applications of (AI) capabilities that assist people in performing well-defined tasks of needs by exploiting and wide range of (AI)-based services. We also use the term " cognitive computing" it is mean a comprehensive net of capabilities based on technology. It comprises the fields of machine learning, reasoning and decision technologies, language, speech and vision recognition and processing technologies, high performance and high efficient functions for any industries or individual consumers needs. For example, robotics, which are usually very good at doing what which are supposed to in any environment, much have public shopping center, factory etc. places which need simply services from the robot (machine man), such as cleans the floor of our houses to the robot that can work together with humans in production chains, passing through the warehouse, robots can take care of the tasks of an entire warehouse and the companion robots like Nao, Pepper, Aibo and Giraff, who can entertain use, talk to use and help elderly people to stay connected to their friends, relatives and doctors.

Google company is building automatic machine (self-driving cars) and has acquired more than 10 robotics companies. Facebook had opened whole new research facility only on (AI) research. Apply computer has developed Siri. Microsoft computer company has built a similar personalized assistant. Google has Deep mind, a UK company whose long term aim is to build general (AI) and has already great potential to win game to the world champion and IBM is investing a huge amount of resources in applying its Watson cognitive computing system to the medical domains to finance and to personalized education. In Europe, IBM is establishing new centers in Munich and Milan focused in the application of cognitive computer capabilities to the internet of things and healthcare respectively.

For example, automatic machine man (self-driving cars) are all about (AI), which used to be able to see what happens in the street (signals ,lanes, other cars, pedestrians, traffic lights, which need to able predict what other cars and pedestrians will do, and who need to be able to cope with unforeseen situations. Since, most car accidents are due to human fault, it is estimated that the adoption of self-driving cars will save about half of the lives that are usually last in car accidents.

IBM Watson company has to understand spoken language, make sense of massive amount to text , respond correctly to questions in many categories, as well as assess its own confidence in responding to such questions. In the future, (AI) technology can own question/answering capabilities that would be very useful, for example, in assisting a doctor when trying to some to the correct diagnosis for a patient and to propose the best therapy .

Intelligent machines can also rely on huge amounts of data to be used to learn how to make better decisions. This data comes from all of us over the years Facebook users have uploaded more than 250 billion pictures and every day who upload about 350 million more. Every second, we submit 40,000 google search queries. So, (AI) technology will be connected through the web from appliances to traffic lights from cars to watches. Other tasks that are very easy for humans are physical and manipulation tasks, such as walking , running, picking up an object to make its shape and location, restricted environment. But (AI) machine man technology still not able to have the general physical and manipulation capabilities even of a 6 year old.

So, it brings this question: Why do (AI) scientists need to concern ethics? Because (AI) technology is complex, information into insight has the potential to reveal long held secrets and help solve some of the world's most difficult problems. (AI) systems can potentially be used to help discover insights to treat disease, predict the whether, and manage the global economy. So, ethic issues is important to and (AI) scientists . If any one new (AI) technology research investigation could success, it will be a secret to and the (AI) scientists can not permit to their loyalty to any competitors to damage the fair (AI) technology products trading market. The country (countries) (AI) technology scientists need to concern ethic issues, who need to keep secrets for their countries economic or/and social benefits. This is moral issues to any countries/country loyalty is whose countries intangible assets. They can not sell (AI) loyalty to any their countries to assist whose economic benefits immorally.

How can (AI) technology influence to global
health care economy development?

According to (AI) lecturer analysis, when combined key clinical health (AI) application can potentially create $150 billion in annual savings for the US healthcare economy by 2026 year. (AI) technology is re-winning modern conception of healthcare delivery. It enables machines to sense, comprehend, act and learn. So which can perform administrative and clinical healthcare functions (Accenture, 2017).

It will help health care service organizations to reduce health care cost, will improve and raise service quality and access. So, (AI) health market size will be predicted growth. (AI) applications in health care include robot-assisted surgery, virtual nursing assistant, administrative workflow assistant, fraud detection, error reduction connected machines, clinical trial participant identifier, preliminary diagnosis, automated image diagnosis and cybersecurity.

What kind of benefits (AI) technology can contribute to healthcare service? (AI) technology can deliver what many health care organizations need, such as financial and operational of labor costs, digital expectations from patient consumers how to use (AI) technology to solve interoperability challenges in any healthcare organizations. Also

(AI) technology can be applied to wellness an d lifestyle management, diagnostics, delivers financially but also way of organizational and workflow improvement. So, (AI) technology will be continue to become most prevalent and adoption to healthcare organizations , which must need to enhance structure to be position to take full advantages of new (AI) technological capabilities. (AI) technology can change the nature of work and employment is rapidly changing to make the best use of both humans and (AI) talent in healthcare industry in the future. For example, (AI) technology offers a way to fill in gaps and the rising labor shortage in healthcare. According to Accenture analysis, the physicians shortage is increasing. However, (AI) technology will manufacture healthcare machine men to replace physicians in future one day(2017). Hence, (AI) technology will be invented to raise health care service staffs work efficiency and performance in any hospitals or clinics in the future.

In conclusion, (AI) technology will raise efficiency for any service or manufacturing industries in the future, although, it is possible that it will also rise low skillful workers unemployment numbers. But, the most important influence to human technological innovation will be risen and it will influence human life will be changed to be better, e.g. self drive cars, health care physician machine men, machine man cleaners etc. intelligent machine men will be manufactured to serve for our daily life. Furthermore, (AI) technological products will influence countries trading, some low technological development countries manufacturing businessmen can choose to buy any (AI) products to raise whose productivity and efficiency and reducing cost to achieve economic cost saving result. Also, GDP of trading growth income will increase to the (AI) products sale countries. Hence, it will be beneficial to economic development to both developed and developing countries both in the future as well as (AI) scientists time and money spending will be valued to continue to invest (AI) technology development for human life and economy benefits for long term.

In conclusion (AI) technology will raise macro economy growth and it can create many (AI) jobs , but it also raise the low level technological worker unemployment change. In the future, (AI) technology can be applied to digital technology to attempt to invent any new undiscovered (AI) and digital technology. So, it needs any scientists to continue to research how digital and (AI) technology can be mixed to satisfy human's future undiscovered needs.

2.2Artificial intelligence education development

or the future of defense choice

Nowadays, artificial intelligence (AI) is widely knowledge to be one kind of the dramatic technology. However, it is expected to continue, to have a disruptive impact on human's private and public life, so defense and security will be no exception. But how exactly will these be affected ? How will (AI) defense and security is incremental in nature?

To research why artificial intelligence (AI) has possible to be used to cause autonomous weapons by human. We need to understand these three aspects of relationship. They include cybersecurity and artificial intelligence and machine learning and autonomous weapon systems relationship between of them.

Firstly, we need to know what is the mean of artificial intelligence and cyber defense/offense? It means defense of critical networks: real time, pattern finding, anomaly seeking, it must utilize machine (AI) learning algorithms to efficiently, and instantaneously respond to potential network threats as well as it means human on or out of the loop. On the loop : it means anomaly detection: human notified, IT analysis, response. Out of the loop: it means anomaly detection: (AI) decides best method of response: quarantine, honey pot monitoring, hack-back. Thus, it is possible that (AI) can be used , such as autonomous cyber weapon.

What is artificial intelligence and autonomous weapons? Autonomous weapons mean one kind of weapon that can be selected and engaged a target, without intervention by a human operator. Are these machines artificially intelligent? I believe the answer is not, because present weapons systems are not capable of human level reasoning. But, (AI) algorithms are presently employed to process sensor data, monitor system health, take and respond to vocal commands manage data, navigate. This, future autonomous weapons systems will require stronger (AI) to be secure and operationally and cost effective. Moreover, self-aware autonomous cyber systems are crucial.

What is cybersecurity mean? It means the ability to control access to networked systems and the information they contain. It is acted to prevent , detect, recover, react. It is application objects concern people, process, technology and it's application goals are confidentiality, integrity and popular availability. Thus, what is cyber weapon mean? Walware means viruses, Trojans, zero-days, worms ransomware, spyware etc. Does it require a particular objective? E.g. military paramilitary or intelligence. Does it require physical harm? E.g. functional harm or interruption? Mental harm? Is (AI) a technological weapon that it is an object or tool? What about when it is an weapon agent?

In simplicity, (AI) can be one of scientific weapons platform. When one day, it is invented to be applied to control war planes to fly to any countries to attack enemies or it is invented to be seemed to human to replace soldiers to bring guns or any weapons go to other countries to attack. So, it is possible that future any war defense planes, (AI) technological automatic control weapon can be replaced of human soldiers or war plane pilots to control any war defense planes to go to different enemy countries to attack them easily. It is very horror matter to threaten global human's ourselves life in the future , if (AI) automatic control war defense planes or (AI) automatic control machine soldiers were invented successfully.

Hence , when (AI) can be applied to weapons platforms, it structures that launch weapons, i.e. jets, ships, vehicles. (AI) platform and weapon and software architecture components are be done one (AI) technological weapons systems. Thus, human will encounter any (AI) benefits or risks (threats) causes in the same time as soon as possible. If we can predict when (AI) weapon system will be manufactured or invented successfully. Then, we can reduce (AI) weapon systems risks , if we can threaten any (AI) scientists continue to invent any undiscovered (AI) weapons in any time to avoid the future first time (AI) weapon war occurrence in possible.

The (AI) weapon system risk means autonomy: the ability to problem solve technological war , when (AI) weapon system is manufactured successfully, the power to act, how to damage the (AI) weapon system. The power to chance to stop (AI) weapon system manufacturing processes, ability to create a new goals, how to change the (AI) weapon system inventors' or scientists' minds to avoid to apply (AI) tools to achieve attack goals to change to another positive goal. Due to human can't know a prior what an autonomous (AI) weapon system will do.

Although, human is known what (AI) is , but human is also known when (AI) scientists whose emergent behaviors will do to change to do any negative behaviors from positive behaviors. Whatever (AI) weapon system design we use, there will be cybersecurity, problems arising from computation design/complexity. Due to any one (AI) scientist can manipulate the system to act against itself, or who can utilize traditional " cyber weapons" against the (AI) weapon system, or who can manipulate the system to lie to humans, but also due to complexity, there is no way to know if it is lying or not or bounded rationality : satisficing.

Finally, the most serious (AI) technological invention risks are human is unknown these aspects of (AI) absolutely: They are not simple automatic systems, learning reasoning, communication of " self-aware" systems. Thus, human will face (AI) technological invention risks or threats. We need to find any methods to avoid (AI) weapon system is manufactured successfully to avoid (AI) technological war can occur in future anyone day. Consequently, why (AI) scientists do not choose to invent (AI) machine men own human reading, writing, speaking, judgement, analyizing abilities to develop human's future education industry, but they choose to invent (AI) machine men own human weapon to attack enemy ability.

Hence, (AI) scientists have moral responsibilities to avoid to invent (AI) machine men to own human's attack abilities. I shall indicate future what aspects of (AI) machine men can be applied to different education industry aspects as below:

2.3 Online technology and online book technology influences artificial intelligence mind development

Nowadays, online technological invention bring online book technological development. Also, artificial intelligent technological machine men had been invented to link internet to do any jobs, e.g. children can find any data from artificial intelligent machine men when the artificial intelligent machine man had been installed internet and computer function, then children can find any online books to read from the artificial intelligent machine man. Such as Japan artificial intellgent machine men had installed computer and internet function, the Japan family children can find any online books to read from the artificial intelligent machine man at Japan any families' homes conveniently. Hence, it implies that future one day, artificial intelligent machine has possible to be invented to own human's reading and/or writing abilities.

For example,online book publishing is one kind of popular internet technology. For example, Amazon publish is as a business model with many potential advantages, relative to a physical operation. It held out the potential of lower book inventing and distribution costs and reduced overhead. Consumers could find the books, they were looking for more easily and a variety book topic choices could be offered for sale. It can accept and fulfill orders from almost any domestic location with equal ease. And most purchasers made on its site would be exempt from sales tax. One Amazon strategy hand, it would have to make its returns and redress processes transparent and reliable, and offer other ways for clients to learn, as much about the book possible before buying. Future online book market development trend, such as Amazon, Barnes & Noble etc. online book shops.

Hence, online book store technology can be applied to artificial intelligent technology. Such as artificial intelligent machine men can apply computer technology to learn the abilities of reading and/or writing any books either on paper or on computer. Hence, it is possible that artificial intelligent machine men will have similar human's writing and/or reading books ability when they own human's mind ability. However, it bring this questions: Can artificial intelligent machine men own human's mind abilities? If they own human's mind abilities, is it mean that they can write and/or read any books? Can artificial intelligent machine men own human's mind abilities to create to write any books? Can artificial intelligent machine men own human's mind abilities to read and make any judgements or decisions more accurate than human's judgements or decisions? To answer these questions? I shall indicate that online book reading and writing technology can be applied to artificial intelligent machine men reading and writing technology. Because they are similiar computer mind technological development. So, I believe that future artificial intelligence machine men can be invented to own similar human's reading and writing's mind abilities in future one day.

I believe artificial intelligence and online technological reading abilities are very similiar. Nowadays, computer can be invented to attempt to read and write any books by human. Why can not artificial intelligent machine men replace computer to read and write any books? Artificial intelligent machine men can replace human to attempt to write or/and read books, due to artificial intelligent machine men had invented to own human mind to do some jobs and their mind had been invented to be similiar to human behavioral abilities to do these behaviors, e.g. cooking, driving, playing games, singing songs, speaking, listening, frighting etc. different human's abilities. So, it seems that artificial intelligent will be possible to be invented to own human's mind abilities to do any writing or reading behaviors or functions.

2.4 Prediction of artificial intelligence reading and writing abilities

development

What is future trend of artificial intelligence reading and writing abilities development? To answer this question, we need to know what benefits of artificial intelligent machine men can attribute to human's needs when they can own any human's mind to read or/and write any books.

I shall indicate e-books reading and writing example, if artificial intelligent machine men can be invented to own human's mind to write and/or read e-books on computer. Then, it brings this question: Can artificial intelligent machine men assist human to learn to do judgement to solve any challenges?

I believe that when artificial intelligent machine men can be invented to own human mind to write or/and read any books, then they will own human's mind ability to make judgement to solve any challenges more accurately, even their decisions can be more accurate to compare to human's decisions. So, artificial intelligent machine mens' writing and reading ability is the main factor to cause their mind to do any judgement in order to make any decisions more accurately. Consequently, in future one day, artificial intelligent machine mens' writing and reading ability will be invented to similar human's reading and writing abilities as well as their minds can also be invented to similar human's minds as well as their judgement abilities can be invented to similar to human's judgement abilities to make any decisions more accurate.

2.5The influences when AI is invented to own human's mind and judgement abilities

Finally, I shall discuss what are the influences when AI is invented to own human's mind and judgement abilities in our future job market. The achievement of artificial intelligent (AI) machine men achievement requirement of owning human's mind and judgement abilities which requires extensive manual labor, and by augmenting the calling process with machine learning, the process where speed and accuracy are needed to close to human's mind and judgement abilities. Expert human race callers now have better information at artificial intelligent machine men at their fingertips faster.

Hence, if the above those requirements are achieved to satisfy artificial intelligent machine men ind and judgement abilities demand to close or exceed humans' mind and judgement abilities. Then, I believe that future human's some simple jobs must be replaced by (AI) machine men. Even, human's some professonal jobs, e.g. lawyer, accountant, administator, typing etc. professional skillful jobs, which will be either replaced or will be assisted by (AI) machine men. For example, (AI) machine men learn how to type english or other language words to do typing job ; they can learn how to apply accounting knowledge to record any firm's income and expenditure record of accounting job; they can also learn how to assist architects to design any architectural building drawing plans to do architect jobs; they can learn how to analyze any court evidences to judge any criminal or civil cases and assist lawyers to give legal advices to achieve more reasonable judgement for any legal cases; they can also learn how to assist firm's managers or administrators to manage any organization teams efficiently.

Consequently, when (AI) machine men can be invented to achieve to exceed human's mind and judgement abilities level. Then, I believe that they can do instead of human' simple jobs, which can do even human's more difficult and more judgement requirement of professional skillful jobs. So, (AI) machine men must need to achieve to do any jobs, they are same, even exceed to human professionals' abilities. Then, it will cause a lot of human's jobs to be disappeared or some human's jobs will be replaced by owning judgement and mind abilities of (AI) machine men to do.

Hence, future many human's jobs will be replaced by technological labors. Employers choose to buy (AI) machine men to replace human labors. The reasons include (AI) machine men have none unhappy, angry emotin to influence their low efficiencies and low productivities. Their judgement and mind abilities can exceed human's abilities or do any jobs to compare better performance to human's abilities. Consequently, different occupation labors need to prepare to learn how to co-operate with (AI) machine men to let future employers feel (AI) machine men will be human's assistant to assist human to do jobs efficiently when human and (AI) machine men work together. It aims to avoid future employers feel (AI) machine men's judgement and mind abilities can exceed any low knowledgeable and skilful occupation labors, even high knowledge and skilful occupation labors. It means that (AI) machine men are only labors' assistant if (AI) machine mens' judgement and mind abilities are below under to human labors' judgement and mind abilities.

Consequently, to avoid (AI) machine men can replace human to do any simple or complex jobs to cause any future any occupation labors' competitiors. I recommend that it is right time labors ought prepare to learn different skills. So, every individual labor does not only concentrate on one kind of skill. Because supposing one kind of the occupation labor's job duties are replaced by (AI) machine men. If the employee had owned more than one kind of occupation skill. Then, I believe that who can avoid the unemployment threat more easier than the employee only owned one kind of occupation skill, when (AI) machine men had invented to own human's mind and judgement abilities in future one day. The most important, I believe that (AI) invention will be applied to be teach how to learn human's skills and mind ability. Such as education industy, teacher won't be replaced by (AI), otherwise, (AI) will be teacher's assistant to help them to do education data gather or teaching jobs. So, teachers won't be replaced by (AI), otherwise, teachers will depend on (AI) data gather or teaching job to give them opinions how to solve student's teaching challenges as well as teachers can concentrate on researching education jobs for schools' benefits if (AI) technology can be invented to on human's mind and judgement and reading and writing abilities in the future.

2.6Artificial intelligence and the future of defense or teaching choice

Nowadays, artificial intelligence (AI) is widely knowledge to be one kind of the dramatic technology. However, it is expected to continue, to have a disruptive impact on human's private and public life, so defense and security will be no exception. But how exactly will these be affected ? How will (AI) defense and security is incremental in nature? If (AI) technological machine men are applied to teach students in education aspect, is it better to my next generation learning develpment more than they are applied to war attack aspect.

To research why artificial intelligence (AI) has possible to be used to cause autonomous weapons by human. We need to understand these three aspects of relationship. They include cybersecurity and artificial intelligence and machine learning and autonomous weapon systems relationship between of thcm. Basic on (AI) machine can be invented to learn any new knowledge, so if (AI) machine men are taught how to attack enemy, which will be such as human soldier function. But, if (AI) machine men are taught how to learn university knowledge to teach students. Then, they will be such as human lecturer function. So, when (AI) is invented to own human mind and judgement and learning abilities, then they will be either human's enemy or human's assistant, such as university lecturer's assistant.

Firstly, we need to know what is the mean of artificial intelligence and cyber defense/offense? It means defense of critical networks: real time, pattern finding, anomaly seeking, it must utilize machine (AI) learning algorithms to efficiently, and instantaneously respond to potential network threats as well as it means human on or out of the loop. On the loop : it means anomaly detection: human notified, IT analysis, response. Out of the loop: it means anomaly detection: (AI) decides best method of response: quarantine, honey pot monitoring, hack-back. Thus, it is possible that (AI) can be used , such as autonomous cyber weapon. If (AI) is applied to make the decision best method of response to learning aspect, such as univeristy different subject knowledge. Then, it will be one good technological educational tool to teach university students.

In simplicity, (AI) can be one of scientific weapons platform or one of university teaching tool. When one day, it is invented to be applied to control war planes to fly to any countries to attack enemies or it is invented to be seemed to human to replace soldiers to bring guns or any weapons go to other countries to attack. So, it is possible that future any war defense planes, (AI) technological automatic control weapon can be replaced of human soldiers or war plane pilots to control any war defense planes to go to different enemy countries to attack them easily. It is very horror matter to threaten global human's ourselves life in the future , if (AI) automatic control war defense planes or (AI) automatic control machine soldiers were invented successfully. Otherwise, when one day, (AI) machine lecturer is invented to be applied to learn university different subjects knowledge to replace lecturers to copy lecturer's every prepared lecturer course to speak to let students to listen when they are sitting in university halls as well as the (AI) machine lecturer can make analysis and judgement response to answer every student's enquire immedicately after it had speaking all courses to students to listen in lecturer hall every time. Then, it can let human lecturer does any education job duty, e.g. research education work. So, (AI) machine lecturer will be future human lecturer's assistant in future one day.

Finally, the most serious (AI) technological invention risks are human is unknown these aspects of (AI) absolutely: They are not simple automatic systems, learning reasoning, communication of " self-aware" systems. Thus, human will face (AI) technological invention risks or threats if human invent (AI) machine man to learn how to attack enemy. Otherwise, if human invent (AI) machine man to learn how to teach univerity student. I believe that my future university students can raise learn ability and writing ability and reading ability from (AI) machine lecturer teaching more than human lecturer teaching.

2.7Online technology and online book technology influences artificial intelligence mind development

Nowadays, online technological invention bring online book technological development. Also, artificial intelligent technological machine men had been invented to link internet to do any jobs, e.g. children can find any data from artificial intelligent machine men when the artificial intelligent machine man had been installed internet and computer function, then children can find any online books to read from the artificial intelligent machine man. Such as Japan artificial intellgent machine men had installed computer and internet function, the Japan family children can find any online books to read from the artificial intelligent machine man at Japan any families' homes conveniently. Hence, it implies that future one day, artificial intelligent machine has possible to be invented to own human's reading and/or writing abilities.

For example,online book publishing is one kind of popular internet technology. For example, Amazon publish is as a business model with many potential advantages, relative to a physical operation. It held out the potential of lower book inventing and distribution costs and reduced overhead. Consumers could find the books, they were looking for more easily and a variety book topic choices could be offered for sale. It can accept and fulfill orders from almost any domestic location with equal ease. And most purchasers made on its site would be exempt from sales tax. One Amazon strategy hand, it would have to make its returns and redress processes transparent and reliable, and offer other ways for clients to learn, as much about the book possible before buying. Future online book market development trend, such as Amazon, Barnes & Noble etc. online book shops.

Hence, online book store technology can be applied to artificial intelligent technology. Such as artificial intelligent machine men can apply computer technology to learn the abilities of reading and/or writing any books either on paper or on computer. Hence, it is possible that artificial intelligent machine men will have similar human's writing and/or reading books ability when they own human's mind ability. However, it bring this questions: Can artificial intelligent machine men own human's mind abilities? If they own human's mind abilities, is it mean that they can write and/or read any books? Can artificial intelligent machine men own human's mind abilities to create to write any books? Can artificial intelligent machine men own human's mind abilities to read and make any judgements or decisions more accurate than human's judgements or decisions? To answer these questions? I shall indicate that online book reading and writing technology can be applied to artificial intelligent machine men reading and writing technology. Because they are similiar computer mind technological development. So, I believe that future artificial intelligence machine men can be invented to own similar human's reading and writing's mind abilities in future one day.

I believe artificial intelligence and online technological reading abilities are very similiar. Nowadays, computer can be invented to attempt to read and write any books by human. Why can not artificial intelligent machine men replace computer to read and write any books? Artificial intelligent machine men can replace human to attempt to write or/and read books, due to artificial intelligent machine men had invented to own human mind to do some jobs and their mind had been invented to be similiar to human behavioral abilities to do these behaviors, e.g. cooking, driving, playing games, singing songs, speaking, listening, frighting etc. different human's abilities. So, it seems that artificial intelligent will be possible to be invented to own human's mind abilities to do any writing or reading behaviors or functions.

2.8Prediction of artificial intelligence

reading and writing abilities

development

What is future trend of artificial intelligence reading and writing abilities development? To answer this question, we need to know what benefits of artificial intelligent machine men can attribute to human's needs when they can own any human's mind to read or/and write any books.

I shall indicate e-books reading and writing example, if artificial intelligent machine men can be invented to own human's mind to write and/or read e-books on computer. Then, it brings this question: Can artificial intelligent machine men assist human to learn to do judgement to solve any challenges?

I believe that when artificial intelligent machine men can be invented to own human mind to write or/and read any books, then they will own human's mind ability to make judgement to solve any challenges more accurately, even their decisions can be more accurate to compare to human's decisions. So, artificial intelligent machine mens' writing and reading ability is the main factor to cause their mind to do any judgement in order to make any decisions more accurately. Consequently, in future one day, artificial intelligent machine mens' writing and reading ability will be invented to similar human's reading and writing abilities as well as their minds can also be invented to similar human's minds as well as their judgement abilities can be invented to similar to human's judgement abilities to make any decisions more accurate.

2.9The influences when AI is invented to own
human's mind and judgement abilities

Finally, I shall discuss what are the influences when AI is invented to own human's mind and judgement abilities in our future job market. The achievement of artificial intelligent (AI) machine men achievement requirement of owning human's mind and judgement abilities which requires extensive manual labor, and by augmenting the calling process with machine learning, the process where speed and accuracy are needed to close to human's mind and judgement abilities. Expert human race callers now have better information at artificial intelligent machine men at their fingertips faster.

Hence, if the above those requirements are achieved to satisfy artificial intelligent machine men ind and judgement abilities demand to close or exceed humans' mind and judgement abilities. Then, I believe that future human's some simple jobs must be replaced by (AI) machine men. Even, human's some professonal jobs, e.g. lawyer, accountant, administator, typing etc. professional skillful jobs, which will be either replaced or will be assisted by (AI) machine men. For example, (AI) machine men learn how to type english or other language words to do typing job ; they can learn how to apply accounting knowledge to record any firm's income and expenditure record of accounting job; they can also learn how to assist architects to design any architectural building drawing plans to do architect jobs;

they can learn how to analyze any court evidences to judge any criminal or civil cases and assist lawyers to give legal advices to achieve more reasonable judgement for any legal cases; they can also learn how to assist firm's managers or administrators to manage any organization teams efficiently.

Consequently, when (AI) machine men can be invented to achieve to exceed human's mind and judgement abilities level. Then, I believe that they can do instead of human' simple jobs, which can do even human's more difficult and more judgement requirement of professional skillful jobs. So, (AI) machine men must need to achieve to do any jobs, they are same, even exceed to human professionals' abilities. Then, it will cause a lot of human's jobs to be disappeared or some human's jobs will be replaced by owning judgement and mind abilities of (AI) machine men to do.

Hence, future many human's jobs will be replaced by technological labors. Employers choose to buy (AI) machine men to replace human labors. The reasons include (AI) machine men have none unhappy, angry emotin to influence their low efficiencies and low productivities. Their judgement and mind abilities can exceed human's abilities or do any jobs to compare better performance to human's abilities. Consequently, different occupation labors need to prepare to learn how to co-operate with (AI) machine men to let future employers feel (AI) machine men will be human's assistant to assist human to do jobs efficiently when human and (AI) machine men work together. It aims to avoid future employers feel (AI) machine men's judgement and mind abilities can exceed any low knowledgeable and skilful occupation labors, even high knowledge and skilful occupation labors. It means that (AI) machine men are only labors' assistant if (AI) machine mens' judgement and mind abilities are below under to human labors' judgement and mind abilities.

Consequently, to avoid (AI) machine men can replace human to do any simple or complex jobs to cause any future any occupation labors' competitiors. I recommend that it is right time labors ought prepare to learn different skills. So, every individual labor does not only concentrate on one kind of skill. Because supposing one kind of the occupation labor's job duties are replaced by (AI) machine men. If the employee had owned more than one kind of occupation skill. Then, I believe that who can avoid the unemployment threat more easier than the employee only owned one kind of occupation skill, when (AI) machine men had invented to own human's mind and judgement abilities in future one day.

2.10Why does AI machine lecturer can raise education quality?

When (AI) machine men can own human reading and writing and judgement and analytical abilities, then they can replace university lecturers to teach students to raise students' learning abilities absolutely. Then, it bring this question: Why does I machine lecturer can raise education quality? Why do universities prefer to apply (AI) machine lecturer to teach teachers more than human lectuer in university lecturer hall learning environment? Will (AI) university lecturers replace human lecturers to teach students to learn at university lecturing halls popularly? Can (AI) university lecturers replace university human lecturers to teach students more easily and it can let students feel more easily to learn when they are listening what (AI) university lecturers are teaching to them every time university lecture.

In university today, nearly all students need to attend university lecturing hall to listen their lecturer's teaching in every time course. However, many students do not feel interesting to attend university halls to listen human lecturer's teaching. The reasons include, they are busy, so no time to attend lecturer's hall to listen lecturer's teaching; or they feel bore to listen their lecturer's teaching; they feel difficulty to learn; they have confidence to exam and do their assignments, so they feel that they do not need to go to lecturing halls to listen their human lecturer's teaching. However, if one day, (AI) machine lecturers are invented to teach university students to learn and solve their learning difficulties. Can it raise student individual learning interest, due to (AI) machine lecturers' education quality is better than human lecturers' education quality?

What will influence to university students if (AI) machine lecturer can invented to replace human lecture? The influences will include such as below:

First reason: the only way is going to be useful to university lecturers are if all (AI) machine lecturers are well-informed and fully supported to assist human lectuers to teach whose students to let them to listen whose teaching absolutely. So, human lecturers can concentrate on doing any education research and data gathering jobs to prepare for (AI) machine lecturers to help them to explain human lecturers' every time prepared course contents more efficiently. So, (AI) machine lectuers can help human lecturers to share whose teaching time in lecturing halls. Human lecturers' can spend whose hall lecturing time to do whose educational research or other educational gathering jobs absolutely.

The second reason, the human lecturer (Human capital) has ability and efficiency of concentrating on education data gatehering research jobs to prepare to write whose books. When (AI) machine lecturer replace the human lecturer to spend time to attend lecturing hall to teach students. Fo long term, the human lecturer can raise education productivity growth and education quality raising, due to who only concentrate on searching or gathering data to prepare to write whose books to raise their education level.

In macro and micro economic view, the well (AI) machine lecturer educated labor (human capital) is often replaced to human lecturer as one of the critical factors to influence rapid education productivities and educational quality growth to the Asia developing countries' any regions or cities. Because any of these Asia developing countries, such as China, Korea, Philippines etc. countries which need have well educated and knowledgeable lecturer labors to raise any universities' educational productivities and educational qualities growth. So (AI) assistant lecturer factors which ought have close relationship to cause the good or bad future student learning effectiveness and education or learning qualities raising in these any one of Asia developing countries.

The third reason, for the big population of student growth number example, China's student growth rate is larger than school growth rate. If China expect every students have enough chance to study in schools, but university human lectuer numbers are not enough to supply to universities to teach their students. I believe that (AI) machine lecturer is only one kind of teaching method to solve these big population countries' university lectuer number shortage challenge.

In conclusion, in long term, (AI) machine lecturers can solve university human lecturer shortage challenge as well as they can attract many students to attend lecturing halls and human lecturers can raise education quality when they can concentrate on searching or gathering data to prepare their education career, when (AI) machine lectuers replace them to spend time to attend univesity halls to teach students in every university lecturing time.

2.11 Future AI machine education market

I believe that when AI (artificial intelligent machine men) which can invented to own to similar to human mind, learning, language, analytical, judgement abilites. Then, which can be applied to any education market service industy. (AI) potential education market service industy includes such as below:

2.12(AI) university lecture assistant

Future (AI) machine men can assist univerity lectuers to attend university halls to attempt to teach university students for different subjects, e.g. english, math, economic, math, engineering, art, architect etc. different subjects. It depends on the human lectuter who prepares to spend time to teach the (AI) machine lecturer to remember whose teaching subject. For example, the economic lecturer spend one year time to teach the (AI) machine lecturer to learn all economic knowledge. Then, the (AI) machine lecturer can use its machine brain to remember all the human lecturer's economic concepts and prepared teaching economic contents within the one year. Hence, after one year the (AI) machine lecturer can remember all the human lecturer's economic concepts and economic theories and economic contents to prepare to attend university lecturing halls to teach all first year undergraduated first year economic students confidently. It means that the human lecturer's job duties will change to teach (AI) machine lecturer to learn whose economic knowledge to prepare to let the (AI) machine lecturer to replace whom to teach whose university students; so the human lectuer can spend more time to do other research job for whose university education development. Hence, the (AI) machine lecturer can share the human lecturer teaching job as well as the human lectuer can concentrate on spending time to do whose research jobs for whose university education development. This is one both win strategy to university and the lecturer if (AI) machine lecturer is invented to assist future university lecturer's teaching jobs.

2.12.1(AI) secondary and primary teacher assistant

In the future (AI) technolgical development, instead of (AI) machine men can be applied to university education aspect. Future (AI) machine men can also be applied to secondary and primary teaching aspect. For example, primary and secondary schools do not need attend classroom to teach students. (AI) machine teachers can replace them to attempt to do teaching job. They only need to spend one year time to prepare to teach (AI) machine teacher to learn how to apply their teaching skill concern their subjects who need to teach to their students, e.g. english language writing and reading and spelling skill, sing song skill, drawing picture skill, calculation skill etc. different studying skill. Then, the (AI) primary or secondary machine teacher can apply the primary or sendary human teacher skills to attempt yo teach whose students. Hence, the primary and secondary human teacher whose duties will change to learn how to teach whose teaching skills to let the (AI) primary or seondary machine lecturer to remember how to apply human skills to teach whose students for different subjects, such as, english writing and reading and spelling language skills, singing songs language skills, math calculation skills etc. Hence, future primary or secondary school teachers who responsibilities will change to learn how to teach (AI) machine teacher teaching skills to prepare to replace them to teach their students in classroom.

2.12.2 (AI) scientific research assistant

Future (AI) machine men can be applied to science research aspect, instead of school education job. For example, (AI) machine men can be any scientist's assistant, e.g. space scientist, earth or ocean scientist, human or animal behavioral psychological scientist, climate scientist, chemical scientist, drug scientist etc. How can (AI) machine men can be any kind of scientist to assist scientists to do research jobs ? I shall indiate such as below:

For space science example, the (AI) machine space scientist can assist human space scientist to gather space data to assist space scientist to research any undiscovered material to cause our earth, even space. Hence, the space scientist only need to teach the (AI) machine scientist to learn how to help them to apply space technological tools to gather data and then enter all data to computer to record, even the (AI) machine scientist can store all space data discovered record to their machine brain every day. Hence, the human space scientist does not need to spend much time to do gathering data job. The (AI) machine space scientist can help whom to do these space data gathering job, then the human space scientist can concentrate on spendin time to do space research job in whose space science laboratory every day.

For earth science example, the (AI) machine earth scientist can help the earth scientist to go to anywhere to gather earth or ocean natural activity data in our earth every day. Then, the earth scientist only need sit in whose earth laboratory to wait the (AI) machine earth scientist to come to whose laboratory to give whose gathering every day earth or ocean natural activity data to do future research job. Hence, the earth scientist does not need to leave whose laboratory to do any data gathing jobs concern earth or ocean natural activities. The (AI) machine earth or ocean scientist had helped him/her to go to our earth or ocean anywhere to do any earth or ocean activities data gathering jobs every day. Hence, the earth or ocean scientist can concentrate on spending whose time to do any research jobs in laboratory. It means that the (AI) machine earch or ocean scientist had replaced whom to do all outdoor original gathering data jobs.

For these human or animal behavioral psychological scientist, climate scientist, chemical or drug scientist, scientist all examples, the (AI) machine human or animal behavioral psychological scientist can help them to do any data gathering job, e.g. the (AI) machine scientist can learn how to help human or animal behavioral psychological scientist to contact human or animal to observe their daily activities and record all their activities data to transfer all these daily activites data to let the human or animal behavioral psychological scientist to do psychological researching analysis only. The (AI) machine climate scientist can help the human climate scientist to arrive anywhere to observe climate changes and record climate changes daily. Then, the human climate scientist only need to wait the (AI) machine climate scientist's gathering climate change data record from whose machine brain to do climate changing predict research job in climate laboratory every day. The (AI) chemical or drug machine scientist can help the drug or chemical scientist to gather data of new drug or chemical from internet channel every day. So, the human chemical or drug scientist only need to do researching job after the (AI) machine scientist transfers all daily chemical or drug information to let them to know from internet channel. It means that the chemical or drug human scientist does not need to spend much time to gather drug or chemical new data development trend from internet. The (AI) machine chemical or drug scientist had helped them to do data gathering job every day.

Consequently, future (AI) machine men can do education and research aspects of jobs duties and their role are only human scientists or primary or secondary teachers or university lecturers whose assistants either to share scientist's data gathering job or share teachers or lecturers' teaching job.

2.12.3Artificia intelligent future education market development

Artificial intelligent robots invention

negative impacts

Indeed, artificial intelligence, computing can learn to something that effectively reasons, thinks, if (AI) learns more powerful and valuable complement to human capabilities; improving medical diaguoses, weather prediction, supply-chain management, transportation and even personal choices about where to go on vacation or what to buy, how to learn teaching any subjects knowledge to assist school teachers to teach students, e.g. accounting, law, architecture, language etc. subjects knowledge It can bring benefits to human it (AI) robots can learn teacher's any subjects to teach students or skillful knowledge, e.g. driving, taking care old people at home, manufacturing vehicles in factories. Otherwise, if (AI) robots learn how to be applied to be weapons to attack enemy. It will bring harm to human's life safety. As a result, technology can assist human's development when it can be applied to do meaning jobs, but it can also damage human's development when it can be applied to do harmful human's behaviour, e.g. attacking enemy to cause robot technological war. Consequently, the negactive impact will be depending on how humans teach (AI) robots to learn when some humans intends to teach (AI) robots to attack enemy. Thus, scientists need to know to educate (AI) robots to learn positive knowledge to attribute to us to raise our standard of living, if it is a tool in the service of humans, making our lives better. Otherwise, who ought not educate (AI) robots to learn negative knowledge to attribute to influence our's life safety when they are applied to attack enemies.

However, some scientists believe (AI) robots will have negative impact to influence our economy and society. Such as (AI) robots will destroy most jobs, it will make humans foolish, due to humans depend on (AI) robots to assist us to do any jobs; it will destroy people's privacy and it will enable bias and abuse and it will eventally exterminate humanity. Hence, when time comes to develop computers really think, intelligence is the same things as consciousness, the brain is a computer. Then, scientists must have responsibilities to concern how to teach (AI) robots to learn useful or attributable human's knowledge, not harmful human's knowledge to avoid future invented (AI) robots are taught to learn how to attack ourselves.

2.12.4Future AI tutoring system potential

development market
Humans can learn (AI) robots how to educate our next generation after it has be taught any knowledge from human. Thus, it brings this question: How can human teach new knowledge to (AI) robots to learn successfully? I shall indicate some scientists' evidences to explain that it is possible (AI) robots had abilities to learn human's mind, judgement and analytical abilities, reading, writing, speaking abilities in future one day absolutely. I shall indicate what is intelligent tutoring systems (ITS) example as below:
When are computer-based tutors which act as a supplement to human teachers. The major advantage of an (ITS) is, it can provide personalized instructions to students according to their cognitive abilities. In this scenario, an intelligent tutoring system can be quite relevant to solve unavailability of skilled teachers challenges. Such as India has many students who demend teachers to learn to them, but India is facing skilled teachers shortage challenge. (ITS) are computer-based tutors, which act as a supplement to human teachers. An intelligent tutoring system is educational software containing an artificial intelligence component. The software tracks students work, tailoring feedback and hints along the way. By contenting information on a particular student's performance, the software can make interences about strengths and weaknesses, and can suggest addition work.
The ITS's one of main advantages is individualized instruction delivery to the group of same learning ability of student in evey classroom, which means the system ill adapt itself to different categories of students. A real classroom is usually heterogeneous where these are different kinds of students, from slow learners to fast learners. It is not possible to provide attention to them individually. Thus, the teaching may not b beneficial to all students. An ITS can eliminate this problem, because in this virtual learning environment, the tutor and the student has a one-to-one relationship. When the school applies TIS intelligent tutoring systems to teach its students, the students can learn in whose own method. Another advantage is their using this system teaching can be accomplished with there is trained teachers. Hence, the functionalities of this intelligent tutor system can be divided into three major tasks: (1) organization of the domain knowledge, (2) keeping track of the knowledge and peformance of the learner, (3) planning the teaching strategies on the basis of the learner's knowledge state. Hence, to carry out these tasks, the ITS have different modules and interfaces for communication (Wenger, 1987; Freedman, 2000; Chou et. at, 2003).
The criteria of robots in education include domain of the learning activity, location of the activity, the role of the robot, types of robots and types of robotic behavior. Scientists indicate that robots are primarily used to provide language, science or technology education and that a robot can take in the role of tutor, tool or peer in the learning activity. However, robotics can include these kinds, such as social robotics, pedagogy, human robot interaction and educational robotics.
Early, industrial robots are invented to apply to manufacturing industry only in 2008 beginning. robots are slowly beginning a process to everyday, lives both at home and at school (IFR, 2008). Nowadays, the most popular countries accept to apply robots to replace human's some jobs, include Japan, Korea, USA, Australia, Germany, Holland.
What is the domain of the learning activity to robots? To develop robots to education industry, the first criterion of the two main categories are robotics and computer educaion (the awareness of technology that could be referred

as technical education) and non-technical education (science and language). The technical education means giving students the knowledge of robots and technology. For example, introducing computer science and programming and to familiarize undergraduate students with technology and schol students were gradually exposed to technical subjects using robots. A lesson plan usually involves first an initial introduction to programming the robot (introduction phase) and then the students apply their knowledge practically by making their robots work (intensive phase. The second observed domain in the area of robots in education are non-robots in education are non-technical subjects (such as the sciences), where schools witness the employment of robots as an intermediate tool to impact some form of education to students in classrooms, such as mathematics. The third common domain is the use of robots to teach a second language. For example, English was taught to Asia countries children by robots in by researchers from the robotics laboratory. For another example, the implication of using robots to teach a second language have been well documented by computer science researchers in Taiwan, where it is stated that children are not as hesitant to speak to robots in a foreign language as they are talking to a human instructor. So, it seems, future robots can be a language teachers to the learning foreign language students. However, the language robots require having accurage speech recognition ability and how to learn in acknowledging the use of robots for language instruction ability in future robots language education market.

2.12.5How can potential social teaching robots
assist to teacher in school?

What benefits do (AI) robots provide to education industry? Artificial intelligence can indicate how to improve courses, when teachers may no always be aware of gaps in their lecturers and educational materials that can let students confused about certain concepts. Different students have different learning styles, abilities, interests and needs. For classroom situation example, on teacher in a classroom of 20 to 30 students will rarely be able to cater to each of those needs. Homework and classes could be customized based on a student profile, interests can be cultivated based enhanced by exposing students to different course and content.

Artificial intelligence can offer a way to solve that problem. For online or non-online course providers cases, will have already benefits if these apply (AI) robots to educate. When a large number of students are found to submit the wrong answer to a homework assignment, the system alerts the teacher and goves future students a customized message that offers hints to the correct answer.

This type of system helps to fill in the gaps in explanation that can occue in online or non-online courses, and helps to ensure that all students are building the same conceptual foundation. Rather than waiting to either hear back from the professor in lecturng hall or classroom from classroom education method or receive back professor's feedback message from thc internet online education channel. So, classroom students or online learning students can get immediate feeback that helps them to understand a concept and remember how to do it correctly the next time around if (AI) robots can be applied to assist university professor or primary/secondary teachers to teach whose students either in classroom teaching learning environment or online teaching learning environment. Thus, (AI) educational and social robots can be attempted to accepted to teach primary school, high school or university students.

How to apply (AI) education robots to teach students in which different educational functional aspects?

Firstly, on grading system hand, artificial intelligence can automate basic activities in education, like grading. In, college, grading homework and tests for large lecture courses can be for much grading activites to secondary teachers or university lecturers to spend much time to do grading jobs for every student. Even in lower grades, teachers often find that grading takes up a significant amount of time, time that could be used to interact with students, prepare for class, or work on professional development. When, (AI) may not every be able to truly replace human grading, it's getting pretty close. it's now possible for teachers to automate grading for nearly all kinds of multiple choice and fill-in-the blank testing and automated grading of student writing may not be far behind. Today, essay grading software will improve over the coming years, allowing teachers to focus more on in class activities and student interface then grading.

Secondly, on (AI) tutor's support hand, students could get additional support from (AI) tutors. When, there are obviously things that human tutors can offer that machines can't. The future could see more students being tutored by tutors that only exist in zero and ones. Some tutoring programs based on artificial intelligence already exist and can help students through basic, mathematics, writing, accounting, law and other subjects. (AI) tutors can teach students fundamentals for helping students learn high-order thinking and creativity, something that real-world teachers are still required to facilitate. It should not rule out the possibility of (AI) tutors being able to these things in the future. With the rapid technology advancement that has marked the past few decades, advanced (AI) tutoring systems will be popular to be applied to teach students.

Thirdly, on (AI) driven program educators helpful feedback hand, (AI) can't only help teachers and students to craft courses, that are customized to their needs, but it can also provide feedback to both about the success of the course as a whole. Some schools, especially those with online offerings are using (AI) systems to monitor student progress and to alert professors when there might be an issue with student performance. These kinds of (AI) systems allow students to get the support they need and for professors to find areas where they can improve instruction for students who may be given feedback how to learn subject matter. (AI) programs at thes schools aren't just offering advice on individual courses. However, some are working to develop (AI) systems that can help students to choose majors based on areas where they succeed.

Fourthly, on (AI) changing the role of teachers hand, there will always be a role for teachers in education, but what role is and that it entails may change, due to new technology in the form of intelligent computing systems. As (AI) can take over tasks like grade, can help students improve learning, any may even be a substitute for real world tutoring. (AI) systems could be programmed to provide expertise, serving for students to ask questions, and find information or could even potentially replace the teachers for basic course materials. In most cases, however, (AI) will shift the role of the teacher to that of facilitator. Teachers will supplement (AI) lessons, assist students who and provide human interaction and hands-on experiences for students. Hence, (AI) technology has already changed in the classroom teaching method, specially in schools that are online lessons.

Fifthly, on (AI) trial-and-error learning hand, trial and error is a critical pasrt of learning, but for many students, the idea of failing, or even not knowing the answer. An intelligent computer system, designed to help students to learn, to deal with trial and error. Artificial intelligence could offer studrnts a way to experiment and learn in a relatively judgement, free environment especially when (AI) tutors can offer solutions for improvement. In fact, (AI) is the perfect format for supporting this kind of learning as (AI) systems themselves often learn by a trial and error method. Sixthly, on changing student individual learning hand, (AI) has the potential to change where students learns, who teaches them, and how they acquire base skills, using (AI) systems, software and support. Students can learn from anywhere in the world at any time and with these kinds of programs taking the place of certain types of classroom instruction. So, (AI) robots may replace teachers in some instances (for better or worse). Educatonal programs is powered by (AI). They are already helping students to learn basic skills, but as these programs grow. Consequently, as (AI) technology can give above advantages to educational organizations. So, in the future, it seems that (AI) can be popular to be used in online or non-online classrooms to assist teacher individual job to raise educational quality.

● Psychological resarch (AI) eduational

social robots and students relationship

Whether can (AI) educational robots bild good social relationsip to students? Some scientists had attempted to do experiments to prove whether (AI) educational robots can do good or bad social relationshp to students.

For example, Knox, W.B. el. (2012) had ever attempted to do two experiments to research whether (AI) robot educational robot can build better or worse social relationship to compare human robot. Their two experiments aim to ask how differing conditions affect a human teacher's feedback frequency and the computational agent's learned performance. The first experiment considers the impact of a self-perceived teaching role in contrast to believing one is critiquing record. The second considers whether a human trainer will give more frequent feedback if the agent acts less (i.e. choosing actions believed to be worse). When the trainer's recent feedback frequency decreases. From the results of those experiments, they draw three main conclusions that inform the design of agents. More broadly, these two studies indicate as early examples of a nascent technique of using agents as highly specifiable social entities in experiments on human behavior. Thus, it implies (AI) educational robots have ability to learn human teacher to teach students in good social relationship learning environment with students. Even, (AI) educational robots can build better learning relationship to compare human teachers between students, it seems (AI) robots have attractive ability t raise student individual learning interest, after which can applied to assist teachers to teach whose students in classrooms or lecture halls or online classroom channels.

Other scientist had ever attempted to do experiments about " reinforcement learning" (RL) to research how result of interactive supervisory input between human teacher and both robot and software agents relationship. M. Mataric (1997) attempted to do one experiment concerns that reinforcement learning is designed for interactive supervisory input from a human teacher, several works in both robot and software agents have adapted it for human input by letting a human trainer control the reward signal. He aimed to examine the assumption, namely that the human-given reward is compatible with the traditionanl RL reward signal. He described an experimental platform with a simulated

RL robot and present an analysis of real time human teaching behavior found in a study in which untrained subjects taught the robot to perform a new task. For the experiment, who reported three main observations on how people administer feedback when teaching a robot a task through reinforcement learning : (a) they use the reward channl not only for feedback, but also for future directed guideance, (b) they have a positive bias to their feedback, possibly using the signal as a motivational channel, and (c) they change their behavior as they develop a mental model of the robotic learner.

Thus, whose experiment concluded that machine learning shall play a significant role in the development of robotic assistants that operate in human learning environment. (e.g. homes, schools, hospitals, offices). Considering the difficulty of hard-coding all information needd for the robot to play a long term role in az dynamic world, human users will need to be able to easily teach such robots. However, various works have addressed some of hard problems robots face when learning in the real-word.

In robots learning process, what difficulties which will face, the scientist indicated this question concerns how to influence robot's learning abilities: Has RL certain desirable qualifties, such as the learning abilities possibility to explore and learn from unsupervised experience? Many also queation RL as a variable technique for learning in complex real-world environments because of practical problems, such as long training time requirements, non-scaling state representations, sparse rewards (resulting in slow utility propagation) and safe exploration strategies. As a result, reinforcement learning has been utilized for teaching robots and game characters, incorporating real-time human feedback by having a person supply reward and/or punishment as an additional input to the reward function. Consequently, the scientist discovered human's teaching method is the most important factor to influence the robot's learning abilities amonf all other environment factors. He also assumed and argued that reinforcement based learning approaches should be reformulated to move effectively incorporate a human teacher. To do this properly, the educational robot must understand the human teacher's contribution; how does the human teach? and what does the educational robot try to communicate from a robot learner? The scientist suggested human trainers ought use these methods to educate robot learners to learn more easily. His main findings indicates reward factor can influence the human robot teachers' motives to teach robot learners to learn, due to more reward can encourage the human robot trainers to teach robots to learn their knowledge and skill. He also found that robot users read the behavior of the robot machine learners and adjust the human robot trainer whose training strategies as whose mental model of the different robot human trainer education method changes. Viweing the human input as a traditional RL reward signal does not take advantage of the fact that a teacher adjusts hose training behavior to best suit the robot educational learner.

In addition to the related RL works mentioned above. Every human robot trainer needs to consider the topic of human input for machine learning systems. Personalization agents and adaptive user interfaces are examples of software that learns by observing human behaviors modeling humann preferences or activities. It empathizes how human teaches the robot learner through interaction, various works address trainable software and robotic agents, exploring explicit human input: learning classification tasks and navigation tasks via natural language, robots that learn by demonstration or/and software agents that learn or training. It seems how to design the robot machine learning software technology will also influence the robot's learning abilities. Thus, human trainer's software learning machine and how to give reward to encourage the human trainer's teaching behavior to let the robot to learn, these factors will influence the robot's learning ability to be applied to education industry to assist human teacher's teaching job successfully. Because how much knowledge and skill, the robot can learn from the human trainer, how much educational knowledge that the robot can own to prepare to teach any students to learn easily. Hence, the human trainer's knowledge and skill will quality to satisfy its primary, secondary and university students learning need.

● Can robots be teachable agents to students really?

In the future, I believe robots have potential to contribute to education by acting as subordinate learners for students teaching. The benefits that the act of teaching provides for one's own learning have long been recognized, tutoring associated improvements in measures like achievement for the tutor role than the lecturer role. However, scientists had confirmed that human teaching robots has been concerned with learning for the benefit of the robot rather than that of the human.

Intelligent autonomous robots are making their way into an increasing range of application areas: Manufacturing, transportation, surveillance and monitoring, rehabilitation, agriculture, service. Hence, if teaching robots can be confirmed to assist teachers to teach students in any schools. It seems that if can be applied to teach manufacturing workers how to produce any products in manufacturing process; it can be applied to teach drivers to drive cars, or teach pilots to control plane engineering machines to fly to sky. So, it can be applied to teach any occupation learners to learn how to operate any engineering machines to replace any human machine training teachers in possible. Hence, it is possible, future one day, robots can be any mahine operating occupation job trainees' teachers (tutors) or trainers.

In education industry aspect, for computer subject example, robotic systems have potential to increase studetn involvement and motivation and to improve the effectiveness of learning. Possible ways in which they could do so range from small personal robots used as teaching tools for areas like programming and computational thinking to move science-fictional future scenanios wirh humanoid robots supplement or even replacing teacher role in schools.

Recently " teachable agents" have been used as a tool to help students learn, e.g. s student is tasked with training a simulated computer agent on course material, which can lead to a deeper and more committed understanding on the student's own part. For example, a robotic presence in classrooms may one day help to solve problems of teacher shortage, as learning-by-teaching systems have historically been used to do. And the data about human teaching styles that will be generated by widespread use of teachable robots in classroom settings will be invaluable in developing approaches to help robots learn more effectively from humans, where it is rapid and natural instruction of a robot in a new task.

Consequently, whether future robot role is teacher role better or teacher's assistant role or tutor role better in education industry. It depends on the general student's preferable teaching choice in the school. Such as if the school's students prefer to be applied to be taught by human teachers. Then, robots can be choosed to be the school teachers' teaching assistant role to assist the school's teachers' teaching jobs only. Otherwise, if the school students prefer to be accepted to be taught by robots. Then, robots can be choosed to be the school teachers' role to replace human teachers to teach students in the school. Thus, future robots can be either teacher role or teacher's assistant or tutor role for child age, young age or adult age student learning consumers in any primary or secondary or university in future robot computer educational machine development.

Reference

Chou, C. Chan T., & Lin, C. 2003 Redefining the learning companion. The past, present and future of educational gents, computers & education, v.40 n.3, pp. 255-269. April 2003.

Freeman, R. 2000, What is an intelligent tutoring system? Published in Intelligence 11(3): pp.15-16.

IFR, Statistical Department, World Robotics Survey, 2008.Knox, W.B. Breazeal , C.Stone,.O: Learning from feedback on actions part and intended : In proceedings of 7th ACM/ZEEE International conference on human-robot interaction, late- breaking reports session (HRI 2012).

M. Mataric, " Reinforcement learning in the multi- robot domain," Autonomous robots, vol.4, no 1, pp.73-83. 1997.

Wenger, E. 1987. Artificial intelligence and tutoring systems. Los altos, CA: Motgan Kaufmann.

CHAPTER THREE

AI human behavioral learning stage

3.1Artificial intelligence and the future of defense

Nowadays, artificial intelligence (AI) is widely knowledge to be one kind of the dramatic technology. However, it is expected to continue, to have a disruptive impact on human's private and public life, so defense and security will be no exception. But how exactly will these be affected ? How will (AI) defense and security is incremental in nature?

To research why artificial intelligence (AI) has possible to be used to cause autonomous weapons by human. We need to understand these three aspects of relationship. They include cybersecurity and artificial intelligence and machine learning and autonomous weapon systems relationship between of them.

Firstly, we need to know what is the mean of artificial intelligence and cyber defense/offense? It means defense of critical networks: real time, pattern finding, anomaly seeking, it must utilize machine (AI) learning algorithms to efficiently, and instantaneously respond to potential network threats as well as it means human on or out of the loop. On the loop : it means anomaly detection: human notified, IT analysis, response. Out of the loop: it means anomaly detection: (AI) decides best method of response: quarantine, honey pot monitoring, hack-back. Thus, it is possible that (AI) can be used , such as autonomous cyber weapon.

What is artificial intelligence and autonomous weapons? Autonomous weapons mean one kind of weapon that can be selected and engaged a target, without intervention by a human operator. Are these machines artificially intelligent? I believe the answer is not, because present weapons systems are not capable of human level reasoning. But, (AI) algorithms are presently employed to process sensor data, monitor system health, take and respond to vocal commands manage data, navigate. This, future autonomous weapons systems will require stronger (AI) to be secure and operationally and cost effective. Moreover, self-aware autonomous cyber systems are crucial.

What is cybersecurity mean? It means the ability to control access to networked systems and the information they contain. It is acted to prevent , detect, recover, react. It is application objects concern people, process, technology and it's application goals are confidentiality, integrity and popular availability. Thus, what is cyber weapon mean?

Walware means viruses, Trojans, zero-days, worms ransomware, spyware etc. Does it require a particular objective? E.g. military paramilitary or intelligence. Does it require physical harm? E.g. functional harm or interruption? Mental harm? Is (AI) a technological weapon that it is an object or tool? What about when it is an weapon agent?

In simplicity, (AI) can be one of scientific weapons platform. When one day, it is invented to be applied to control war planes to fly to any countries to attack enemies or it is invented to be seemed to human to replace soldiers to bring guns or any weapons go to other countries to attack. So, it is possible that future any war defense planes, (AI) technological automatic control weapon can be replaced of human soldiers or war plane pilots to control any war defense planes to go to different enemy countries to attack them easily. It is very horror matter to threaten global human's ourselves life in the future , if (AI) automatic control war defense planes or (AI) automatic control machine soldiers were invented successfully.

Hence , when (AI) can be applied to weapons platforms, it structures that launch weapons, i.e. jets, ships, vehicles. (AI) platform and weapon and software architecture components are be done one (AI) technological weapons systems. Thus, human will encounter any (AI) benefits or risks (threats) causes in the same time as soon as possible. If we can predict when (AI) weapon system will be manufactured or invented successfully. Then, we can reduce (AI) weapon systems risks , if we can threaten any (AI) scientists continue to invent any undiscovered (AI) weapons in any time to avoid the future first time (AI) weapon war occurrence in possible.

The (AI) weapon system risk means autonomy: the ability to problem solve technological war , when (AI) weapon system is manufactured successfully, the power to act, how to damage the (AI) weapon system. The power to chance to stop (AI) weapon system manufacturing processes, ability to create a new goals, how to change the (AI) weapon system inventors' or scientists' minds to avoid to apply (AI) tools to achieve attack goals to change to another positive goal. Due to human can't know a prior what an autonomous (AI) weapon system will do.

Although, human is known what (AI) is , but human is also known when (AI) scientists whose emergent behaviors will do to change to do any negative behaviors from positive behaviors. Whatever (AI) weapon system design we use, there will be cybersecurity, problems arising from computation design/complexity. Due to any one (AI) scientist can manipulate the system to act against itself, or who can utilize traditional " cyber weapons" against the (AI) weapon system, or who can manipulate the system to lie to humans, but also due to complexity, there is no way to know if it is lying or not or bounded rationality : satisficing.

Finally, the most serious (AI) technological invention risks are human is unknown these aspects of (AI) absolutely: They are not simple automatic systems, learning reasoning, communication of " self-aware" systems. Thus, human will face (AI) technological invention risks or threats. We need to find any methods to avoid (AI) weapon system is manufactured successfully to avoid (AI) technological war can occur in future anyone day.

3.2 AI system immoral intention

Why (AI) system can be invented to damage our society ? IS it possible to achieve this (AI) damage system successfully? ON (AI) attribution hand, it can be applied to cars, aircraft, which are subject to regulation designed to protect the public from harm and ensure fairness in economic competition. Thus, (AI) safety issue is important to scientists to consider.

IN general, the approach to regulation of (AI)-enabled products protect public safety issue should be informed by assessment of the aspects of risk that the addition of (AI) way reduce any respects of risk that it may increase. Also, where regulatory responses to the addition of (AI) threaten to increase the cost of compliance, or slow the development or adoption of beneficial innovations, policymakers should consider how those responses could be adjusted to lower costs and barriers to innovation without adversely impacting safety or market fairness.

For example, regulatory challenges that (AI) enabled present are found in the cases of automated vehicles. (AI)s, such as self-driving cars and (AI)-equipped unmanned aircraft systems. IN the long run, self-driving cars will likely save many lives by reducing driver error and increasing personal mobility, it will offer many economic benefits. Thus, public safety must be protected as these technologies are tested and begin to mature. Creating safe spaces and test beds for experimentation , and working with industry and civil society to evolve performance based regulations that will enable more uses as evidence of safe operation accumulates. Thus, it implies that any scientists can also invent (AI) system to control weapon defense planes or (AI) automatic machine human to do any soldier's behaviors to attack to any countries easily, instead of none driver automatic control vehicle invention. Thus, (AI) system can be applied to harm to human or achieve to damage our society aim by ourselves in possible.

The rapid growth of (AI) has dramatically increased the need for people with relevant skills to support and advance the field. AN (AI) –enables would demand a data literate citizenry that is able to read, use, interpret and communicate about data and participate in policy debates about matters affected by (AI). Thus, if (AI) technology is applied to assist human's social development and raising life enjoyment or benefits. It will bring positive impact to influence human's future life. Otherwise, if (AI) technology is unsafe to be applied to threaten human's society. It will bring negative impact to influence human's future life. Thus, (AI) scientists need to consider how to apply (AI) technology.

As (AI) technologies move toward deployment, technical expects, policy analysts and ethicists have raised concerns about unintended, consequences of adoption. Use one (AI) to make consequential decisions about people, often replacing decisions made by human –driven bureaucratic processes, leads to concerns about how to ensure justice, fairness, and accountability, the same concerns of human's safety issue. Thus,)AI) expects have cautioned that there are challenges in trying to understand and predict the behaviors of advanced (AI) systems.

Use of (AI) to control physical-world equipment leads to concerns about safety, especially as systems are exposed to the full complexity of human environment. A major challenge in (AI) safety is building systems that can safety transition from the closed world of the laboratory into the outside open world, when unpredictable things can happen. Adapting to unforeseen situations are difficult necessary for safe operation. Experience in building other types of safety artificial systems and, such as aircraft, power plants, bridges and vehicles has much to teach (AI) practitioners about verification and validation, how to build a safety case for a technology, how to manage risks, and how to communicate with stakeholders about risk. The risk means the harm of human's safety of (AI) damage system control machine invention. Thus, any (AI) scientists need consider moral responsibility when who decide to invent what kind of (AI) system machine to aim to bring human's benefits or attribute to human's welfare intention.

Thus, (AI) products safe invention matter will need any scientists' considerations. Because , if (AI) any products are unsafe or harm human's invention in the manufacturing process, it will bring any human's life danger when the (AI) system damage tools are invented successfully and are provided weapons to humans to use to attack other countries easily. It will cause future global human (AI) technological war occurrence.

I shall recommend the solution is necessary of ethical training for (AI) practitioners and students. Ideally, every student learning (AI) , computer science, or data science would be exposed to curriculum and discussion on related ethics and security topics. However, ethics alone is not sufficient. Ethics can help practitioners understand their responsibilities to all stakeholders, but ethical training should be methods for deciding good intentions into practice by doing the technical work needed to prevent unacceptable or immoral (AI) invention outcomes.

Hence, global human needs to concern (AI) weapon system invention security issue. Nowadays, (AI) has important application is increasing role for both defensive and offensive cyber measures. Currently, designing and operating secure systems requires significant time and attention from experts.

Challenges issues are raised by the potential use of (AI) in weapon systems. The United States has incorporated autonomy in certain weapon systems for decades, allowing for greater precision in the use of weapons and safer, more humane military operations. Nonetheless, direct human control of weapon systems involves some risks and can raise legal and ethical questions concern (AI) manufacturing process intention.

The key to incorporating autonomous and semi-autonomous weapon system into American defense planning is to ensure that U.S. Government entities are always acting in accordance with international humanitarian law, taking appropriate steps to control , to develop standards related to the development and use of such weapon systems. The United States has activity participated in ongoing international discussion on Lethal autonomous weapon systems and anticipates continued robust international discussion of those potential weapons systems. Thus, (AI) scientists have responsibilities to manage the potential to be a major driver of economic growth and social progress only, their (AI) intentions are not the global dominance aims absolutely, if (AI) product industry , civil society, government and the public work together to support (AI) positive development of the technology with thoughtful attention to its potential and to managing its invention threat risks to avoid (AI) products to manufacture to be used weapon tools.

Finally, I recommend that as the technology of (AI) continues to develop, practitioners must ensure that (AI) enables systems are governable, that what their inventions need to be openness to let public to know clearly and understandable; that they can work effectively with people and that their operation will remain consistent with human values and aspirations. Researchers and practitioners have increased their attention to these challenges , and should continue to focus on their future any (AI) inventions.

Hence, (AI) safe system ought to be applied to solve the biggest challenges that society faces, such as mobility for the elderly and those with disabilities, smart buildings may save energy and reduce carbon emissions, precision medicine may extend life and increase quality of life, smarter government may solve citizens more quickly and precisely., better protect those at any immoral invention risk and save money.

Moreover, (AI) enhanced education may help teachers give every child on education that opens doors to a secure and fulfilling life. Thus, these are the future human's potential benefits if the (AI) technology is developed to its benefits and scientists ought avoid to manufacture (AI) tools to cause weapon risks and challenges.

Consequently, the main point is that how experts invent (AI) systems. (AI) systems ought not be advanced weapon systems, it doesn't seem to be thought similar human soldiers mind and behaviors. (AI) system ought be systems that think like humans. (e.g. cognitive architectures and neural networks), systems that act like humans (e.g. pass the test via natural language process, knowledge representation, automated reasoning, and learning), systems that think rationally , e.g. logic solvers, inference and optimization and systems that act rationally e.g. intelligence software agents and embodies robots that achieve goals via perception, planning reasoning, learning , communicating, decision-making and acting function.

In conclusion, it is horror (AI) scientists will invent (AI) systems to be owned human's (soldier's) mind and attack strategic behavior to attack other countries easily, who must need to consider (AI) system ought be invented to own scientists' creating mind and non manual assistance functions for positive attribution to human's society. I expect that (AI) system can only be invented to create human's welfare in our future.

3.3(AI) soldier weapon ethical, social and economic negative
impact

In the future, how human can avoid (AI) technological ethical, social and economic negative impact. Scientists need to concern these questions: how to develop of a good (AI) society, how the role and responsibility of the government, the private sector, and the reserch community(including education), in pursuing such a development, whether how the recommendation to support , such a (AI) system development may be in need of improvement.

However, none appers to deliver a comprehensive explicit vision of the role that (AI) system should play in mature information societies. Thus, (AI) 's potential contribution to social good shoud include an in-depth plan for linking in a comprehensive socio-political design questions of responsibility of the different stakeholders, of cooperation between them and of sharable values to understand of a good (AI) positive impact society, not a bad (AI) negative impact society.

Thus, the notion of mature information societies is introduced to stree the importance of addressing the current ethical challenges that (AI) poses in a comprehensive fashion.

It seems (AI) wil invention will be human's moral societal consideration issue. It concerns our (AI) scientists' moral issue, how who invent (AI) system to apply to which kind aspects. IF (AI) system was one direction on war weapon tools to similar to soldier's personal mind or attacking behavior. Then, it will bring poor social safety and poor economy growth our world, due to (AI) scientists' moral is low level.

Thus, the developed country US (AI) technological leader needs to focuse on the impacts of (AI)-driven customatin on the US job market and economy. It represents three specific policy responses to the perceived impact of (AI) on the US economy. They include these three aspects such as: How to invest in and develop (AI) for its many benefits, how to educate and train Americans for the jobs of the future and how to aid workers in the transition and empower workers to ensure broadly shared growth.

The future of (AI) influenced cyber conflicts need more than just the application of current and past solutions in order to ensure security and stability of societies, and avoid risks of escalation. To achieve this end, efforts to regulate cyber conflicts require an in-depth understanding of this new phenomenon, identify the changes brought about by cyber conflicts and the information revoluation, and defines a set of shared values that will guide the stakeholders operating to avoid the international (AI) war occurrence. This becomes clear when considering for example, cyber deterrence. Deploying conventional (cold war) strategies to deter (AI)-influenced cyber conflicts proves highly problematic and the urgent need to foster and coordinate new solutions able to account for the any kinds of conflicts of the cyber demain and of mature information societies to avoid (AI) technological war occurrence in the future.

We hope that in the on-going international conversations and reviews, the US government with further specify how " (AI) system invention law" fit into their vision of the future of society in this case the future of (AI) technological war and conflicts. Hence, (AI) scientists need to concern ethical issues related to (AI), like fairness, accountability and social justice can be addressed through increasing needs. Such as: how the creation of a new body focused on robotics and related (AI) system development to avoid to intent to apply weapon tools to provide advice on the policy, legl and consumer protection issues arising in these fields should be considered.

How to achieve ethical training of (AI) staff and ethical education of the public is certainly important responsibility for (AI) tools ethical behavior and design to the private sector and the citizens : of unique challenges that (AI) brings to society in terms in fairness, social equity and accountability are addresses. Thus, the development of the (AI) technology and defining good (AI) remains problematic. In particular, the US government's innovation driven approach to defining the potential, positive impact of (AI) shows that more could be done to ensure that the opportunities and advantages brought about by (AI) are shared by all society.

An initial on Robotics, based upon the ethical framework and guiding principles is proposed. It should be complementary to legislaton and comprise ethical codes of conduct for Robotics researchers and designers, codes for research ethics committees as well as licenses (rights and duties) for designers and users. Thus, (AI) robotics invention of safety issues is very important considertion to any (AI) inventions or researchers. Every country's government ought have legal guiding to control their robotics' manufacturing intention. If their robotics (AI) is applied to seem to be soldiers to attack other countries to threaten their people's safety. Then, those (AI) inventors or researchers need to be punished by law.

In conclusion, I believe (AI) technology will be applied to weapon, when it's technological development is nearly mature to able to learn human's mind to do any behavior. During (AI) technology reachs thie mature stage, I predict the (AI) weapon tool , e.g. (AI) soldiers will have chance to be caused. This (AI) invention mature stage has these characteristics such as:

When (AI) invetion reachs this mature stage, computers and robots will develop conscious, intelligent, personified minds. Further, information technology devices and (AI) systems will be implanted into humans, enhancing, psychological and behavioral abilities and allowing for direct communication with artificial intelligent minds. There will be both artificial intelligence (AI) and intelligence amplification (AI) in the relatively near future stage.

During the (AI) invention reachs this mature stage, these will be an ongoing mulit-faceted integration of information technologies and human life. Humans and information technology will cooperate. Humans will increasingly immerse their lives and minds in (AI) systems of technological intelligence and virtual reality. The distinction between humanity and technology will increasingly close dependence.

During the (AI) invention mature stage reachs that the environment will be infused with information technology, becoming animated, communicative and more intelligent. The destinction between the artificial and the natural will increasing close dependence.

During the (AI) invention mature stage will expand through virtual reality, simulated and virtual reality will increasingly into normal reality, e.g. the (AI) weapons is virtual reality to seem to be soldier weapon.

Finally, during the (AI) invention mature stage is as the global expression of the evolving human-technology integration a " world brain" and " world mind" will emerge on the earth. This psychophysical (AI) weapon system will enhance and enrich the capacities of both individual and collective cogniton. This (AI) weapon system is a potential starting point toward the evolution of a cosmic brain and cosmic mind.

Thus, it is possible that the workship raw data was a unique way in which (AI) could be weaponized to cause war, during the (AI) invention stage reachs the invention mature stage. However, (AI) weapon manufacturing factory will be built possibly. In the future, how will we defins and locate (AI) weapon factories. Especially, as these factories are no longer solely buildings , but a mil of virtual and substantially different facilities, particularly as it shifts from a physical assemly and development model to a distributed and flexible network. Needing minimal raw materials to develop (AI) weapons, the phsysical location of their (AI) factories could be anywhere and their identification from the outside, nearly impossible. Given the expanding uses for intelligent and super-intelligent (AI). How will we tell the different form a location that is manufacturing (AI) for the creation of weapons versus creating (AI) for an innovative new gaming platform?

In conclusion, human needs to consider every (AI) scientist's personal ethical or moral mind and research intention and (AI) system invention of (AI) weapon factories cause. During (AI) invention reachs the mature stage if human expects to avoid (AI) technological war occurrence in future one day. The technological development on autonomous military robots, ideally among relevant social groups and actors including human-rights, activists, researchers developers, engineers, philosophers, policy-makers, military authorities, lawyers, journalists and the publis need to consider when human has effort to invent autonomous military robots successfully in the future one day. Finally, some ambitious countries or dominant global countries must like to apply (AI) autonomous military robots to be machine soldiers more than human soldiers if (AI) technology had reached the mature stage. So, future (AI) autonomous military robots will be the next choice of weapon to follow nuclear weapon. If civilians were used as a human (AI) soldiers, the weapon simply ignored them and targeted anyway. This scenario highlighted the dangers of proliferation and quick replication of autonomous weapons. Unlike nuclear weapon, a piece of code for (AI) artificial intelligent soldier could be obtained on the black market and replicated at little cost and the hardware for this type of weapon doesn't require costly or hard to obtain components and materials. Thus, (AI) artificial intelligent soldiers can be manufactured many at cheaper cost. Otherwise, manufacturing one nuclear bomb weapon will spend too much cost. Hence , it is possible that (AI) artificial intelligent soldier will be future new technological weapon to follow nuclear bomb weapon. Hence, any country government needs to legislate to control any (AI) scientists' inventions whether they are attributed benefits or welfares to human or damage human's safety.

● 3.4How does (AI) robots' brain invention influence our lives?

(AI) research modeling the human brain has developed important technologies, and has overcome significant barriers. How will (AI) affect humanity in the near future? How will (AI) change our lives and our societies? Is the evolution of (AI) to humanity, or it represent a threat?

On white collar workers (AI) job replacement aspect, University of Tokyo, Institute of informatics, lecturers who had attempted to do experiments to take (AI) exams over a two year period. The (AI) achieved standard scores of around 50 in each subject, exceeding the norms for humans attempting the tests. The (AI)'s results in subjects emphasizing memorization, such as world history and Japanese history subjects were comparatively high, and the results of the study suggested that an appropriate selection of subjects would give at an 80% chance of passing the entrance exams of 80% of Japan's private universities.

So, if (AI) is applies to human white collar workers' job duties aspect, at this level, if white collar workers were replaced by (AI) in the future, around 30% of current staff would be replaced. Whatever, the outcome, large companies will be represented with two choices. One choice will be to protect their employees, but as a result lose their international competitiveness. The latter choice will enable them to reduce the cost of general duties, financial management procedures, accounting etc. general administrative job duties of cost in offices. Hence, it seems that (AI) will be possible to be invented to own human's brain ability to do some mind jobs in future on day.

However, the method called " deep learning" must be developed to cause (AI) to match human's brain ability as well as these were dramatic advances in technologies, such as image recognition and voice recognition, which form the foundation for (AI). Nowadays, this new method called" deep learning" does not reach the matured and stagnated stage. It needs to wait human to continue to invent to let (AI) to match human brain to achieve 100% owning human's mind ability. Nowadays, (AI) industry product include cleaning robots, smart TVs and future (AI) product development market. It will include self-driving vehicles, drones, and nursing robots.

On (AI) weapons applied aspect, if (AI) can be invented to own human's brain judgement and analytical abilities. Then, it is possible that it can be applied to attack enemy to cause war effect. For example, if weapons such as missiles were equipped with (AI) in the future, they would become able to decide on their own targets. Hence, human needs to apply restrictions when necessary.

On (AI) applied to analyzing information collected technological aspect, nowadays, every one will use wearable terminals to connect to the internet to obtain various types of information as well as computers will collect and analyze information on people. Our lives will probably be more reliant on these internet technologies than they are on smartphones today. When, (AI) can match human brain to own mind ability.

Then, (AI) can be applied to do any analyzing information and collection job duties aspect to raise large information restoring and remembering efficiency. For example, (AI) will be generally used and will be extremely useful in analyzing the information collected from wearable devices and stored in the cloud. (AI) will enable wearable devices to be of real assistance in our lives offering their users more intelligent support.

Rather than allowing (AI) to develop on serves, as something separate from humanity. It will be more meaningful to encourage its development via wearable devices, situating it under the control of human intelligence. The intelligence of (AI) will increase rapidly in the future. If this increase in (AI) occurs under human control, enabling humans to increase their own abilities, then surely it will be possible for us to put up a degree of resistance to the opposite scenario, the domination of (AI) over humanity. Hence, if (AI) can be invented to remember and store and make analytical judgement to collect any information from internet. Then, it will bring the effect, such as large international organizations‘ (AI) internet storage robots can bear in mind factors, such as competitors' privacy or business secret information, such as the loss equality between people and threats to privacy that will be stolen form the owning (AI) storing internet information remembering robots.

Consequently, what is the effect of successful invention of (AI) matching human brain's mind ability? (AI) present computers are adequately able to reproduce the emotional, conceptual and intuitive abilities of humans. Because of this, it is important that we should envision potential future problems that may manifest when we consider how to employ wearable devices. It will be essential to enhance our technologies in order to ensure that we can use (AI) under human control.

However, when a goal has been set. (AI) will implement an appropriate means for its realization. (AI) will be need as a tool by human society. If the capacities of analytical and judgement mind abilities of (AI) brain exceed those of human brain, it is difficult to imagine the type of technological, then singularity is represented by the creation of an (AI) by another (AI). It is important that we rapidly and accurately predict these developments, when image recognition and other individual technologies are functioning at a high level. There will be a considerable matter in different sectors of (AI) industry development.

Today, however, machines have become able to decide for themselves what they will learn, making it difficult to copy human's mind ability. What we must consider when machines exceed humans and (AI) surpasses human capabilities. May technologies exceed human capabilities, cars are faster than humans, planes are able to fly. Consequently, it brings a question that human needs to consider: When does (AI) brain technology be invented to reach the most reasonable stage to be accepted or stopped by humanity?

- 3.5What is artificial intelligence

human brain invention?

A machine is likely to achieve the ability of a human brain. Does it a scientific story? Some scientists has predicted that a US$1,000 personal computer will match the computing speed and capacity of the human brain by around the year 2020 year. With human reverse engineering, human should have the software insights before 2030 year. it is possible that of machine intelligence and exotic new technology for faster and more powerful computational machines from cellular automata and DNA playing cheese game competition case example, it proves that (AI) had been invented to own human's analytical and judgement ability to exceed the best cheese game human player's brain analytical and judgement ability. Then, it seems that (AI) will have possible to be built machine brains to achieve the exceed level of human brain's analytical and judgement ability in the future one day.

Supposing we scan someone's brain and restate the resulting " mind file" into suitable computing medium. Will the entity that emerges from such an operation be conscious? How have advances in electronic communications changes power relationship? For electronic book publishing case example, a book that looks at the principles companies must adopt to meet the needs and desires of this new kind of client. So, such as paper book can be changed to electronic book for human to read. Why can't human brain be changed to (AI) machine brain to do human's analytical mind and behavioral mind of activities to replace to do any human's daily analytical and behavioral mind activities?

Over the next few decades, machine achieve super intelligence, human will encounter a dramatic phase. Will it be a "WALL" a barrier as conceptually the event of a black hole in space. Such as (AI) brain invention case, an " AI singularity" ruled super-intelligence AIs, or a gentler " surge" into a post human era of agelessness and super-intelligence brain. Will future technology, such as bio-engineered pathogens, self replicating nan robots, and super smart robots run and accelerate out of control, perhaps threatening the human race?

If one day, (AI) brain is invented to achieve agelessness possibility. It means human's brain will be old to lose mind and analytical ability when human's age is increasing. Otherwise, (AI) machine brain age won't lose mind and analytical ability, due to (AI) machine is no age increasing possibility. It is a machine brain. If (AI) machine brain can be built successfully. Scientists need to consider technological ethic matter, such as the challenge of guiding nanotechnology in a constructive direction, advances in nanotechnology and related advanced technologies can not be inevitable, any broad attempt to relinquish nanotechnology would interfere with the benefits. When actually making the dangers worse.

Keeping in mind that intelligence machines are already making their way into our blood stream. There are dozens of projects underway to create blood-stream based " biological micro electronic- system" (bio MES) with a wide range of diagnostic and therapeutic applications BioMEMS devices are being designed to intelligently pathogens and deliver medications in very precise ways. For example, a researcher at the University of Illinois at Chicago has created a ting capsule with pores measuring only seven nanometers. The pores let insulin out in a controlled manner, but prevent antibodies from invading the pancreatic Islet cells inside the capsule. These nano- engineered devices have cured rated with type I diabetes, and there is no reason that the same methodology would fail to work in humans. Similar systems could precisely deliver dopamine to the brain patients, provide blood-clotting factors for patients with hemophilia and deliver cancer drugs directly to tumor sites. A new design provides up to 20 substance-containing reservoirs that can release their cargo at programmed times and locations in the body.

Another brain health technological related invention case, such as Kensall Wise, a professor of electrical engineering at the University of Michigan, who has developed a tiny neural probe that can provide precise monitoring of the electrical activity of patients with neural disease. Future designs are expected to also deliver drugs to precise locations in the brain. Also, kazushi Ishiyama at Tohoku University in Japan has developed micro machines that use microscopic-cancer tumors.

A particularly innovative micro machine developed by Sandia National labs has actual micro teach with a jaw that opens and closes to trap individual cells and then implant them with substances, such as DNA, proteins or drugs. There are already at least four major scientific conferences on bio MES and other approaches to developing micro- and nano-scale machines to go into the body and bloodstream. All these inventions are related to how to apply machines to copy human's brain knowledge in order to achieve to do any human's brain functions.

Finally, for Freitas envisions micron-sized artificial platelets invention case example, who could achieve hemostasis (bleeding control) up to 1,000 times faster than biological platelets. Freitas describes nano-robotic microbivores (white blood cell replacement) that will download software to destroy specific infections hundreds of time faster than antibiotics, and that will be effective against all bacterial, and fungal infections with no limitations of drug resistance.

Consequently, such as above machine health scientific invention cases, there were many scientists had invented any health machines to apply drugs to transfer to human's brain to attempt to reduce human's disease causing risks, such as reducing cancer cell increasing number. Why it is no possible that scientists can attempt to invent (AI) brain which can own human's mind ability to judge or analyze any matters to give opinions in order to exceed human's judgement and analytical ability.

3.6How can artificial intelligent brain satisfy to human beneficial and natural needs?

Nowadays, new scientists' most familiar form of this vision in our times is genetic engineering. Specifically, the prospect of designing better human beings by improving their biological systems of a small, serious and accomplished group of tailors in the field of artificial intelligence and robotics. Their goal is a simply new age of post-biological life, a world of intelligence without bodies, immortal identity without the limitations of disease, death and unfulfilled desire. If human can understand why this fate is presented as both necessary and desirable, human might understand modern science can help us to enter the good life and good society stage when (AI) brain is invented by scientists successfully in our future life.

How can (AI) beneficial brain satisfy to human natural need? For relatively recent example, similarly as a long term trend beginning with the first mechanical calculators, the evaluation of computing capacity increases in speed over time and decrease in cost. From biological evolution has been invented to influence human brain, an electronic chemical machine with a great, but finite number of computer neuron connections, the product of which we call mind or consciousness. As an electro-chemical machine, the brain obeys the laws of physics, all of its functions can be understood and duplicated. And since computers already operate at far faster speeds then the brain, they soon will rival or surpass the brain in their capacity to store and process information. When happens, the computer will at the vary least, be capable of responding to stimuli in ways that are indistinguishable for human responses. At that point, we would be justified in calling the machine intelligent, we would have the same evidence to call it conscious that human now have when giving such a label to any consciousness other than our own.

At the same time, the study of human brain will allow us to duplicate its functions in machine circuitry. Advances in brain imaging will allow us to " map out" brain functions, allowing individual minds to be duplicated in some combination of hardware and software. The result, will be a world that is remade and reconstructed at the atomic level through nanotechnology, a world whose organization will be shaped by an intelligence that surpasses all human comprehension.

Whether or not today's humans are willing or able to " download" their brains into machines, there will come a time when all human beings will be intelligent machines in the future. Computer hardware will continue to get faster, cheaper and more powerful computer software will increase in sophistication. Brain research will continue to explore the " mechanics" of consciousness. Nanotechnology will continue to develop.

There are powerful incentives, commercial, military, medical and intellectual that will drive many of the advances that the extinctions desire if for very different reasons. Much of the work in artificial intelligence and robotics is open to the same defense that is made on behalf of biotechnology: If we don't do it, they will and why suffer or be unhappy when some new agent or invention is available that will solve the problem.

Finally, we already accept significant artificial argumentation and replacement of natural body parts when those parts are missing or defective. Over time indistinguishable from or " superior" to their biological counterparts as they employ increasing computer processing power. There are powerful incentives, commercial, military, medical and intellectual that will drive many of the advances that the extinctions desire, if for very different reasons. Much of the work in artificial intelligence and robotics is open to the same defense that is made on behalf of biotechnological if we don't do it, they will and why suffer or be unhappy, when some new agent or invention is available. That will cure the problem.

Finally, we already accept significant artificial augmentation and replacement of natural body parts when those parts are missing or deductive. Over time, such replacements are only likely to get more useful and perhaps eventually indistinguishable from or superior to their biological counterparts, as they employ increasing computer processing power. Nor is there an obvious distinction between using manufactured chemicals to fight disease and using " smart" nanotechnology. The extinction project is begun by offering new routes to fulfilling old promises about doing good for human beings. But, it doesn't necessary end.

In connection with machine intelligence, it does not seem very promising to try to limit the power or ability of computers. The danger (or promise) that computers might develop characteristics that lead some people to call them conscious and that this age of intelligent machines would mean our extinction seems remote when compared with their practical benefits. We already rely so heavily on computers that the incentives to make them easier to use and more powerful are very great. Computers already do a great many things better than we can, and there seems to be no natural place to enforce a stopping point to further abilities. Certainly mechanistic and reductionist assumptions about society, ethics and psychology the notion that we are atoms or animals, driven by chance or instinct, run deep in the present world.

3.7Artificial intelligent brain future
innovation and attribution

● (AI) brain invention successful factors

(AI) brain will bring what attribution to influence human's positive impact. How (AI) brain will be invented to apply to any businesses' needs. By how much the (AI) brains might exceed us remain unknown, but it could potentially be by a very significant degree. Future (AI) brain invention will have noted similar growth in everything from hard-drive storage density to the price and speed of DNA sequencing. On key feature of this technological growth that has not been adequately measured in the degree to which technology is becoming more intelligent.

3.8 (AI) brain test experiment

When there is an intuitive sense that (AI) programs/brains today are more capable than those of age, and that those were considerably " smarter" than the serial instructions that passed through the first supercomputers. Scientists will carry on testing (AI) to do any experiments to improve (AI) brain development. They will assess the progress of artificial (general) intelligence, but the need for intelligence tests and tests for other cognitive abilities will be tested in the forthcoming decades for bots, robots, avators, " animats" etc. and any collective system of these and biological systems (humans and non-human animals).

When (AI) brain technology is invented successfully, the idea of a super intelligent computer means invention successfully also. Whether super intelligent computer or (AI) brain can be invented successfully. Similarly, many think that the future beyond the technological singularity is unknowable or even unimaginable. Since its conception, the idea has been examined and explored by technologists. (AI) brain invention will be mean human-equivalent (AI) vs human-level(AI). Many machine intelligence tests is the exclusive focus on identifying systems that achieve human equivalence. Considering our experience with studying non-human animal intelligence.

The need to distinguish human equivalent (AI) from human level (AI) seems critical. Perfect human intelligence , such as (AI) brain invention is likely to be extremely difficult to achieve. Potentially every aspect of the biological processes involved would need to be translated with very high fidelity.

Human level (AI), such as (AI) brain invention is another matter. Achieving capabilities that are equivalent to those of the human mind could be very feasible if it is not limited to perfectly processes involves. For instance, some pattern recognition algorithms are already superior to human abilities. This machine ability is not achieved by duplicating the processes our brains use, through some of the methods have been inspired by them. If researchers had been limited to replicating the brain's mind processes, We would still be waiting for the development of a (AI) brain machine equivalent.

Tests that would seen to have a reasonable chance of successfully testing non-human intelligence are those that use mathematics to define the value of a given challenges for (AI) brain invention. Such as Capability-test has some potential to generate meaningful data about (AI) machine intelligence, e.g. others in complexity theory test, it presents a series of abduction and prediction problems, similar to those in standard IQ tests to (AI) brain. Hence, IQ test and C-test will be potential tests to test (AI) brain ability.

(AI) brain test goals include that to identify a range of possible types of mind such as: super-fast human mind, mind with operational access to its source code, any mind capable of general intelligence and self awareness, general intelligence without self-awareness, self-awareness without general intelligence, super-logic , machine without emotion, mind capable of imaging greater mind or creating greater mind to compare human's brain abilities. Thus, any IQ or Capability test experiments aim to evaluate whether (AI) brain mind ability which can exceed to human brain mind ability. Thus, if future one day, scientists could prove (AI) brain mind ability can exceed to human brain mind ability. Then, they believe (AI) brain invention has ensured to achieve success.

3.8.1(AI) brain invention successful factors

Hence, scientists want to invent (AI) brain successfully. They need to solve these challenges. Such as How robots and computers have progressively supplemented humans, initially only in relatively simple computational and manipulation tasks, but more recently in higher cognitive tasks that used to be the pre negative of the human brain, including language, mathematics, probabilistic reasoning and decision making.

An important challenge is how to enhance the productive interactions between humans and artificial intelligence? The important challenge include these major successful factors to invent (AI) brain technology, such as:

What is the state of the art in (AI) software and machine learning?

Can all aspects of brain function be manufactured by artificial system?

What is the proper form of mathematics that may capture the operation of minds and brains?

How to make (AI) brain feels consciousness?

What would it be taken for a machine to pose a sense of art in (AI) brain software and (AI) brain machine learning by artificial system?

Will machines soon surpass us in all domains of human competence?

What is the proper form of mathematic that may capture the operation of minds and brains?

What is consciousness to (AI) brain invention?

Could a machine be endowed with an artificial consciousness?

What would it take for a machine to posses a sense of self?

Will intelligence machines soon pose a danger to humanity of (AI) brain is invented to reach the mature stage successfully?

Is it possible to design and construct an intelligent robot with an artificial brain sense of ethics?

How can we enhance the humanitarian uses of artificial intelligence brain and owning mind ability of robotics, in particular in the field of education, health and emergencies?
Consequently, above all these challenges, I recommend scientists need to solve to achieve (AI) brain invention in order to reach (AI) brain invention mature stage easily.

3.8.2Artificial intelligence brain invention opportunities and challenges

If scientists focus wrong direction to invent (AI) brain, it will bring wrong marketing development to attribute any benefits to human. So, they need to reduce a mismatch of timescales between the pace of commercial innovation and (AI) brain invention process, reduce an underappreciation of the fundamental unpredictability of (AI) brain autonomous systems and reduce a lack of a university agreed upon conceptual framework for any (AI) brain invention and reduce a disconnect between the (AI) brain design of any kind of (AI) autonomous robots. Thus, scientists need examine these gapes, provide a roadmap of opportunities and challenges and identify areas of any (AI) beneficial functions to be attributed to human to use for our daily life needs.
Future (AI) brain market opportunities, it is rapidly growing innovations in digital -electronic and information technology had development of new intelligence, surveillance, and reconnaissance platform and battle management capabilities, precision-strike weapons, stealth aircraft, smart weapons and sensors and tactical exploitation of space (e.g. GPS).
Any one of these aspects will be (AI) brain future marketing development opportunities. Future (AI) brain invention of so called " narrow AI", (i.e. non-sentient artificial intelligence, whose problem-solving capability is confined to one narrow task. For example, (AI) brain needs to find the best method to win any one of chess player in any both human and (AI) robot chess playing game.
In smart weapon strategy industry, (AI) brain is needed to design how to analyze or mind to protect whose country to avoid enemy attack in any war by the best weapon protection strategy. In education industry, (AI) brain is needed to design how to analyze or mind how to assist teachers to educate whose students by the best education method. In aircraft industry, how to design (AI) brain to analyze or mind to assist pilot to make the most correct flying direction judgement to fly in the most safe way. In space exploitation industry, (AI) brain is needed to design how to find undiscovered natural resources to supply to human to use in anywhere space.
Thus, future (AI) brain invention needs have these features/characteristics to be designed. They include: (AI) learned on its own, where to find the information it needs to accomplish a specific task, (AI) can predict the immediate future from studying any matter, (AI) automatically needs to be inferred the rules that govern the behavior of individual robots within a robotic swarm simply by watching, (AI) needs to be learned how to navigation the acquired memories and experiences, much like a human brain, (AI) speech recognition needs to be reach human parity in conversational speech, (AI) communication system needs to be invented its own encryption scheme, without being taught specific cryptographic algorithms (and without revealing to researchers how its method works,

(AI) translation algorithm needs to be invented to remember fluent language to more effectively translate between any two languages (without being taught to do so by humans), (AI) brain system interacted with its environment (via virtual environment) to learn and solve problems in the same ways that a human child can do, (AI) based medical diagnosis system needs to be achieved 99% percent accuracy in any medical reviewing researches (at a rate minimum 30 times faster than humans), (AI) poker playing program brain development needs to be defeated some of the world's best human poker players during a minimum three-week-long tour, (AI) brain development needs to be effectively " read minds" of human test subjects looking at pictures of faces, via functional magnetic reasonable images of brain activity.

Consequently, (AI) future brain development needs to follow above directions to be invented to attribute to human's satisfactory needs.

3.9 (AI) brain legal remembering attribution

Future, (AI) robots can assist lawyers to deal any legal cases more efficient. If human understands that smart (AI) technology is not to replace human lawyers, but to make a better lawyer that forces who to use, emotional intelligence, and capital on lawyers' mind, then human lawyer have made the first step in future, proofing whose legal service business from (AI) legal robots' assistance. (AI) promises to be a real advantage for today and tomorrow' lawyers having to deal with the rate of legislative evolution and technological change.

In future, for the better with regard to technology in any law firms. According to the ALM 205 law tech. survey 95% of firm leaders and technologist respondents agreed with recent decisions by management regarding the firm's technology in legal service profession.

How can (AI) robots be applied to legal service industry by legal service firms? The (AI) reality in the legal world, it includes in relation to the four key elements of legal service provision, such as commodity, research, reasoning and judgement, exist and can support or replace certain aspects of every lawyer individual jobs both fee earning processes and business processes can be supported and/or replaced by expert systems, cognitive computing, robotics automated systems, (AI) and the machine learning, clients demand and expect more speedy, accurate, expert, creative, intuitive and accessible legal advice, it can assist young lawyers to innovate / tech. focused firm, reducing pressure both from within law firms (or in house teams) and from clients to respond to the demand for client-designed service from (AI) robots assistance, technology related projects that are both user and client -centric need to be implemented successfully.

Due to the deployment of (AI) robots in the legal ecosystem where lawyers, firms, general counsel and clients are beginning to believe (AI) capability technologies, (AI) robots can assist lawyers to increasingly become more productive, efficient, accurate, better quality, less labor intensive and time intensive and the role of the lawyer is gradually changing. If we break down a lawyers' tasks in a legal project from beginning that can handle the majority of these four tasks far more quickly and accurately than human lawyer. (AI) robots can handle legal task in the four aspects as below:

First in legal aspect, it can be used for deep research and processing, such as extracting specific pieces of information from land registry documents, (AI) technology is placed top of a document set including client guidelines and similar forms. It searches through documents and extracts key data points to provide a report of data for improved coordination with clients.

Second on managed services technology aspect, (AI) platform which could have a huge advantage for general counsel and law departments in corporations and for clients of all company sizes.

Third on reading aspect, (AI) brain program that reads and analyzes , e.g. clauses in loan agreements. Its program helps its lawyers through transactions and points. Then toward the correct precedents of each stage of a process.

Fourth, on academics aspect, (AI) robots can assess the merits of personal injury cases. It can automatically review high volumes of contract documents to identify provisions that could potentially be impacted by contract law regulation.

Thus, all of these systems can handle large quantities of structured and unstructured data, and assist with the process management, research, and reasoning elements related to legal issues. Thus, in future, (AI) brain development can be invented to apply to knowledge research job, such as legal industry.

Artificial legal intelligence presents a thought-provoking approach to both computational models of legal reasoning and the use of evolutionary thinking about the law. The visions of computerized artificial legal intelligence , a vision of developments in both technology and legal history. A number of creative research projects have applied artificial intelligence techniques to the domain of legal reasoning.

Consequently, (AI) brain for legal industry marketing development ought concentrate on those three fields of artificial intelligence at most relevant to work in the legal areas in order to achieve the excellent attribution. Such as case-based reasoning, expert systems and neural networks. Artificial intelligence program, such as the legal reasoning programs. Thus, (AI) brain invention needs to own these human legal concept knowledge in order to achieve (AI) legal brain program development successfully.

3.9.1 Whether human mind can create to (AI) brain mind

How can (AI) scientists build a machine that think? In fact, there was general agreement that minds can be existence on non-biological substrates and that algorithms are of central importance to the existence of minds. However, there are much debate about the raw hardware power present in organic brains, such as (AI) brain.

I think (AI) scientists need to invent powerful hand ware, e.g. commercial digital signal processing might be, giving an appearance even to digital operations, but nothing would ever make up the intellectual runaway that is the essence of the singularity.

I also think raw hardware power is not be able to organize the parts to behave in a super-human way as well as I also think powerful software complexity is the main factor to solve (AI) brain mind invention challenge.

Hence, future super-human (AI) brain invention will ought consider how to invent superhuman software more than hardware, because software can store any memory, i.e. human mind. When, (AI) brain invention which can achieve to own human mind ability. Then, (AI) scientists need to consider ethic matter: Does the future of (AI) pose an existential threat to humanity? How do we present learning algorithms from morally objectionable biases? Should autonomous (AI) be used to kill in warfare? How should (AI) systems be in our social relations? Is it permissible to fall in love with an (AI) system? What sort of ethical rules should (AI) like a self-driving car use? Can (AI) systems suffer moral harms? All those ethic matters. I think (AI) scientists need to consider after (AI) brain owns human's mind ability because it is possible that (AI) robots will harm human if they are educated to do any wrong or illegal or immoral mind ability. Thus, (AI) scientists need to consider (AI) robot's moral mind and judgement behavior.

3.9.1 Brain-inspired intelligent robotics

How to solve fundamental problems in the areas of brain sciences and brain-inspired intelligence technology? One way scientists seek to accomplished the mission is to develop brain-inspired hardware including intelligent devices, chips, robotic systems and brain inspired computing systems. (AI) scientists ultimate goal, but since the robot's memory and learning after the human brain, there is still much to learn about neurobiology before that goal is attached.

In (AI) brain university research aspect, two schools of thought have emerged in robotics: bio-logically robots that include a body, sensor and actuators, and brain-inspired computing robot.

Robots have found increasing applications in industry, service and medicine, due in large part to advances achieved in robotics research over the past decades, such as the ability to accomplish complex manipulations that are essential for automated product assembly. However, robots still have these weaknesses which need to be solved if (AI) scientists expect (AI) brain invention can be success. Robots still lack truly flexible movement, have limited intellectual perception and control, and not yet able to carry out natural interactions with human. These deficits are especially critical in service robots. A critical concern of government, academia, and industry is how to advance research and development for the key technologies that can bring about the next generation of robots. Developing robots with more flexible manipulation, improved learning ability and increased intellectual perception will achieve the main goals for (AI) scientists‘ solutions.

Consequently future (AI) brain -inspired intelligent robotic invention needs have these competitive or attractive abilities or strengths to compare computer storage ability. Such as (AI) brain needs have perception to exceed computation ability, adaptation exceeds computing speed, flexibility exceeds, computer memory access speed, cognition exceeds computer memory lifetime, learning exceeds computer memory capacity and innovation exceeds computer memory storage abilities. Hence, (AI) brain innovation must need to exceed general computer storage, lifetime, capacity, learning abilities if (AI) scientists expect (AI) robots will be popular to be applied by any service, manufacturing, education industries.

3.10How can web intelligence need (AI) brain informatics?

Brain informatics (BI) invention will be a new inter-disciplinary field that systematically studies the mechanisms of human information processing from both the macro and micro view points by combining experimental cognitive neuroscience with advanced information technology. (BI) studies human brain from the viewpoint of informatics (

i.e. human brain is an information processing system) and uses informatics (i.e. WI centric information technology) to support brain science study. It seems that (AI) scientists need to further understand how human intelligence and brain sciences development through brain sciences fosters innovative web intelligence research and development because innovative web intelligence research will have ability to assist (AI) scientists to research how to invent (AI) brain robotic technology more easily. The synergy between (web informatics) (WI) and (brain informatics) (BI) advances our ways of analyzing and understanding of data, knowledge, intelligence, and wisdom, as well as their interrelationship, organizations and creation processes. Web intelligence is becoming a central field that information technologies and artificial intelligence to achieve human level web intelligence.

(WI) may be viewed as applying results from existing disciplines , e.g. artificial intelligence (AI) and information technology (IT) to a totally new domain the world wide web. (WI) may be considered as an entrancement or an extension of (AI) and (IT), (WI) introduces new problems and challenges to the established disciplines.

Thus, developing human-level web intelligence will be seem to develop brain level artificial intelligent technology. Because brain informatics (BI) is an interdisciplinary field to systematically investigate human information processing mechanisms from both macro and micro points of view by cooperatively using experimental, computational, cognitive neuroscience, and advanced (WI), centric information technology. It attempts to understand human intelligence in depth, towards a holistic view at a long term, global vision to understand the principles and mechanisms of human information processing system (HIPS).

So, I recommend (AI) scientists needs to research how to invent brain informatics technology and web informatics technology to achieve how to apply (AI) brain to analyze and judge or mind web informatics ability to compete internet (web site) communication tool product industry. Hence, if (AI) brain can be applied to web informatics industry will increase attraction to an internet user market in the future.

3.11Why model of sustainable development environment industry be (AI) robot attractive market

In the world scientific literature various conceptions of sustainable development are found, however, their basis are formed by three dimensions: environmental, economic and social development. The biggest attention is concerned to the environmental dimension which forms the basis of existence of social environment and economy.

The reason is emphasized that each person must preserve and manage natural resources as the basic of economic and social development. However, in the sustainable development strategy, the sustainable development is understood as among environment protection, economic and social society that form the basis to achieve the universal welfare for present and future generations, it is difficult to let human to adapt to live in pollution environment. Thus, environment pollution will be human's concerning issue. It implies how to protect environment pollution which will be human's future challenge. If (AI) brain invention can be applied to how to solve environment pollution challenge. It is very attractive attribution to human (AI) brain environment protection function can be invented to include such as : how to apply (AI) brain to do mind to give opinions or do any environment protection behaviors/activities to assist human how to effective use of natural resources, how to effective use of universal economic society's welfare, do strong social guarantees during the period of strategy's implementation (until 2020 year to achieve global (AI) robots environment protection mission from (AI) robots' behavioral assistance. Because environment pollution will influence world's climate to be worse to cause our food or vegetable can not grow up easily. Then, human will face food / vegetable shortage challenge. If (AI) brain invention can be applied to solve environment pollution aspects, then human will avoid food / vegetable shortage crisis.

3.12 How to invent (AI) brain's environment protection ability?

All similar problems significantly promotes scientists to research for new technologies of data extraction progressive software of data extraction operating on the basis of artificial neural networks allow finding the relations among various types of data in the huge data. Due to the data extraction technologies, it is possible to prove empiric observations to group, to process and model big amounts of data, distinguishing unknown schemes in data and using them in future activities (Rotman M. J., 1995).

It seems scientists believe gather every country's climate environment data to predict environment climate change will have chance to avoid environment pollution challenge. In addition, the traditional statistic methods applied to process digital data of the indicators of sustainable development environmental dimension are not able to analyze the present situation of environmental dimension in the context of sustainable development to present possible reasons of change of environmental dimension problems to generate future forecasts characterized by a high level of accuracy.

Consequently, if (AI) scientists can apply (WI) web informatics technology and (BI) brain informatics technology both to apply to (AI) brain technology to gather global climate environment daily change data. Then, I believe (AI) brain invention can assist human to solve future environment pollution challenge Then, it is possible that (AI) brain can attribute to environment protection or how to give opinions or choose to do any environment pollution activities to avoid global warming crisis.

3.13 (AI) human behavioral learning Asia market

When (AI) brain is successful invention, I think Asia will be a new market to need (AI) brain attribution for Asia consumer needs. I believe Asia people expect (AI) can attribute to let them to use. The (AI) ability includes the ability of machines and systems to acquire and apply knowledge, and to carry out intelligent behavior.

This includes a variety of cognitive tasks (e.g. sensing, processing, oral language, reasoning, learning, making decision) and demonstrating an ability to move and manipulate objects according). So, future Asia people (AI) consumers expect (AI) robots can attribute to whose society's needs, such as: how to apply intelligent systems to use a combination of big data analytics, cloud computing, machine-to-machine communication and the internet of things (IOT) to operate and learn. Asia people expect (AI) robots can give beneficial attribution to them, e.g. talking or playing a game for Asia young entertainment market; (AI) robots need to reflected by physical substance (such as any talking or playing game robot player).

In this sense, (AI) is like a human brain. For Asia (AI) robot service industry need, Asia (AI) robot clients expect to use soft robotics (robotic process automation) can be used to meet Asia (AI) robot service consumers' expectation of automation repetitive tasks and common processor needs, such as client servicing and sales without the need to transform existing IT system maps (e.g. (AI) salespeople robots, or (AI) service robotic).

In (AI) office task aspect, Asia office consumers expect algorithmic game theory and computational social choice of (AI) robots to be attributed to replace some office human workers' tasks. Such as (AI) systems tat address the economic and social computing dimensions of (AI), such as how systems can handle potentially incentives, including self-interested human participants or firms, and the automated (AI) -based agents representing them, e.g. complex or simple office administrative tasks, e.g. typing, accounting, filing, etc. general office tasks which need human office workers who use computers to work to be replaced by (AI) robots to do. So, Asia office (AI) robots users who expect any office human administration tasks can be replaced by (AI) robots to do.

In Asia computer vision market, Asia computer vision (image analytics), users expect (AI) robots can be replaced to human computer image workers to shorten time to work, or raise image quality to be more clear in the process of pulling relevant information from an image or sets of images to advanced classification and analysis. Such as hospital or clinic x-ray image vision (AI) robot invention, photo image (AI) robot invention etc. any Asia image industry (AI) robot market need.

In Asia collaborative systems work with human (AI) robot market, Asia autonomous systems robots users who expect (AI) robots can be applied its models and collaborative systems to help them to develop autonomous systems that can work collaboratively with other systems and with humans, e.g. car manufacturing, computer manufacturing or any machine manufacturing products. So, Asia machine related manufacturing product industry manufacturers who expect to apply (AI) robots who can assist factory human manufacturing workers to manufacture any products in the short time efficiently.

In Asia language teaching (AI) robot market, language educators expect (AI) robots own natural language processing ability, algorithms that process human language input and convert it into understanding representation, such as Asia translation education market (PWC).

Thus, Asia language teaching businessmen expect (AI) brain invention which needs to be designed to own these above abilities of (AI) robot's manufacturers expectation to provide to them to use from any (AI) robots import.

3.14Is the brain a good model
for machine intelligence?

The actions of a human " computer" using paper and pencil to perform a calculation (as the world meant), into a formalized machine, manipulating symbols on an infinite paper tape. But I believe it still has challenges to influence human brain can be invented to machine intelligence successfully.

I think (AI) scientists need to solve these further challenges to influence (AI) brain invention success. The limitations include such as below:

Computation is based on functions of integers is limited. They must let computer data can change to words, then words can change images, then any images can change to storage to let (AI) brain to remember to do any analytical and judgement able tasks to make any actions in the short time finally. It is (AI) brain behavioral and analytical mind speed limitation.

Moreover, anther limitation concerns biological systems clearly difference, they must respond to varied stimuli over long period of time, those responses any changes alter their environment and subsequent stimuli. The individual behaviors of social insects, for example, are affected by the structure of the home, they build, and the change their behaviors. Nowadays, (AI) brain invention is called computational neuro science, which have assured that the brain is a computer, it means a machine that is algorithms and architectures. Second, neuro science findings may validate the energy ability of existing algorithms being integral parts of a general (AI) system. It means (AI) robots change adapting environment limitation. It means how (AI) brains adapt to choose to make any analytical mind as well as how to be influenced by external environment to do their behaviors or actions in the efficient way, e.g. how to manufacture many cars efficiently in one factory in the short time.

Consequently, to solve these limitations, we need to know how to apply correct conceptual knowledge to let (AI) robots to learn, e.g. for example, if we know how conceptual knowledge was formed from perceptual inputs, it would crucially allow for the meaning of symbols in an artificial language system to be grounded in sensory " reality". When (AI) scientists can achieve how to solve all above limitation challenges, then (AI) brain invention will achieve more easily.

Reference

PWC, Sizing the prize, see: https:// www. pwc. com/gx/en/issues/data-and- analytics/publications/artificial-intelligence- study.html.

Rotman M. J., Data mining-a practical approach to database marketing (1995). IBM.

CHAPTER FOUR

Artificial intelligent tools predict travelling consumer behavior in airline and air agent travelling market

I believe that applying (AI) big data tool to predict vehicle buyer consumption choice behavior, it is similar to predict traveler consumption choice behavior. In this chapter, I shall indicate how to apply (AI) big data gathering tool to predict vehicle buyer consumption choice behavior. Then, I shall its what its similar points to be applied to predict traveler consumption choice behavior.

Nowadays, many vehicle manufacturers hope their vehicles can attract to vehicle buyers to choose to buy their vehicles. However, there are many different brands of vehicles to provide to them to choose, so the vehicle market competition is very serious.

How to judge their different kinds of vehicle price which is reasonable acceptance to attract vehicle buyers to choose to buy the brand of vehicle manufacturers‘ any kinds of vehicles, e.g. fast speed sport style vehicles, comfortable and slow speed common cars, for four passengers common small size or more than four passengers common large car size?

How to evaluate the vehicle prices issue is important factor to influence vehicle buyers' choices. Either if the brand of vehicle price is too high to compare other brands of similar vehicle price, it will influence many vehicle buyers choose to buy other brands‘ vehicles or if the brand of vehicle price is too low, it will influence vehicle buyers feel this brand's vehicle machine quality or safe driving level or manufacturing steel material or speed or not comfortable sitting etc. different factors is worse to compare to other vehicle brands' similar vehicle products.

Thus, if the brand of vehicle manufacturers can predict how to design vehicles which can attract many vehicle buyers to choose to buy whose any vehicle products. What are future vehicle buyers‘ favorable vehicle styles? Then, the vehicle manufacturer can concentrate on manufacturing the kind style of vehicle products to sell already. It will reduce its vehicle manufacturing investment risk.

How to apply (AI) tools to predict vehicle buyers' behavioral consumption model? Whether artificial intelligent tools can predict automotive buyers‘ behavioral consumption model and predict future vehicle design trend. In fact, automotive brands and dealerships are facing an increasingly competition when attempting to manually gathering the vast quantities of data required to create customer focused programs that increase retention, ultimately new sales and service automotive business.

Building a based on that client's intrinsic needs and interests to any kinds of automotive vehicles at any given time. This is especially true in the automotive industry where the time span between purchases is measured in years. Because vehicle buyers would not like often to change their old vehicle to another new one. So, their decisions to buying another new vehicle, the time is usually after one year, even longer time. Hence, it seems any vehicles won't be frequent consumption products to the owned at least one vehicle family consumers (vehicle buyers). It implies that why vehicle manufacturers ought need to spend time to predict future vehicle buyer design choice for whole year vehicle buyer number growth because they won't often change preferable vehicle design to change another new vehicle more easily.

Hence, how to predict vehicle consumers' taste or preferable which styles of vehicle choices issues is very important. If the vehicle manufacturers can not manufacture any attractive vehicles to sell easily in this year. Then, it will lose time, money in this year because it won't know when the owned least one vehicle users or non-owned any vehicle users who will decide to buy one new vehicle or change another new vehicle ensure. The different brand vehicle dealers will possible wait more than one year to attract them to buy their vehicles if their styles are not attractive to compare other brands of vehicle competitors.

However, artificial intelligence and machine learning can help any vehicle manufacturers to find solution to solve patterns in highly to solve patterns in highly complex data-sets that are beyond the capability of a human brain, and then building and automatically acting on the customer insights it generates.

Given the automotive customer need for individualized communications, this technology is positioned to become a critical component of any successful vehicle retailer's domestic or/and overseas vehicle markets. How can vehicle manufacturers and retailers use (AI) to enhance their vehicle marketing campaigns? How will (AI) affect their vehicle sale marketing strategy? What criteria would they use when selecting on (AI) solution?

Vehicle consumers today are able to quickly access different brands of vehicle information, research vehicle products and reviews, negotiate prices and compare one vehicle brand or retailer to another resulting of the brands of vehicle customers. At the same time, the rise of " big -data mining", wearable devices that track user's every move and preference and greater contextualization in advertising and social media has resulted in consumer expectations of individualized. Thus, it seems that (AI) tools can be used to gather " big-data" and then they can make human's mind to analyze how to design kinds of vehicles to satisfy vehicle buyers‘ needs.

As automotive vehicle marketers can apply (AI) tools to achieve messaging strategies to meet the needs of this new generation of informed vehicle consumers, using data from a variety of sources to move from a variety of sources to move from mass- messaging to more personalized messages aimed at particular vehicle buyer segments, e.g. fast speed sport vehicle buyer segment, slow speed comfortable small size or large size of buyer segment. However, when

90% of vehicle marketers believe having a single vehicle buyer view is important, only 6% have achieved it.

However, one of the main issues vehicle marketers are facing the lack of capacity to efficiently sift through and analyze the massive vehicle buyer amounts of data required to create vehicle buyer individualized vehicle customer experiences easily. This is especially difficult for automotive dealers, the long periods between purchase cycles, and the highly considered nature of the vehicle purchase means that each vehicle dealer needs to not only track a large number of potential vehicle customers for an extremely long period of time, but each of those vehicle customers will generate a huge amount of different kinds of vehicle behavioral consumption data as they research their next vehicle purchase. However, by choosing the right (AI) technological tools and programs , vehicle dealers can solve this big data gathering challenge into a major advantage.

For Forrester vehicle brand example, vehicle consumers have more power over the Forrester vehicle brand's reputation than ever before. Mayne, L. (2014) indicated that Forrester calls this new (AI) tools is the " age of the vehicle customer", a 20 year business cycle in which the most successful vehicle enterprises will reinvent themselves to systematically understand and serve increasingly powerful vehicle consumers. To win in this new age, Forrester declares companies must become vehicle customer obsessed and the only sustainable competitive advantage is knowledge and engagement with customers, such as (AI) gathering data knowledge.

Thus, the biggest challenge vehicle businesses currently face is not the collection of a large quantity of vehicle consumer data, but what to do with that data once they have it. Even at a large vehicle data research firm, the data sets are often too big for a single analyze, or even a team of analysts to sort through and draw conclusion from. However, enter artificial intelligence and machine learning , an efficient technology solution that can continuously find patterns in highly complex data sets that are way beyond the capacity of a human brain and then automatic drive action based on the customer insights is generated.

What is (AI) machine learning tool? Machine learning is a type of (AI) that learns from data and is not explicitly program. Think Amazon, face book. Machine learning serves up relevant content based on an individual vehicle purchase behavior and experiences. More simply, machine learning is a computer program that can learn relationships between data, subject those learnings to errors functions, and then learn from its errors. The program in effect, trains itself.

Lee, T. (2016) explained that "Thus, (AI) tools can learn deep a more advanced branch of machine learning inspired by how our brain's nervous function, has also been found to be especial effective in identifying patterns from data."

When this way sound is complicated from a vehicle dealer perspective, the implementation of a marketing program driven by artificial intelligence can take care of these tasks in an automatic vehicle fashion with little to no manual intervention required from the staff at time vehicle stores.

In practice at a vehicle dealership, the program will continue track vehicle customer behavior online, merging that data with any offline source (like CRM or DMS data) and then analyze this aggregated vehicle buyer data set to predict what vehicle customer may be shopping for and what information they might like to relevance from different kinds style of vehicle design photos.

4.1 Why does travelling market seem to similar to vehicle market which can apply (AI) learning tool to predict travelling consumer behaviors?

Artificial intelligence refers to complex in vehicle market and travelling entertainment market which is very seem to be applied to predict consumer behaviors.

(AI) machine learning that posses the same characteristics of human intelligence and that have all our sense, all our reason and think just like human vehicle buyer who prefer vehicle purchase choice or travelling consumer who prefer travelling package or travelling destination and airline choice. Besides, machine learning is the practice of using algorithms to collect and examine data, learn from it, and then make a determination or prediction about something in the world.

So, it can be attempted to gather data concerns that travelling consumer past travelling destination choice and air ticket price choice and different travelling package, e.g. high, middle, or low class hotel and foods supply and entertainment places choice in their past travelling journeys.

The machine is " trained" using large amounts of data and algorithms that give it the ability to learn how to automatically perform a task with increasing accuracy. Otherwise, deep learning is primarily based on artificial neural networks inspired by our understanding of the biology of human's brains.

Thus, (AI) big data can gather all these past traveler consumption behavioral choice data to make reference to analyze whether how many travelers will choose to go to the specific travelling destination in any time by the past traveler number record to different travelling destinations, then it can gather the past air ticket sale price to different destinations and past travelling package design to different destinations in order to analyze whether it is the cheap airline ticket price factor or attractive travelling package factor or attractive travelling entertainment etc. in order to predict which factor is the most potential influential factor to they choose to go to the destination to travel in different time within one year. Then, traveler agent or airline can collect these big data to judge how to design their package to attract travelers to go to anywhere to travel or what the main factor influence most of them to choose to visit the destination to travel.

For example, travel agents or airlines can apply "Deep learning" breaks down tasks in ways that enables machines to assist them to predict when travelling consumer choice will be changed and why their travelling choice will change and how their travelling choice will change with increasingly complex tasks.

So, such as why (AI) technology can be applied to predict how travelling consumer behavior changes to bring to judge whether anywhere will be many travelling consumers who will prefer to choose travelling hot destinations next year or next month.

Then, travel agents and airlines can gather overall past travelling consumer data to analyze and conclude the more accurate prediction of different travelling destinations to the number of traveler. Then, they can choose how much air ticket price is more reasonable to charge to the travelling destination or how to design the travelling package which can bring more attractive to the prediction number of different travelling destination travelers in order to achieve to raise the different travelling destination number next year.

Thus, (AI) big data machine learning can help airlines or travel agents to solve how to design any attractive travelling package challenge. A travelling package is both one of the most important and carefully considered travelling entertainment consumption the majority of travelling people will ever make in their lifetime at least one travelling time.

It is also a prediction how travelling package will be designed that tends to be fundamentally tied to a travelling person's travelling destination choice identify and travelling package view of themselves. As the same time, travelling consumers' travelling choice changing lifestyles result in changing travelling destination needs, e.g. the country's young travelers can choose to change non-extreme exciting travelling entertainment package from past extreme exciting travelling entertainment package. Due to personal feeling factor in general. However, I believe that (AI) big data can also be attempted to predict when the country's young travelers will choose to change non-extreme exciting travelling behavior.

It is similar to automotive dealers need to remember that vehicle customers and prospects are individual human beings with risk, complex and ever-changing lives factors, these factors will influence every vehicle consumer why who feels has vehicle purchase need, and how who choose to buy the first vehicle if who decided to buy the first vehicle.

It seems that travelling agents or airlines need to remember that travelling consumers and different features or designs are very traveler beings with risk, complex and ever-travelling package attitude personal changing factors in different travel season, these factor will influence every individual traveler why who feels has travel entertainment need, and how who choose to buy different feature or design travelling package if who decide to travel.

The (AI) big data technological travelling customer behavioral prediction tool seems to be the best travelling behavioral prediction tool in the world are those that know every one of different country's traveler need. Their likes and dislikes which style of travelling package, preferences and travel destination changing tastes to travelling destination choices.

The capacity of the human brain, however, limits us from achieving these different type of travel package sales. In this competitive travelling destination choice entertainment environment, (AI) big data machine learning enables platforms to assist the air ticket and travel package sales team by tracking the travelling consumer behaviors of each travelling customer, learning and memorizing their preferences and predicting their future travelling destination choice and travelling package design needs.

Finally, I recommend that for a travel agent or airline travelling marketing platform to make their travelling customer engagement efficient and fully-functional, I should be able to: applying (AI) tools to track every travelling customer behavior across the web, connecting to a society of data sources, CRM, DMS, third-party, web travelling brands, social traveler email, click etc., aggregating and accurately cross-reference data from a variety of sources, leveraging this data to drive insights on a mass scale, as well as on an individualized basis, driving actions and automatically direct travelling customer engagement via multiple channels based on where each customer is in their travelling individual lifecycle.

4.2 Why is (AI) big data gathering tool better than psychological and survey methods to predict traveler individual travel choice behavior?

Prediction travel behavioral consumption from psychology and survey methods.

How to predict travel consumption? It is one question to any travel agents concern to use what methods which can predict how many numbers of travelers where who will choose to go to travel more accurately. I think that who can consider how to predict travel behavioral consumption from psychology and survey travel choice prediction method, but it is better to apply (AI) big data gathering method to predict travel consumer's destination choice more accurate. The reason is as below:

The first reason is that traveller individual travel psychological desire is difficult to predict accurate more than (AI) big data gathering method, it is due that the data is past traveler's destination choice and travel package and ticket price actual data from (AI) big data gathering method. Otherwise, survey investigation is only traveler psychological thinking method. It lacks enough past actual traveler data gathering.

The second reason is that on the weakness of traveler individual psychological thinking view of survey investigation. It has evidence to support the relationship between self-identify threat and resistance to change travel behavior to any travelers, controlling for whose past travelling behavior, resistance to change if a psychological phenomenon of long standing interest in many applied branches of psychology.

Past travelling behavior has been acknowledged as a predictor of future action. Such as travelling behavior that is experienced as successful is likely to be repeated and may lead to habitual patterns. Some psychologists differentiate habit between two concepts, such as goal oriented and automatic oriented both. Although repeated past travelling behavior is addition goal oriented and automatic oriented. Further non-deliberative nature of habit may make appeals to judge and to predict future individual traveler's behavior accurately.

However, repeated one traveler will choose the destination to repeat to travel without a necessary constraint of goal orientation and automatic oriented both. So, it seems that psychological factor can influence any individual traveler why and how who choose to decide to repeat to choose the destination to travel.

So, survey investigation is only the traveler's thinking to answer the travel firm. It is not sure that the traveler's past travel experience is real answer. Otherwise, (AI) big data gathering method is computer gathering method which gather past traveler consumption actual data to analyze and conclude future traveler possible repeated travel destination choice and travel package choice more accurate.

The third reason is that on the strength of (AI) big data gathering method computer statistic view to predict future traveller consumer's destination and travel package choice. It is structural equation modeling is an extremely flexible linear-in-parameters multivariate statistical modeling technique. It has been used in modeling travel behavior and values since about 1980 year. It is a software method to handle a large number of variables, as well as unobserved variables specified as linear combinations (weighted averages) of the observed variable.

4.3 Can (AI) big data gather data to predict when climate will change to influence poor travelling behaviours?

(AI) big data tool can predict the flexibility of human travelling behavioral change is at least the result of one such mechanism, our ability to travel mentally in time and entertain potential future. Understanding of the impacts is holidays, particularly those involving travel.

Using focus groups research to explores tourists' awareness of the impacts of travel own climate change, examines the extent to which climate change features in holiday travel decisions and identifies some of the barriers to the adoption of less carbon intensive tourism practices.

The findings suggest many tourists don't consider climate change when planning their holidays. The failure of tourists to engage with the climate change to impact of holidays, combined with significant barriers to behavioral change, presents a considerable challenge in the tourism industry. In the future, computer (AI) big data tool can attempt to predict when the country's climate change to influence travelers to choose to go to the country to travel, e.g. next month or next half year or next year hot travelling destinations.

Tourism is a highly energy intensive industry and has only recently attracted attention as an important contributions to climate change through greenhouse gas emissions. It has been estimated that tourism contributes 5% of global carbon dioxide emissions. There have been a number of potential changes proposed for reducing the impact of air travel on climate change. These include technological changes, market based changes and behavioral changes.

However, the role that climate change plays in the holiday and travel decisions of global tourists. How the global tourists of the impacts travel has on climate change to establish the extent to which climate change, considerations features in holiday travel decision making processes and to investigate the major barriers to global tourists adopting less carbon intensive travel practices.

It will bring this question: Will tourists aware the impacts that their holidays and travel have on climate changes to influence their travelling decision?

When, it comes to understand individual traveler's behavioral change, wide range of conceptual theories have been developed, utilizing various social, psychological, subjective and objective variables in order to model travel consumption behavior. These theories of travel behavioral change operate at a number of different levels, including the individual level, the interpersonal level and community level. Whether pro-environmental behavior can be used to predict travel consumption behavior in a climate change. However, the question of what determines pro-environmental behavior in such a complex one that it can not be visualized through one single framework or diagram.

Despite the potentially high risk scenario for the tourism industry and the global environment, the tourism and climate change ought have close relationship.

However, (AI) big data tool can be applied to find what factors to influence the time of travelers' travelling choices. What are the important factors and variables which can limit tourism? e.g. money, time, family problem, extreme hot or cold weather change, air ticket price, journey attraction etc. variable factors.

Mention of holidays and travel were deliberately avoided in the recruitment process, so as not to create a connection factor to influence traveler's individual mind. However, the dismissal of alternative transportation modes can be conceived as either a structural barrier, in the sense that flying is perhaps the only realistic option to reach long-haul holiday destination, or a perceived behavioral control barriers in that an individual perceives flying as the only option open to whom.

The transportation tool factor will be depend to extent on the distance to the destination. This can also be interpreted in a social perspective as an intention with the resources available where much international tourism is structured around flying. To increase the availability of different transportation modes, tourists could choose holiday destination closer to home.

Finally, also how to predict future travel behavioral consumption. I feel that travel agents need to predict whether any country's random daily variation of weather factor is also important to influence travel behavior. e.g. in weather, temperature, rainfall and snowfall with traffic accidents factors will have relationship to cause travel demand.

Some scientists estimate suggest that when warmed temperatures and reduced snowfall are associated with a moderate decline in non-fatal accidents, they are also associated with a significant increase in fatal accidents. Thus increase in fatalities and temperature. Half of the estimated effect of temperature on fatalities is due to changes in the exposure to pedestrians, bicyclists and motorcyclists as temperature increase.

So, if any countries have rainfall, snowfall and low temperature to cause traffic accidents, whether this accident occurrence will influence the travelers who liking climb snow hills, riding bicycle, running sports who will avoid to travel to these countries‘ bad weather after occurs. So, why I feel that this natural climate factor will also be one serious factor to influence travel behavioral consumption. However, (AI) big data tool can predict more accurate than survey method when climate change to influence the country's climate to be poor, then it can predict when which countries are not popular acceptable to global country consumers' travel choice next month.

CHAPTER FIVE

(AI) predicts traveller behaviors with better-informed decisions

I shall explain how (AI) big data gathering technology can provide travelling businesses with better-informed decisions to drive top-line growth, deliver meaningful experience for travelling customers and smooth their path along the travelling consumer journey. The widely understood definition of (AI) involves the ability of machines or computers to learn human thinking, reasoning and decision-making abilities.

So, such as (AI) learning machine system can attempt to learn travelling consumer's travel destination or travel package thinking, judgement of their reasons why they choose to go to the destination to travel or why they choose to buy the travel package and learn how and why they make their past travelling decisions from their past travel big data gathering.

A Narrative science study in 2015 year identified that (AI) was being used primarily in voice recognition, machine learning virtual assistants and decision support. This study also highlighted the many branches of (AI) and that techniques and their definition are used interchangeably. It is possible that (AI) can be used to gather big data , then to analyze to help travel businesses to predict travelling consumer travel destination and travel package choice behaviors. For example, one of the most common techniques is traveler machine learning, where algorithms are used to perform tasks by learning from the airline or travel agent whose past all travelers' travelling destination choice and travel package choice historical data.

However, during 2017 year, search engines will begin to find what additional factors can influence past traveler personal travelling destination and travelling package travelling behavioral data into prediction of future travelling customer behavioral results, such as the online traveler (user's) history of travelling data searches, such as anywhere are the most popular travelling locations or travelling destinations and previously captures conservations.

Artificial intelligence will use this past travelling destinations and travelling package information to power predictive search results, e.g. predictive future travelling consumer's choice behavioral processing for where will be their preferable travelling destination choice and how to design travelling package to satisfy future travelling clients' needs. Predictive search will improve the quality of online travelling search results, and provide new insights into travelling consumers‘ travelling destination and package behavior and the moments which matter to them. Search will give recommendation into tailored how travelling consumer individual travelling destination choice in travelling decision making process. Several of the largest online platforms already use (AI) travelling machine learning to improve predictive travelling consumer behavioral search results.

For example, Google's rank brain technology adds research by understanding the context in which the travelling consumer has entered it. Over time, rank brain will learn further from user behaviors Amazon's DSSTNE (pronouned destiny) learns from shoppers' purchasing habits and consumption behavior to offer better product recommend actions, which Amazon can offer before a consumer has entered anything into the search bar.

Such as (AI) big data can gather past online travelers‘ e-ticket purchase transactions to conclude that online traveler's travelling choice habits and online traveler consumption behavior to offer better travelling destinations and travelling package opinions to travel agents or airlines. However, this technology is not independent of human input. For example, Google engineers will periodically retain the rank brain system to improve the models it uses.

For another example, in 2016 year , Apple computer revamped its travelling scene photos app to allow travelling consumers to search for specific travelling destinations in the travelling scene phots, they want to find anywhere travelling destination photos, not just dates and locations. Each travelling photo that an intelligent phone or intelligent pad user takes goes through 11 billion computations, so that travelling scene photos can understand exactly where is the travelling destination photography to let online travelling consumer to feel anywhere they plan to go to the location to travel. So, (AI) learning machine can make online travelling photos more attractive to influence potential travelers choose to the destination to travel after they see the travelling destination scene photos from internet.

It seems that in future, (AI) machine learning will allow online travelling search to evolve even further. Search engineers will deliver refined recommendations to airlines' online traveler e-ticket search users and use less human input to predict travelling consumers‘ needs from internet channel. For IBM computer example, it indicated 90% of the data that exists today has been created in the last two years.

This huge explosion of past traveler's e-ticket consumption data gives the opportunity to quickly spot and react to the latest trends, fashion and fads among its travelling clients and potential clients. This will allow airline or travel agent companies to better engage with younger travelling consumers, who gain influence access to the latest travelling destination and package trends.

They associate with to help define who they are as individuals. Thus, travelling company brands have to identify and make use of them before travelling consumers move on, but the vast quantity of past e-ticket purchase data available makes from internet channel. This a resource-intensive task. For next example, Lesara, a based online clothes store, uses this machine learning to inform its product decision often gathering information from internal and external sources.

When its trends -spotting shoes. Lesara has a range of over 20 styles and sells hundreds of pairs a day. It focus on giving consumers, the very latest trends allow Lesara to develop on average of 50,000 new items each year.

It compared to 11,000 old items each year. Thus, travelling agents or airlines can attempt to apply (AI) big data gathering method to gather all past e-ticket purchase data, concerns where they prefer to choose to go to the destinations to travel and what travelling packages are the most attractive to the travelers to choose to buy. It aims to help them to predict where future travelers will prefer to choose to go to travel or what travelling package they will prefer to choose to buy next year.

For another (AI) big data prediction example, Lesara is one online clothes store, uses machine learning decisions after gathering information from internal and external sources. One of its most popular products, shoes with LED started life when its trend spotting software flagged up a blogger wearing similar shoes. Now Lesara has a range of over 20 styles and sells hundreds of pairs a day. Its focus on giving consumers the very latest trends allows Lesara to develop an average of 50,000 new items each year, compared to 11,000 for its competitor Lara.

It seems (AI) big data gathering machine learning can help Lesara business to predict what kinds of shoes design or style that shoe consumers will prefer choose to buy in future shoe market trend. Thus, Lesara can predict shoe consumers' taste successfully and it can manufacture many attractive style of shoes.

(AI) machine learning can gather global past shoe consumer's shoe shopping experiences, then analyzes to make conclusion to give lesara recommendation successfully. This will make the experience more enjoyable for shoe consumers and allow Lesara to advert whose different new style or design of shoes to deliver them move relevant messages by understanding the context of the experience.

So, online travel agents or online airline can also attempt to apply (AI) big data gathering method to predict where travelers will prefer to go to travel and how they ought design travelling packages to attract them to choose to buy next year. Hence, (AI) big data gathering technology can conclude how to design traveler agents' travelling package products to be the most attractive to excite many travelers choose to buy their travelling package, due to it has more accurate to predict travelling consumer destination and travelling package choice behaviors to compare human themselves prediction judgement effort, e.g. travelling survey or marketing research, or telephone enquire. It seems that (AI) machine judgement effort is more accurate to compare to human judgment effort in travelling industry.

5.1 Future travel consumption behavior

Can (AI) big data gathering tool predict traveler individual habitual behavior , e.g. renting travel transportation tools ?

Can (AI) big data gathering tool can predict past traveler destination and travelling package choice habit and it can be intended to predict of future traveler behavior to people are creatures of habits judgement of future anywhere travelling destination choice next year or next month or next half year destination prediction ?

Many of human's everyday goal-directed behaviors are performed in a habitual fashion, the transportation made and route one takes to work, one's choice of breakfast. Habits are formed when using the some behavior frequently and a similar consistency in a similar context for the some purpose whether the individual past travel consumption model will be caused a habit to whom. e.g. choosing whom travel agent to buy air ticket or traveling package; choosing the same or similar countries' destinations to go to travel ; choosing the business class or normal (general) class of quality airlines to catch planes.

Does habitual rent traveling car tools use not lead to more resistance to change of travel mode? It has been argued that past behavior is the best predictor of future behavior to travel consumption. If individual traveler's past consumption behavior was always reasoned, then frequency of prior travel consumption behavior should only have an indirect link to the individual traveler's behavior. It seems that renting travel car tools to use is a habit example. So, a strong rent traveling car tools useful habit makes traveling mode choice. People with a strong renting of traveling car tools of habit should have low motivation to attend to gather any information about public transportation in their choice of travelling country for individual or family or friends members during their traveling journeys.

Even when persuasive communication changes the traveler whose attitudes and intention, in the case of individual traveler or family travelers with a strong renting travel car tools habit. It is difficult to change whose travel behaviors to choose to catch public transportation in whose any trips in any countries. However, understanding of travel behavior and the reasons for choosing one mode of transportation over another. The arguments for rent traveling car tools to use, including convenience, speed, comfort and individual freedom and well known.

Increasingly, psychological factors include such as, perceptions, identity, social norms and habit are being used to understand travel mode choice. Whether how many travel consumers will choose to rent traveling car tools during their trips in any countries. It is difficult to estimate the numbers. As the average level of renting travel car tools of dependence or attitudes to certain travel package policies from travel agents. Instead different people must be treated in different ways because who are motivated in different ways and who are motivated by different travel package policies ways from travel agents.

In conclusion, the factors influence whose traveler's individual traveler destination choice behavior The factors include either who chooses to rent traveling car tools or who chooses to catch public transportation when who individual goes to travel in alone trip or family trip. It include influence mode choice factors, such as social psychology factor and marketing on segmentation factor both to influence whose transportation choice of behavior in whose trip. So, (AI) big data can be attempted to gather past traveler transportation tool choice, rent travelling car tools choice or catching public transportation tools choice to predict where destination can provide what kind of transportation tool to attract many travelers to choose to go to the place to travel.

How (AI) big data determine future travel behavior from past travel experience and perceptions of risk and safety for the benefits to travel consumers?

How (AI) big data determine future travel behavior from past travel experience and perceptions of risk and safety for the benefits to travel consumers? Why does individual traveler avoid certain destination(s) is(are) as relevant to tourist decision making as why who chooses to travel to others?

Perceptions of risk and safety and travel experience are likely to influence travel decisions. If travel agents had efforts to predict future travel behavior to guess whether travelers will feel where is(are) risk and unsafe to cause who does not choose to go to the country to travel. Then, the travel agents will avoid to choose to spend much time to design the different traveling package to attract their potential travel consumers to choose to travel. The reason is because in the case of individual traveler's tourism experience, the traveler whose past disappointment travel experience (psychological risk) will be a serious threat to the traveler's health or life (health, physical or terrorism risk). The past safety or unhealthy risk to the country(countries) will influence the traveler decides to choose not to go to the countries(country) to travel again in the future.

5.2 What is push and pull factors to influence any traveler who chooses where is whose preferable travelling destination ?

How to apply (AI) big data to predict individual traveler's behavioral intention of choosing a travel destination? Understanding why people travel and what factors influence their behavioral intention of choosing a travel destination is beneficial to tourism planning and marketing. In general, an individual's choice of a travel destination into two forces.

The first force is the push factor that pushes an individual away from home and attempt to develop a general desire to go somewhere, without specifying where that may be.

The other force is the pull factor that pull an individual toward in destination, due to a region-specific or perceived attractiveness of a destination. The respective push and pull factors illustrate that people travel because who are pushed by whose internal motives and pulled by external forced of a destination. However, the decision making process leading to the choice of a travel destination is a very complex process.

For example, a Taiwanese traveler who might either choose new travel destination of Hong Kong or another old travel Asia destinations again or who also might choose any one of Western country, as a new travel destination. The travel agents can predict where who will have intention to choose to travel from whose past behavior and attitude, subjective and perceived behavioral control model. When (AI) big data gather past every country traveler number who chose to go to which countries to travel in order to judge where destinations will be the country travelers' travelling choice destinations in the future.

The factors influence where is the traveler choice, include personal safety, scenic beauty, cultural interest, climate changing, transportation tools, friendliness of local people, price of trip, trip package service in hotels and restaurants, quality and variety of food and shopping facilities and services etc. needs. So, whose factors will influence where is the individual travel's choice. It seems every traveler whose choice of travel process, will include past behavior. e.g. travelling experience, travelling habit, then to choose the best seasoned travelling action to satisfy whose travel needs. This process is the individual traveler's psychological choice process, who must need time to gather information to compare concerning of different travel packages, destination scene, climate change, transportation tools available to the destination, air ticket price etc. these factors, then to judge where is the best right destination to travel in the right time.

Hence, (AI) big data can gather past different countries' climate changing data, transportation tool changing data, destination scene environment changing etc. different data to give opinions to travelling businesses whether any country's these above factors will influence about how many traveler number will be increase or decrease in the future.

5.3 Why can expectation, motivation and attitude factor influence travelling behavior?

Social psychology is concerned with gaining insight into the psychological of socially relevant behaviors and the processes. For instance, on a global level bad influence to global warming, it influences some countries extreme cold or hot bad climate changing occurrence, then it ought influence some travelers' behavioral decision to change their mind to choose some countries to go to travel at the moment which do not occur extreme hot or cold climate (temperature). e.g. above than 40 degree in summer or below than 0 degree in winter. Due to the extreme climate changing environment in the countries, it will cause them to feel uncomfortable to play during their trips. So, the global warming causes to climate changing factor will influence the numbers of travel consumption to be reduced possibly. This is global climate changing environment factor influences to bad or uncomfortable social psychological feeling to global travelers' mind of traveling decision. What is individual traveler expectation, motivation and attitude? Tourism sector includes inbound (domestic) tourism and outbound (overseas) tourism both incomes to any countries. According to recent article, a tourist behavior model has been developed, called the expectation, motivation and attitude (EMA) model (Hsu et al., 2010).

This model focuses on the pre-visit stage of tourists by modeling the behavioral process by incorporating expectation, motivation and attitude. Travel motivation is considered as an essential component of the behavioral process, which has been increasing attention from the travel; industry. The economic approach defines "tourism" is an identifiable nationally important industry. It includes the component activities of transportation, accommodation, recreation, food and related service. So, tourism behavioral consumption is concerned the individual tourist's usual habituate of the industry which responds to whose needs, and of the impacts that both the tourist and the tourism industry have on the socio-cultural, economic and physical environment.

However, travel motivation means how to understand and predict factors that influence travel decision making. According to Backman and others (1995, p.15), motivation is conceptually viewed as " a state of need, a condition that services as a driving force to display different kind of behavior toward certain types of activities, developing preferences, arriving at some expected satisfactory outcome." So, motivation and expectancy which has close relationship to any tourist before who decided to do any tourism of behavior.

Some economists confirmed motivation and expectancy which has relations, such as expectation of visiting an outbound destination has a direct effect on motivation to visit the destination; motivation has a direct effect on attitude toward visiting the destination; expectation of visiting the outbound destination has a direct affection on attitude toward visiting the destination and motivation has a mediating effect on the relationship in between expectation and attitude.

Hence, (AI) big data can gather all the country's climate environment change, transportation tool change, entertainment scene change, hotel price and restaurant price change etc. data to give opinions whether the country will attract how many traveler to choose to go to travel in the year.

CHAPTER SIX

(AI) deep learning techniques to forecast travelling environment behavioral consumption

Prediction how many travelers will choose to go to the country to travel. It is similar to apply deep-learning technology to predict how to raise the agricultural farming productivity in the agricultural export country.
The (AI) deep-learning technology leads to performance enhancement and generalization of artificial intelligent technology. It influences the global leader in the field of information technology has declared its intention to utilize the deep-learning technology to solve environmental problems, such as climate change.
So, it will help agriculture farming businesses can raise any plant food: vegetable, fruit, rice which grow up very easily if farmers can apply (AI) deep-learning technology to solve environment problems to influence their plant food grow. If the whole year seasonal change is very good and it is suitable for any plant food to grow in farming land easily, e.g. rain is enough and soil is enough for any plant food to grow in the farm lands. Then, fruit, rice, vegetable etc. agriculture businesses will have much beneficial attribution to global farmers.
The question is how to use deep-learning technologies in the environmental field to predict the status of pro-environmental consumption. We predicted the pro-environmental consumption index based on Google search query data, using a recurrent neural network (RNN model). To certify the accuracy of the index, we compared the prediction accuracy of the RNN model with that of the ordinary least square and artificial necessary network models.

For example, the RNN model predicts the pro-environmental consumption index better than any other model. we expect the RNN model to perform still better in a big data environment because the deep-learning technologies would be increasingly as the volume of data grows. So, deep-learning technologies could be useful in environmental forecasting to prevent damage caused by climate change to influence any rice, vegetable, tomato, potato, fruit etc. different plant food grow in any countries‘ farming land easily.
For South Korea example, over 800 government agencies spent 2.2 trillion Korea won on eco-products in 2014 year.

However, green products are rarely purchased outside these agencies. This phenomenon occurs because there is a gap between consumer attitudes and behavior , that is environmental attitude is a major factor in decision making vis-a-vis the consumption of " green" food and services (Jorea Ministry of Environment, 2015).

Therefore, it is necessary to understand those consumer attitude, that will lead to sustainability-conductive behavior and consumption. (AI) Deep learning system can be applied to attempt understand those traveler attitude to environment protection to fly to which country. For example, (AI) deep learning system can attempt to gather data concerns how many Hong Kong people concern air pollution challenge to influence their health, then it can attempt to predict how many Hong Kong travelers do not choose to go China travel, due to the air pollution challenge to influence their health.

6.1 Environmental travel consumption prediction

Recently, many researchers have studied pro-environmental consumption and household indexes as well as suicide rate predictions using messages posted by internet users on Google trend, Tweets etc. channel.

Whether can environmental consumption be predicted by (AI) deep-learning technological internet channel to influence how many travelers choose to go to the country to travel?

How can impact the pro-environmental consumption attitudes of green policies to influence how many travelers choose to go to the country to travel?

For example, Korea scientists estimated pro-environmental attitudes using search query data provided by Google trend and confirmed through regression analysis, that pro-environmental attitude has a positive correlation with the pro-environmental attitude index. They also explained that environment-friendly attitude of residents plan an important role in policy making. In the past, most household consumption indexed were calculated through surveys, but (AI) deep-learning technological tool " big data" have recently gained research attention (Lee et al. 2016). So, (AI) deep learning technology can attempt to gather whether how many Korea residents who concern environment pollution to influence their eating green food attitude then to judge whether how many Korea residents hope to leave their country to travel anywhere either high risk environment pollution countries to travel or low risk environment pollution countries to travel in the future.

It seems that (AI) deep-learning technology can help agricultural export countries' farmers , e.g. US, UK, Canada, New Zealand, Australia, Japan, China, India etc. they can predict environmental behavioral consumption to any rice, tomato, potato , fruit, vegetable etc. plant food consumers. The beneficial advantages to them include as below:

(a) Assuming they know their countries' weather, when it has less rain to cause drought or when it has more rain in any seasonal time in the year. They can choose not to grow any kinds of above these plant food to avoid loss.

(b) They can make any kinds of above these plant food price raising after their prediction of these bad seasonal time to cause their plant food shortage supply challenge. Because these plant food consumers' demand number is more, but the supply of these above plant food supply number is less. However, due to they had predicted when the bad seasonal time can not allow them to grow these above plant food before. So, they have enough time to grow many these above plant food number in predictive good seasonal time to prepare to supply to their plant food import countries' plant food consumers to eat. Thus, these predictive environmental consumption plant food export countries can raise their plant food price to sell to them. When, the other non-pre-predictive environmental consumption plant food export countries can not supply any one of those plant food to them to eat, due to the bad climate to cause them can't grow any one of these plant food to export to sell.

Thus, (AI) deep-learning technology can be applied to predict how to raise the plant food supply number in order to raise price to the import plant food countries consumers to eat, due to they feel difficult to buy these plant food to eat in the bad climate seasonal time in whole year.

(c) (AI) deep-learning technology can help climate scientists to find what reasons cause their countries; rain sudden increases or cause their countries' rain sudden decreases. After its gathering data analysis, it can assist climate scientists to find solution methods to attempt to control the rain level can be right falling down level to let agricultural export farmers who can grow their plant food to sell to agricultural import countries in whole year.

(d) The agricultural export countries' farmers can apply (AI) deep-learning technology to help them to choose whether growing which kinds of plant food in that whether climate time to earn more plant food consumption number more easily.

Due to the agricultural countries climate will often change, for example, tomato, potato, rice, fruit etc. plant food can be adapt to grow in more rain time, but vegetable can not be adapt to grow in more rain time. If farmers can apply this technology to predict when it will have move rain or when it will have less rain to fall down in their countries. Then, they can choose to grow which kinds of plant food number more, in the suitable seasonal climate time in order to raise plant food growing number productivities to supply to sell to satisfy any agricultural food import countries' demand effectively.

(e) (AI) deep-learning technology can help agricultural import countries to solve agricultural food shortage challenge in long term. When this technology can be popular to base applied by the agricultural plant food export countries. It will solve global agricultural food shortage challenge. For example, when one agricultural export countries' farmers can popular accept to apply this technology to predict when to grow which kinds of plant food more to rise number productivities to sell. e.g. vegetable, fruit, rice Besides another agricultural export countries' farmers can also accept to apply this technology to predict when to grow plant food, e.g. potato, tomato to raise number productivities to sell. Then, they can concentrate on growing the specific kinds of plant food in order to raise the specific plant food number productivities in every seasonal change time every month. Then, global agricultural plant food supply must be raised, due to these predictive environmental change farmers can know who ought grow which kinds of plant food to sell to raise number productivities.

Consequently, (AI) deep learning can gather where countries will have high risk environment pollution to influence health food supply. Then, it can give opinions to travelling businesses when these high risk environment pollution countries will encounter the traveler number to be decreased, due to the environment pollution serious challenge will occur.

6.2 What methods can predict future travel behavioral consumption ?

How to use qualitative of travel behavioral method to predict future travel consumption from (AI) big data ?

I also suggest to use qualitative of travel behavioral method to predict future travel consumption. Methods such as focus groups interviews and participant observer techniques can be used with quantitative approaches on their own to fill the gaps left by quantitative techniques. These insights have contributed to the development of increasingly sophisticated models to forecast travel behavior and predict changes in behavior in response to change in the transportation system. I shall indicate the weaknesses of human travelling investigation methods as below:

First, survey methods restrict not only the question frame but the answer frame as well, anticipating the important issues and questions and the responses. However, these surveys methods are not well suited to exploratory areas of research where issues remain unidentified and the researched seek to answer the question "why?".

Second, data collection methods using traditional travel diaries or telephone recruitment can under represent certain segments of the population, particularly the older persons with little education, minorities and the poor. Before the survey, focus group for example can be used to identify what socio-demographic variables to include in the survey, how best to structure the diary, even what incentives will be most effective in increasing the response rate.

After the survey, focus, focus groups can be used to build explanations for the survey results to identify the "why" of the results as well as the implications. One Asia Pacific survey research result was made by tourism market investigation before. It indicated the travel in Asia Pacific market in the past, had often been undertaken in large groups through leisure package sold in bulk, or in large organized business groups, future travelers will be in smaller groups or alone, and for a much wider range of reasons.

Significant new traveler segments, such as female business traveler. The small business traveler and the senior traveler, all of which have different aspirations and requirements from the travel experience.

Moreover, Asia tourism market will start to exist behaviors in the adoption of newer technologies, a giving the traveler new ways to manage the travel experience, creating new behaviors. This with provide new opportunities for travel providers. The use of mobile devices, smartphones, tablets etc. and social media are the obvious findings to become an integral part of the travel experience. Thus, quality method can attempt to predict Asia Pacific tourism market development in the future. It is such as (AI) big data gathering tool can give traveler quality opinions to any travelling businesses to make the more accurate where will be the popular travel destination choice next month or next half year or next year.

However, improving the predictive power of travel behavior models and to increase understanding travel behavior which lies in the use of panel data(repeated measures from the same individuals). Whereas, cross-sectional data only reveal inter-individual differences at one moment in time, panel data can reveal intra-individual changes over time. In effect, panel data are generally better suited to understand and predict (changes in) travel behavior. However, a substantial proportion was also observed to transition between very different activity/travel patterns over time, indicating that from one year to the next, many people renegotiated their activity/travel patterns.

6.3 How to apply advanced traveler information systems (ATIS) to predict future travelling behavior?

Nowadays, information can impact on traveler behavior and network performance. For example, when steadily growing levels of vehicle ownership and vehicle miles traveled information has been identified as a potential strategy towards man aging travel demand, optimizing transportation networks and better utilizing available capacity. Toward, this goal to predict further tourist behavioral consumption. Many countries, government tourism development institutes has applied advanced traveler information systems (ATIS) which travel behavior models and high-fidelity network performance models made increasingly feasible through the rapid advances in computer power. Crucial components of this problem domain are the modeling of individual tourist drivers' response to travel information and the development accurate guidance of relevance to real would trip makers. So, this advanced traveler information systems (ATIS) can assist the tourist who like to rent travelling car tools to travel in any countries own free traveler information systems service conveniently. Also, this travel information system can be intended to assist travelers to make better travel choices. e.g. this system can improve the decision making of individual traveler rather than improvements of network performance overall. So, we need to understand how tourists make their travel plans. Also, understanding decision process that lead to booking of the trip is equally important, as it allows of a potential behavior.

6.4 How can online tourism sale channel influence traveling consumption of behavior?

Nowadays, internet is popular, it seems that booking air ticket behavior of using internet is predicted to influence overall tourism air tickets payment method. Tourism industry has grown in the previous several decades. Despite its global impact, questions related to better understanding of tourists and whose habits. Using online travel air ticket booking benefits include booking electronic air tickets can be made from entering any electronic travel agents websites in the short time and electronic travel ticket payers do not need leave home, who can pay visa card to pre booking any electronic travel ticket from online channel conveniently.

6.5 How can analyze activity based travel demand ?

Nowadays, human are concerning the traffic congestion and air quality deterioration, the supply oriented focus of transportation planning has expanded to include how to manage travel demand within the available transportation supply. Consequently, there has been an increasing interest in travel demand management strategies, such as congestion pricing that attempts to change aggregate travel demand. The prediction aggregate level, long term travel demand to understanding disaggregate level (i.e. individual levels) behavioral responses to short term demand policies, such as ride sharing incentives, congestion pricing and employer based demand management schemes, alternate work schedules, telecommuting limitation of travel agent traditionally work nature shall influence oriented trip based travel modelling passenger travel demand indirectly.

Finally, online travel purchase will be popular to influence the number of travel behavioral consumption nowadays.

Any travel package products can be sold from websites to attract travelers to choose to pre-book air ticket for any trips conveniently. In the past ten years, the internet has become the predominant carrier of all types of information and transactions. Regarding travel decisions, internet has also become an important sales channels for the travel industry, because it is associated with comparably lower distribution and sales costs, but also because it adapts to high supply and demand dynamics in this industry. Consequently, the travel and tourism industry tries to increase the internet sale specific share of sales volumes. So, internet sale channel has changed travel consumption behavioral pattern and characteristics and travel experience. For example, Switzerland has one of the highest population-to-computer ratio in Europe. It is also one of the most highly internet penetrated countries in terms of use of the WWW on a day-to-day basis, with more than 75 percent of the population older than 14 years using the WWW daily (ICT, 2005).

The reason of booking online tourism may include: convenience, fast transaction, finding traveling package choice easily, more airline seats available. So, online booking tourism will influence the traditional tourism agents visiting of sales and air tickets and travelling package numbers to be decreased. Finally, the online booking tourism market shares will be expanded to more than traditional tourism agents visits sale market in the future one day. So, the travel agents who still use the traditional tourism visiting sale channel which ought raise whose features to compare to differ to online tourism sale channel if these traditional tourism agents want to keep competitive ability in tourism industry for long term.

6.6 What is actively based patterns of urban population of travel behavioral prediction method?

Actively based patterns of urban population. It is a method of motivational framework means in which societal constraints and inherent individual motivations interact to shape activity participation patterns. It can be used to predict one city or urban the numbers of travel demand in the year. It has two elements: First, capability constraints refer to constraints are imposed by biological needs, such as eating and sleeping and/or resources, such as income, availability of cars etc. to undertake the urban or city's family activities in the year. Second, coupling constraints define where, when and the duration of planning activities that are to be pursued with other individuals. So, this method needs to gather information (data) to get the relationship between activities, travel and spending work time and space time to evaluate whether there are how many families who have real needs to spend time to go to travel in the year.

6.7 What is trip based versus activity based approaches?

What is trip based versus activity based approaches? The fundamental difference between the trip-based and activity based approaches is that the former approach directly focuses on trips without explicit recognition of the motivation or reason for the trips and travel. The activity based approach , on the other hand, views travel as a demand derived from the need to pursue travel activities. So, it is better understand the individual or family behavior basis for individual or family travelling decision regarding participation in travelling activities in certain places or cities or countries at given times and hence the resulting travel needs. This behavioral basis includes all the factors that influence the why, how, when and where of performed activities and resulting individuals and household, the cultural/social norms of the community and the travel surrounding environment.

Another difference between the two approaches is in the way travel is represented. The trip based approach represents travel as a collection of trips. Each trip is considered as independent of other trips, without considering the inter-relationship in the choice attributes , such as time, destination and mode of different trips. As tours are chains of trips beginning and ending at a same location , say home or work. The tour based representation helps maintain the consistency across and capture the interdependency and consistency of the modeled choice attributed among the trips of the same tour.

In addition to the tour based representation of travel, the activity based approach focuses on sequences or patterns of activity participation and travel behavior, using the whole day or longer periods of time is the unit of analysis. Such as approach can address travel demand management issues through an examination of how people modify their activity participation, for example, will individuals substitute more out-of-home activities for in home activities in the evening of who arrived early form work due-to a work schedule change?

The major difference between trip based and the activity based approaches is in the way, the time dimension of activities and travel is considered. In the trip based approach, time is reduced to being simply a cost making a trip and a day's viewed as a combination, defined peak and off peak time periods. On the other hand, activity based approach views individuals' activity travel patterns are a result of their time use decisions with a continuous time domain. As individuals have 24 hours in a day or multiples of 24 hours for longer periods of time and decide how to use that travel among or allocate that time to activities and travel and with who, subject to their socio-demographic, transportation system and other and scheduling of trips. So, determining the impact of travel demand management policies on time use behavior is an important step to assessing the impact of such policies on individual travel behavior. The final major difference between this two approaches relates to the level of aggregation. In the trip based approach, most aspect of travel, e.g. number of trips etc. are analyzed at an aggregate level.

Consequently, trip based methods accommodate the effect of socio-demographic attributes of households and individuals in a very limited fashion, which limits the activity of the method to evaluate travel impacts of long term socio-demographic characteristics of the individuals who actually make the activity travel choices and the travel service characteristics of the surrounding environment. So, the activity based models are better equipped to forecast the longer term changes in travel demand in response composition and the travel environment of urban areas. Also, using activity based models, the impact of policies can be assessed by predicting individual level behavioral responses instead of employing trip based statistical averages that are aggregated over defined demographic segments.

6.8 Can apply (AI) big data gathering method predict senior age will be main travelling target?

In the past, Germany government had established tourism survey analysis to analyze survey data in order to arrive at reliable conclusions on future trends in travel behavior. To aim to find how demographic change will influence the tourism market and how the industry can adapt to those changes. The travel analysis provided data on tourism consumer behavior, including attitudes, motives and intentions. Since, 1970 year, it is based on a random sample, representative for the population in private households aged 14 years or older. Then, a continuous high scientific standard combined with a national and international users makes the travel analysis a useful tool and reliable source for tourism industry and policy decisions. It aimed to gather statistical data. e.g. on the age structure and on demographic trends, quantitative and qualitative analysis with time series data from the travel analysis. It shows e.g. not only the future volume , quite different from today's seniors, or how who will travel of family holidays will change, e.g. single parents of low, but grandparents of growing significance for tourism.

Demographic change is said to be one of the important drivers for new trends in consumer traveling change behavior in most European countries (e.g. Lind 2001). Because the growing number of senior citizens in the European Union and other industrialized countries, such as the USA and Japan, looks to become one of the major marketing challenges for the tourism industry. United Nations statistics predict that the share of people being 60 age or older will grow dramatically in the coming future, and is expected to rise from 10 percent of the world population in 2000 year to more than 20 percent in 2050 year (United Nations Population Division, 2001). From its statistic, some data showed that travel propensity increased throughout life until the age of about 50 years of age and was then kept stable until very late in life 75 age. The most important results is that the travel propensity when getting older is not going down between 65 and 75 age of course, the overall development of this variable is influenced by a lot of other factors which are responsible for quite a variation over time. It is now possible to suggest that the general pattern of travel propensity is one of the key indicators for holiday life cycle travel behavior, includes three stages. The growth stage tends to increase from early adult hood until 45 age old or when reaching some 80%. The next stage is stabilization from the ages of around 50 age, until 75 age old, starting with a lower increase. Finally, the decrease stage is a slight decrease occurs once people reach the more advanced age of 75 age to 85 age old (Lohmann & Danielsson 2001).

So, it seems Germany government tourism prediction to future travelers' behavior indicated these findings, such as on how future senior generations will travel, who had used survey data to examine the patterns of travel behavior of a generation getting older and applied the findings to draw conclusions on the future. Also, it predicted that on the future of family trips, family segmentation will be the travel behavior patterns in the future. These findings together with the statistical data on demographic change allowed for a better understanding of the coming tends in family holidays. It's aim developed in consumer behavior related to demographic change and predicted what will happen future of tourism one had to consider other influences and drivers as well, for example, trends on the supply side. e.g. low cost airlines or in travelling consumption behavior in general whether how the past may provide a key to predict travel patterns of senior citizens to the future.

Given the projected growth of the senior citizens market, designing specific marketing strategies to meet the prospective needs of elderly tourists will become increasingly important. It has been an implicit assumption that it will be a close relationship between the travel behavior of today's senior citizens and the those of future ones. The growing number of senior citizens in the world. e.g. China, Hong Kong, Japan, USA etc. countries. Global senior citizen tourism market will be based solely on demographic predictions about the future of the population's age structure. However, many of these seniors won't only live longer but will be fitter and more active until later in life.

Many of the will also have plenty in life. Many of them will also have plenty of time and money to spend on travel. So, will these new seniors behave like today's senior citizens? Will they adopt the same travel behavior as the previous generation or become a new market of oldies for the leisure and tourism industry? However, to determine the actual number of senior citizens who will be travelling and to sought to evaluate and specify certain difficult to predict the actual numbers of senior citizen to any country. However, they can be based on the implicit assumption that there is a close relationship between the travel behavior of past, present and future seniors. But is this a valid assumption? As the revise- analysis travel analysis survey, which was conducted in Germany every year, offered some interesting data possibilities. It was designed to monitor the holiday travel behavior, opinions and attitudes of Germans and has been carried out since 1970 year, questions in the questionnaire. Data are based on face to face interviews, with a representative sample of more than 7,500 respondents, the interviews being carried out in January each year. All results refer to the average for the defined generated, which ranges generally over ten years. The group of people then at the age of 60 to 69 age is described. This corresponds to the same generation ten years ago, when they had an age of 50 to 59 age. When this methodological approach is not necessarily very sophisticated, it does have the important advantages of being cost effective.

6.9 IS (AI) big data gathering method a better psychological method to compare human marketing research method predict travel behavioral consumption?

On the psychological view point, I think individual traveler's character will have those kind of personal characteristics. First, simplicity searchers value above everything ease not transparency in their travel planning and holiday making, and are willing to avoid having to go through extensive research. Second, cultural purists use their travel as an opportunity to immerse themselves in an unfamiliar looking to break themselves entirely from their home lives and engage. Sincerely with a different way of living. Third, social capital seekers understand that to be well travelled is a personal quality, and their choices are shaped by their desire to take maximum of social reward from their travel. They will exploit the potential of digital media to enrich and inform their experiences, and structure their adventures always keeping in mind they are being watched by online audiences. Finally, reward hunters seek a return on the investment who make in their busy , high-achieving lives. Linked in part to the growing trend of wellness, including both physical and mental self-improvement who seek truly extraordinary and often indulgent or luxurious' must have experiences.

Why needs to know the personal character of individual traveler's characteristics? Because if travel agents could feel which kinds of individual traveler's character, then who can predict which kind of travel package to design to them more easily. For example, how to determine future travel behavior from past travel experience and perceptions of risk and safety? We need to concern that the influences of past international travel experience, types of risk associated with international travel and the overall degree of safety feeling during international travel on individual's travelling experiences likelihood of travelling to various geographic regions on their next international vacation trip or avoidance of those regions, due to perceived risk. Because individual traveler's experience of safety risk degree to the countries, it will influence who chooses to go to the countries/country to travel again.

Why travelers avoid certain destinations are as relevant decision making as why who choose to go to the country(countries) to travel. Perceptions of risk and safety and travel experiences are likely to influence travel decisions; efforts to predict future travel behavior can benefit to individual tourist's decision making.

As Weber & Bottorn (1989) defined risky decision is as "choices among alternatives that can be described by probability distributions over possible outcomes" (p.114). Some psychologists judge subjective perceptions of physical reality, i.e. image of a particular tourist destination, whereas value judgement refers to the way individual rank destinations according to whose attributes. i.e. attractiveness, safety, risk etc. factors to form on overall image. So, if the individual traveler had unhappy and worried and unsafe experiences to go to where the place(country) to travel during whose vacation time before. Then, this negative travel experience will influence who is afraid to go to the place (country) to travel again. Risk of place, country, destination or region means the danger is relatively high to the place, i.e. increasing in airplane accidents, crime or terrorist activity targeting citizens of potential traveler's nationality or the probability of occurrence is great , i.e. recent occurrences involving travel regions/destinations under consideration or effective actions to control consequences exist. i.e. selecting safe regions and destinations, taking extra precautions when traveling to risky destinations. These risk factors will influence the individual traveler who chooses to cancel travel plan to go to the country again.

Another interesting research, how to predict behavioral intention of choosing a travel destination, which has focus of tourism research for years, but the complex decision making process leading to the choice of a travel destination has not been well researched. The planned behavior model using its core constructs, attitude, subjective norm and perceived behavioral control, with the addition of the past behavioral variable on behavioral intention of choosing a travel destination.

Understanding why people travel and what factors influence their behavioral intention of choosing a travel destination is beneficial to tourism planning and marketing. Understanding travel motivation is the push and pull model. The idea of the push and pull model is the decomposition of an individual's choice of a travel destination into two forces. The first force is the push factor that pushes an individual away home and attempts to develop a general desire to go somewhere else, without specifying where that may be. The second force is the pull factor, that pulls on individual toward a destination, due to a region specific travel location or perceived attractiveness of a destination. The respective push and pull factors illustrate that people travel because who are pushed by their internal motives and pulled by external forces of a destination. Nevertheless, how push and pull factors guide people's attitude and how these attributes lead to behavioral intentions of choosing a travel destination have rarely been investigated. The decision making process leading to the choice of a travel destination is a very complex process. The planned behavior model is as a research framework to predict the behavioral intention of choosing a travel destination. The model based on the three constructs of attitude, subjective norm, and perceived behavioral control (Fishbein & Ajzen, 1975).

In conclusion, the factors can influence travelers who decide to choose to travel the country, which include personal safety was perceived to the highest motivation factors among the important factors which include, scenic beauty, cultural interests, friendliness of local people, price of trip, services in hotels and restaurants, quality and variety of food and shopping facilities and services. The factors include both push and pull. Push factors include knowledge, prestige, and enhancement of human relationship etc., whereas, the most significant pull factors include high technologic image, expenditure and accessibility etc. For example, Japanese travelers visiting Hong Kong. Push factors are such as exploration dream fulfillment and pull factors are such as benefits sought, attractions and good climate city. It will be the factor of future travel patterns and motivations of sub-cultural and ethic groups for Japanese choice to go to Hong Kong travelling.

6.10 How can apply (AI) digital channel (big data gathering method) predict travelling consumer behaviors?

(AI) big data digital channel can be applied to help travelling businesses to evaluate whether how much the e-ticket price and travelling package price is the most attractive or reasonable to persuade travelling consumers feel it is the most reasonable price to choose to buy the airline's e-tickets or the travel agent's travelling package product from internet channel . It helps travelling consumers to feel which airlines or travelling agents which ought change their e-ticket and/or travelling package price to let travelling consumers to choose to buy the airline e-ticket or the travelling agent's travelling package products from internet channel. It can be applied to predict whether how many travelling consumer numbers can be increased or decreased when the airline e-ticket price is variable or the travelling agent travelling package price is variable . It aims to give opinions to help any online airlines or travelling agents to judge whether which e-ticket or travelling package price is the most reasonable to let travelling consumers to accept to choose to buy which airline's e-tickets or traveling agent's package products more attractive.

Thus, (AI) e-ticket or e-travelling package price measurement technology can be preference to be applied online communication ecommerce and mobile phone internet platform aspect. As traveling businesses can enter their past e-ticket or travelling package prices data and past travelling customer number data into computer or mobile. Then, (AI) price measurement technology can gather these data to analyze these e-ticket or travelling package product prices and past travelling customer number to compare their e-ticket and/or travelling package prices variable changing range level to find their e-ticket and /or travelling package price variable difference to measure to make conclusion about every travelling package or/and e-ticket product's price variable changing will influence how many travelling customer number increase or decrease changing to choose to sell their different kinds of travelling package or e-ticket products more accurate. Then, (AI) price measurement software will help them to analyze all past e-ticket and/or travelling package price variable changing data to compare whether which e-ticket and/or travelling package price range can let travelling customers to feel it is more reasonable and attractive to influence them to choose to buy their e-ticket or travelling package product among different airlines and travel agent choices. Because any e-ticket or travelling package product's price is one important factor to influence travelling consumers to choose to buy the airline's e-tickets or travelling agent's travelling package products.

For example, Amazon publish has applied (AI) price measurement technology to help authors to decide how much every different topic of e-book or paper book price, it can attract the largest number of readers to buy. Any one author only needs to type whose book name to Amazon publish author himself/herself Amazon website. Amazon publish (AI) price measurement learning machine will help them to auto-calculate and judge how much e-book or paper book price is the most attractive and the most reasonable in order to increase reader number to buy their e-books or paper books to read. So, (AI) online price measurement machine will gather past similar book names and past every similar book readers‘ reading times and the number of readers to give opinions to let every author to judge whether his/her very new e-book or paper book ought charge how much price to the e-book or paper book which can attract many readers to choose to buy. Although, it is not ensure that the e-book or paper book price must let readers to feel it is the most reasonable price to choose to buy in reader's view point. However, it has other factors to influence readers' choice to buy the e-book or paper book, e.g. whether the book content is attractive to public, the author's familiarity, the book's page is enough or not to satisfy readers to read etc. factors. But, instead of all these extra factors to influence readers to choose to buy the book to read. (AI) price measurement learning machine can real give opinions to every author to let them to judge the e-book or paper book different price range whether is too high to influence readers to choose to buy to read or tool low to influence readers feel it is possible poor content book to compare other similar content books. Thus, (AI) price measurement machine can help authors to predict every reader's reading behaviors or reading experience and reading habit from online channel in short time easily. The author only enter the book name to let Amazon publish price measurement machine to check, it will follow past reader's reading habit and reading experience to judge whether the similar all book topic sale record to judge how much price is the reasonable price to attract many readers to buy the book.

Hence, (AI) can be applied to digital channel to help travelling businesses to predict travelling consumer behavior in the future. In the future, mobile/smartphone, laptop, desktop will be most frequent used ecommerce channels to develop online business. So, (AI) can be also applied to these platforms to gather data to make analysis to help travelling businesses to predict travelling consumer purchase behaviors popularly. Due to , ecommerce is popular to global, so digital online and instore channels can be one good channel to let (AI) learning machine to make platform to gather past every online travelling consumer purchase (buying) experience data to help travelling businesses to build airline or travelling agent brand personality and having a responsible, positive impact on society.

To apply (AI) learning machine technology to understand travelling customer online purchase behavior, it will raise business e-commerce successful chance: For example, (AI) learning machine can help travelling businesses to gather data to analyze to determine whether short-term or long-term signals in the online travelling consumer behavior that indicate higher purchase intents to let every online travelling business to know. (AI) learning machine can find that online users with long-term purchasing intent tend to save and click through on more content.

However, as online travelling users approach the time of purchase their activity becomes more topically focused and actions shift from saves to searches from online travelling consumption channel. Then, (AI) learning machine will further find that the brand airline and/or travelling agent purchase signals in online travelling consumption behavior can exist weakness before an online travelling purchase is made and can also be traced across different online travelling purchase categories. Finally, (AI) learning machine synthesize these insights in predictive models of online travelling user purchasing intent to the brand of airline or/and travelling agent travelling package product. Taken together, it's work identifies a set of general principles and signals that can be used to model online travelling user e-ticket and/or travelling package purchasing intent across many online content discovery applications. Thus, (AI) learning machine can help online travelling businesses to gather any online travelling users' click online travelling behaviors data to judge whether there are how many online travelling users will choose to find their online travelling business websites to make final decisions to buy their travelling package or/and e-ticket products from online channels. Then, it will give opinions to help the online travelling businesses to let it to judge whether what are the important website factors will help its online travelling business to attract many online travelling consumers, e.g. designing unattractive travelling website issue, online unattractive scene photos issue, unclear website travelling photo color issue, unclear website travelling advertisement message, contents and words impressions issue, lacking image movement frequent attractive seeing issue etc. different website factors. Thus, online digital channel will be one good choice to apply (AI) learning machine to help travelling businesses to predict travelling consumer behaviors.

Thus, (AI) big data technology can also assist travelling consumers to gather different manufacturers' data to compare what their advantages and disadvantages of their travelling package products are. Then, travelling consumers can make comparison to choose which airline or travelling agent is the suitable to whom to buy e-ticket or pre-booking travelling package in online travelling consumption market.

Thus, I believe that artificial intelligent "big data" gathering method can be suggested to be applied to attempt to predict travelling consumer behavioral changes in global online travelling business environment, the reasons are as below:

On the travelling consumer's beneficial hand, travelling consumers can apply this (AI) big data gathering method to attempt to gather any global airline e-tickets and/or travelling agent's package product data to be analyzed by this artificial intelligent learning system to compare human general marketing research method, e.g. survey, questionnaire, marketing plan etc. different human judgement methods to predict traveler consumption behavioral change model. Then, it analyzed all the different data to compare what are the range of the most reasonable e-ticket and/or travelling package online purchase history and sale in order to make more accurate prediction to future traveler change traveling consumption behavioral model in next month, or next half year or next year short term period traveling consumption change prediction. Thus, it seems that future AI tool can be attempted to apply to predict any industries price behavior, e.g. deciding what level of price is the attractive level to attract consumer in these industries, e.g. fuel, education, tourism, health, entertainment, etc. different product purchase. It can give more absolute price suggestion to any merchants to set their price change predict in order to increase many customer numbers to buy their products in every year, or every quarter every month, or month week, even every day etc. different sale period.

Reference

Backman and others “motivation is conceptually viewed as “ a state of need, a condition that services as a driving force to display different kind of behavior toward certain types of activities, developing preferences, arriving at some expected satisfactory outcome.”, 1995, p.15.

Fishbein & Ajzen, “The model based on the three constructs of attitude, subjective norm, and perceived behavioral control”. 1975.

Hsu et al. “A tourist behavior model has been developed, called the expectation, motivation and attitude “ (EMA) model ,2010.

ICT,WWW . “Switzerland has one of the highest population-to-computer ratio in Europe.” Switzerland, 2005.

Jorea Ministry of Environment, “ For South Korea environmental attitude is a major factor in decision making vis-a-vis the consumption of " green" food and services”, Korea, 2015.

Korea Ministry Of Environment. Public Organizations spend 2.2 Trillon Korean Won To Purchase green Products in 2014; Ministry Of Environment: Sejoung, Korea, 2015.

Lind , Lohmann & Danielsson , United Nations Population Division, “Demographic change is said to be one of the important drivers for new trends in consumer traveling change behavior in most European countries”. 2001.

Mayne, Lonnie. " Evolve of die in the age of the consumer". Entrepreneur, N.P. , 16 Apr. 2014. web of Oct. 2016.

Lee, D.; Kim, M. ; Lee, J. adoption of green electricity policies: Investigating the role of environmental attitudes via big data-driven search-queries. Energy policy 2016. 90, 187-201.

Lee, Terrence, " Tech in Asia-connecting Asia’s startup system " Tech. in Asia- connecting Asia’s startup ecosystem, N.p.,4 July 2016.

Weber & Bottorn “risky decision is as choices among alternatives that can be described by probability distributions over possible outcomes" , 1989, p.114.

CHAPTER SEVEN

What does artificial intelligence(AI) development

- What (AI) function is?

Some scientists explain that artificial intelligence means which is an expert system, computer software that embodies a portion of the specialized knowledge of a human portion in a specific, narrow domain, owns decision making ability of human expert. The (AI)technology is based on the premise that what makes a person an expert is years of experience that enables who recognizes certain patterns in a problem as being similar to pattern. For example, in the future artificial intelligence system can be applied to control air traffic, design to computer configuration, medical diagnosis, instruction/training, speech/interpretation, monitoring to (nuclear plant), planning to mission, factory scheduling, prediction weather, repairing telephone, automatic driving etc. different industries.

Artificial intelligence characteristics include: creative, adaptive , common sense, fact processing, quick replication, broad focus permanent and consistent skill. Otherwise, traditional computer expert system disadvantage includes perishable, unpredictable, slow reproduction, expensive, slow reproduction, slow processing lacks inspiration, needs instruction, narrow focus only machine knowledge. So, artificial intelligence is a branch of computer science devoted to creating computer to influence software and hardware to attempt to create human intelligence or human intelligent behavior. It is learning from experience, responds flexibility in situation that are, new or not anticipated.

Thus, (AI) can be learnt programmed knowledge to solve problems, using reasoning in solving problem, understanding and inferring facts and rules, recognizing the relative importance of different elements in a situation.

In summary, artificial intelligence is concerned with two basic ideas mainly: The first idea, it involves studying the thought processes of humans to understand what intelligence is; the second idea, it deals with representing thought processes using companies to create artificially intelligent entities for testing the theories of intelligence.

It brings this question:

Can AI apply these strengths to assist human to raise productivity?

- Can (AI) impact human job nature?

Human need concern these two questions:

Will artificial intelligence (AI) reduce some human jobs in order to instead of replacing machines to do?
If (AI) can replace human some jobs, does it reduce productivity or raise productivity ?
Due to artificial intelligence is the ability of machines to do thing, that people would require intelligence. For example, artificial intelligence machine man driving(self-driver), it (AI) machine man driving research is an attempt to discover and describe aspects of human intelligence that can be simulated by driving machine functions. Alternatively, (AI) mathematical research may be another viewed as an attempt to develop a mathematical theory function to describe the abilities and actions of things (natural or man-made) exhibiting intelligent behavior and server as a design of intelligent calculation machine function.
Can artificial intelligence machines better than manual to replace traditional human service job? For example, can artificial intelligence machine man (self-driving) driver drive to replace human driver?
Is (AI) replaced to human any job, Can it bring positive impact to raise more productivity than human ?
I shall compare the differences between humans and computers function as below:
The characteristics of humans are good at recognizing various things, either seen before or not, recognizing the relationship patterns between things. Human thinking is common sense reasoning, combining all types of sensory input, acting appropriately in novel situations, learning new things and changing behavior patterns, making decisions , even when given incomplete information, working with noisy, incomplete information gathering behaviors . However, characteristics of computers are good at: The tasks humans do naturally are extremely difficult for a computer program as intelligent, which must be able to do the same kind of tack as humans do naturally.
Hence, it seems that (AI) can raise productivity, due to it is manufactured computer software and computer software can do complex jobs to compare human, even human can not do these complex jobs.
Hence, (AI) is an combination of many different success and technologies: Linguistics - computational and socio, philosophy-logic, philosophy of mind and of language, electronical engineering -image and speech processing, pattern recognition, robotics, machine learning, neural networks, optimization scheduling, management information system and decision making. So, it is possible that (AI) can impact human job nature to raise more productivity to do better than human working behavior in the future.

How can (AI) influence labor market?

- How can human society job nature
to be changed to artificial intelligent society?

From the first intelligent perspective reason view point, artificial intelligence is making machines " intelligent" acting as humans expect people to act. Artificial intelligence has ability to distinguish computer responses from human responses, it owns knowledge to solve expert problem. From another research perspective reason view point, artificial intelligence is the study of how to make computers do things which, at the moment, people do better (Rich & Knight, 1991, p.3).
(AI) researchers are native in a variety of domains, e.g. formal tasks (mathematics, games), tasks (perception, robotics, natural language, common sense reasoning), expert tasks (financial analysis, medical diagnostics,

engineering, scientific analysis and other areas).

From the second business perspective reason view point, (AI) is a set of many powerful tools, and methodologies for using those tools to solve business problems. From a programming perspective reason view point, (AI) includes the study of symbolic programming problem solving and search .

From the third human technological perspective reason view point, today's computer can do many well-defined tasks, for example, arithmetic operations, are much faster and more accurate than human beings. However, the computers' interaction with their environment is not very sophisticated yet. How can human test whether a computer has reached the general intelligence level of a human being? Can a computer convince a human interrogator that it is a human? But before thinking of such advanced kinds of machines, human will start developing our own extremely simple " intelligent" machines.

So, it is possible that human society job efficiency and performance and productivity will to be changed better, due to artificial intelligent robots are applied to assist human to do anything when (AI) technology is developed to the mature stage in the future.

● Why does human need artificial intelligence machines?

One of major division in (AI) is between humans who think (AI) is the only serious way of finding out how we (human) work and human who want companies to do very smart things, independently of how we (human) work. This is the important distinction between cognitive scientists vs engineers.

One of another major division in (AI) is between symbolic (AI), which represents information through symbols and their relationships. Specific Algorithms are used to process these symbols to solve problems or deduce new knowledge and connectionist. So (AI) , which represents information in network. Biological processes underlying learning, task performance and problem solving are imitated from human mind behaviors.

Thus, it is possible that artificial intelligence machines can do the better human task behavior to achieve productivity and efficiency raising.

● How does artificial intelligence influence future working changing in automation employment and productivity aspects?

(AI) influences the automation working changing aspect, as companies increasingly use robots on production lines or algorithms to optimize their logistics manage inventory, any carry out other core business functions. Technological advances are creating a new automation age in which ever-smarter and more flexible machines will be deployed on an ever larger scale in the marketplace. However, researching artificial intelligence with how influences human working nature. We need to answer these questions:

How will automation transform the workplace?

What will the implications for employment?

What is likely to be its impact both on productivity in the global economy and on employment?

Advances in robotics, artificial intelligence, and machine learning are growing in a new age of automation as machines match or outperform human performance in a range of work activities, including ones requiring cognitive

capabilities.
What factors are determined the changing in workplace adoption by artificial intelligence innovation?
What advantages are automation?
Automation of activities can be enabled businesses to improve performance by reducing errors and improving quality and speed, and achieving outcomes that go beyond human capabilities.
Some scientists indicated based on their scenario modeling. They estimated automation could raise producing growth globally by 0.8 to 1.4 percent annually. Almost, the activities people are paid almost $16 trillion in wages to do in global economy have the potential to be automated by adopting currently demonstrated technology. According to their analysis of more than 2,000 work activities across 800 occupations. When less than 5% of all occupations have of least 30% of activities that could be automated. They also indicated that technical economic and social factors will determine automation. Continued technical progress, for example, in areas such as natural language processing is a key factor beyond technical feasibility , the cost of technology, competition with labor including skills, and supply and demand dynamics, performance benefits including and beyond labor cost savings and social and regulatory acceptance will affect (alter) the scope of automation.
Other some scientists also indicate U.S. country for example, the anticipate shift in the activities in labor force of a similar order of magnitude as the long term sight away from agriculture and decreases in manufacturing. Share of employment in the United States both which were achieved. So, those factors can influence why artificial intelligence technology needs. So, it is possible that future agriculture and manufacturing both industries will apply (AI) technology manufacturer-kind of job nature to raise productivity instead of farmers, fruit picking workers, farming transportation labours as well as factory manufacturing workers and supervisors etc. human-kind of job nature.

- Is artificial intelligence possible to replace labor ?

Not just intelligence, but also debating, if machines are capable of having a conscious minds. Artificial intelligence has those characteristics as below:
On functionalism aspect, artificial intelligence inputs mental states, sensory inputs, (beliefs, desires being in pain feeling) and behavioral outputs. Since mental states are identified by a functional role, which are thoughts to be manifested in various systems. Even, perhaps computers which are physical devices with electronic substrate that inform computations on inputs to give outputs similar to brains which are artificial intelligence composed of part any intrinsic relationship to each other. Thus, artificial intelligence activities is not the whole itself, but into parts or on external influence on the parts.
On dualism aspect, artificial intelligence is a set of views about the relationship between mind are matter. On materialism aspect, it builds the only thing that exists is matter, including consciousness.
On biological naturalism aspect, it is similar a human brain than feels pains makes mental situation. So, artificial intelligence is similar biologist which might to be excited to human labor work. Hence, it seems artificial intelligence can change (alter) or replace human labor work of nature in order to raise efficiency and productivity in possible

any working environment when it own human mind and effort absolutely.

- Can (AI) technology replace human labour nature of work to raise better productivity and efficiency?

On technological innovation reason view point, the history development of artificial intelligence studying the intelligence is one of most ancient scientific discipline. The history development of artificial intelligence what aims to achieve human use to sense, learn remember and think, logic probability, decision making and calculation develop from mathematics, instead of replacement human labor functions.

Artificial intelligence history development aim is the scientific analysis of skills in connection and practice with the appearance of computers from 1950 year beginning. The artificial intelligence (AI) can deal with the ultimate challenges. How can (either biological or electronic) mind sense, understand and manipulate a world that is much simple and more complex than itself? And what if would human like to construct something with such capabilities?

The general-purpose software of the early period of (AI) were only able to solve simple tasks effectively and failed when which should be used in a wider range or an more difficult tasks. One of the sources of difficulty was that early software had very few or mix knowledge about the problems which handled, and activities successes by simply syntactic manipulation. Moreover, the other difficulty was that many problems that were tried to solve by the (AI) were untreatable.

The early (AI) software whether trying step sequences based on the basic facts about the problem that should be solved, experimented with different combinations till which found a solution. From the end the 1960 year, developing the so-called expert systems were emphasized. These systems had (sue-based) knowledge base about the field which handled. Till to the beginning of the 1970 year, (Prolog) the logical programming language was born, which was built in the computation realization of a version of the resolution calculus. (Prolog) is a remarkably prevalent tool in developing expert systems (on medical, judiciary and other scopes), but natural language parsers were implemented in this language. Then, in 1981 s, the Japanese announced the fifth generation computer system project, a 10 years plan to build an intelligent computer system that use the (Prolog) language as a machine code. Nowadays, (AI) can be applied any industries, such as car manufacturing industry can use (AI) technological machine-men manufacture car, instead of replacing human labors in factory. Even, in the future, using (AI) machine-men drivers can drive any private cars or public transportation tools, instead of replacing human drivers, e.g. bus, train, tram, ferry etc. Also in the future, machine-men can replace housewives to serve families to do housekeeping clean job , e.g. cleaning toilets, bathrooms, kitchens, even cooking functions at home. So (AI) machine-man can reduce housewives works at home. Moreover, (AI) machine man can take care old people , when who are living at homes or elder care centers.

So, it seems artificial intelligence (AI) will be possible developed to manufacture a new generation machine-man to assist (serve) families to do any simply cleaning or cooking jobs at homes. Moreover, the overall demand of (AI) general social needs will also rise, such as security, driving transportation tools, restaurant cleaning, elder centers care service etc. (AI) will have chance often to practise to do its tasks every day. It is possible that it can improve worker individual simple job duty to raise productivity and efficiency to be fast.

● Why can artificial intelligence satisfy human needs?

First, On machine-man satisfactory demand aspect view point, it makes computers that think, it is the automation of activities. We associate with human thinking: like decision making, learning. It is the act of creating machine that perform function that require intelligence when performed by people. It is the study of mental faculties through the use of computational models. It is the study of computations that make it possible to perceive, reason and act. It is a branch of computer science that is concerned with the automation of intelligent behavior. It is anything in computing service that human don't yet know how to do property.

Second, on thought aspect artificial intelligence means systems thank think like humans, systems that think rationally.

Third, on behavioral aspect, artificial intelligence systems that act like human and that systems act rationally. However, the basic objective of (AI) is to represent human's thought processes in computation . These machines are supposed to exhibit behavior that. It is performed by a human being, would be considered intelligent. However, some authors feel (AI) has disadvantages, such as it is not creative, it is excited in the use of sensory devices, it can't make use of a very wide context of experiences and it does not use common sense.

For speech recognition and understanding function needs example, (AI) can be applied in speech recognition and understanding function, which (AI) speech or voice recognition is a data input method. For example, the computer recognizes and understands one (or a few) word commands. Speech understanding on the other hand is the computer's ability to understanding a spoken language. That is , the computer understands the meaning of sentences, an paragraphs through (AI).

So, (AI) can be attempted to learn human language how to speak. It is similar to translate human language skill, instead of actual human speaking skill. Also, (AI) can assist handicap learning or language student how to listen different languages by machine-man sounds from computers more accurately.

So, it seems that it (AI) can replace human language teachers speaking function and can change teaching language nature of job in language speaking and listening education industry. IT will improve its language speaking performance to teach students to raise teaching efficience and teaching performance to satisfy student learning needs in short time.

● Is artificial intelligence one good choice for human future technological benefit?

Nowadays, new technology development is popular. However, artificial intelligence is one kind of new technology choice among different technologies innovation. So it brings this question: Is artificial intelligence technology value to invest? To answer this question. I shall indicate some other new technology developments to compare (AI) technology development to judge which has urgent needs to achieve human expectation nowadays.

For example, why is green peace interested in new technologies? New technologies features prominently in our ongoing campaigns against genetic modified crops and number power. However, which are also an integral part of our solutions to environmental challenges, including renewable energy technologies, such as solar, wind and wave (water) power energy as well as waste treatment technologies, such as mechanical, biological treatment.

It seems humans need concern how to apply (AI) technology to solve environment pollution challenges in our future. So, environment protective, agriculture, natural energy technology will be popular demand to attempt to apply (AI) technology to solve their challenges or apply (AI) to assist to develop their industry. It can raise farming food and fruit number more than farmers. It seems that it can raise farming productivity.

CHAPTER EIGHT

What is relationship between (AI) productivity and economy growth

● How can artificial intelligence technology influence economy?

Advances in artificial intelligence (AI) technology and related fields have opened up new markets and new opportunities progress in critical areas, such as health, education, energy, economic development, social welfare and the environment pollution.

(AI) automation will continue to create wealth and expand the global economy development in the future. However, when many will benefits that growth won't be costless and will be accompanied by changes in the skills, that workers need to increase productivity in the economy and structural changes in the economy. So, in the skills that workers need to succeed in the economy and structural changes.

I shall indicate why aggressive policy action will be needed to help Americans who are disadvantaged by these changes , due to (AI) technology is caused. For automation industry change example, artificial intelligence (AI) capabilities will enable automation of some tasks that have long required human labor. These artificial intelligence technology introduction can increase new opportunities for individuals. The economy and society, but (AI) has also the potential to disrupt be current livelihoods of many Americans. However, (AI) leads to unemployment and increase in inequality over the long run depends not only on the (AI) technology itself, but also on the institutions and policies that are changed.

Thus, it is possible that (AI) technology will raise some countries unemployment number if the employer apply (AI) technology workers to replace human labor in their factories, but it can also raise productivities for these employers, when (AI) can spend less time to compare labor to do any human's same tasks in order to raise productivity.

● Can (AI) influence global economy growth?

Technological progress is main driver of growth of GDP per capita, allowing output to increase faster than labor and capital . However, technology can increase productivity, but also decrease the number of labor hours needed to create a unit of output. So (AI) causes unequal to labor wage decreases, even reduces the number of labor to manufacture, e.g. artificial intelligence technology of automation car manufacturing industry; clothing manufacturing industry; plane manufacturing etc. high technology of artificial intelligence manufacturing method. But (AI) should be potential environment benefit, although it raises unemployment ratio. Moreover, it can rise production , due to many skilled craft were replaced by the combination of machines and lower-skilled labor. The result of (AI) technology introduction , it causes output per hour risen when inequality declined, driving up average living standards, but the labor of some high-skill workers was no longer as valuable in the market. Otherwise, if (AI) technology is continue developed to be success. Some routine intensive occupations will be loss, which focused on predictable, e.g. easily programmable tasks, such as switchboard operators, filing clerks, travel agents, and assembly line workers would be particularly replaced by new (AI) technology. However, at the same time, (AI) technology development will bring these benefits: improvement in education (training (AI) technology scientists) , due to (AI) manufacturing technology needs are raising to businesses and institutional changes, such as the reduction in unionization and raising in the minimum wage to the (AI) manufacturing technology skilled labor in factories.

Because (AI) technology is not a single technology, but rather a collection of technologies that are applied to specific tasks, the effects of (AI) will be felt unevenly though the economy. It will bring some tasks will be most easily automated than others , and some jobs will be affected more than others, both negatively and positively. Finally, new jobs are likely to be directly created in areas , such as the development and supervision of (AI) as well as indirectly created in a range areas though out the economy as higher incomes lead to expanded demand.

However, if (AI) technology could dominate global labor markets. If labor productivity increases, do not influence to wage increases, then the large economic gains brought about by (AI) technology could be increased wealth inequality, due to employers can reduce production cost, but workers (labors) wages will not be increased, even will be decreased. Hence, it seems the (AI) technology will bring disadvantages to labor market to cause unemployment or reduce wages in possible, although it can reduce employer individual salary (wage) expenditure and it can raise productivity.

● How can artificial intelligence impact global economy growth?

Artificial intelligence (AI) technology is a branch of computer science that aims to create intelligent machines that work and react like humans. So, (AI) is a technology that appears to impact (influence) human preference by learning, understanding complex contents, enhancing humans in executing both routine and non-routine tasks. In the future, (AI) technology that can be virtual personal assistant, as well as it may exist, such as robots with human-like processing capabilities.

How can (AI) technology impact global economy growth over the next 10 years? During this time period, (AI) technology is predicted to have wide-ranging applications including: Machine learning that automates analytical model building by using algorithms that allow machines to operate without human assistance.

In global education aspect, potential applications include predicting cause-and-effect relationships from biological data, identifying new drugs, self-driving cars, and protecting against fraud, improved natural language processing that allows computers to continue to better analysis, understand and generate language to interface with humans using natural human languages. For example, transcribing notes dictated by physicians, automatically drafting articles and translating text and speech. So (AI) technology can be applied to education aspect to improve humans' knowledge level.

In visual art aspect, (AI) machine vision that allows computers to identify objects, scenes and activities in images. Current applications of (AI) machine vision include providing objective descriptions for the blind seeing(visual) needs.

We except the economic effects of (AI) technology to include both direct GDP growth from sectors that develop or manufacture. (AI) technology and indirect GDP growth through increased productivity in existing sectors that employ some form of (AI). If (AI) technology is an increasingly critical component of more products, it will become an integral part of many people's lives. Thus, (AI)'s ability to influence economic activity, rather than the economic or development status of the region. (AI) has the potential to impact income classes and to bring significant gains to both developed and developing countries. For example, (AI) has the potential to optimize good production around the world by analyzing agricultural regions and identifying what is necessary to improve crop yields.

In estimating the future economic effects by (AI) technology innovation, it is important to note that it is challenging to accurately predict which applications of (AI) will ultimately be commercially successful. In micro level economic influence, we need to apply methodologies to estimate the economic effects of investment in firms developing (AI) technology since investment levels in a technology are a telling sign of the future potential of that (AI) technology.

- How can (AI) influence GDP of high income countries in the next ten years?

How (AI)'s development may affect the global economy over the next ten years. In fact, (AI) technology has the potential to affect business across the global in a wide range of industries in ways only a number of technologies have done in the parts. For example, (AI) technology's expected to be a useful tool for enhancing human capabilities and in some instances replacing functions, such as driving a car, adoption of broadband internet, mobile telephone, industrial robotic automation have served to enhance human capabilities.

However, significant public debate has focused on projections of (AI) technology's effect on the labor force. However, large companies prefer to invest in (AI) technological industry. For example, face book's (AI) research lab., google machine intelligence lab. and micro soft machine learning and artificial intelligence research division are all making advances in (AI) technology and investing in the industry's top talent. Additionally, between 2010 year and 2015 year, nearly $5 billion in venture capital funding invested in firms across the global developing and employing (AI) technology (Facebook (AI) Research).

- How can artificial intelligence impact on workplace?

Modern information technologies and the labor economy growth of machines is powered by artificial intelligence have already strongly influenced the world of work in the 21 ST century. Computers, algorithms and software simplify every tasks and it is impossible to image how most of our life could be managed without them. How can be the information economy characterized by exponential growth replaces the most production industry based on economy of scales? What will the future world of work look like and how long will it take to get? Will the future world of work be a world where humans spend less time earning their livelihood? Alternatively, are mass unemployment, mass poverty and social distortions also possible scenario for the future, where robots, artificial intelligence systems play an increasingly central role? These questions concern how artificial intelligence further development . Can influence labor economy growth on workplace ? When the labor market has widespread impact on intelligence property, information technology, product liability, competition and labor and employment laws.

How (AI) technology impacts on labor workplace.

The future influence any organizations how labor economies use of (AI) can be analyzed, such as deep machine learning is based on a set of model high level data. Unlike human workers, the machines are connected the whole time in workplace. If one machine makes a mistake, all autonomous systems will keep this in mind and will avoid the same mistake the next time.

Over the long run intelligent machines will win against every human expert. Production robots have been replacing employees because of the (AI) technology. They work more precisely than humans and cost loss. Creative solutions like 3D printers and the self learning ability of these production robots will replace human workers, the automatic data recording and data processing, traditional back office activities are no longer in demand. Autonomous software will collect necessary information and will send it to the employee who needs it. Additionally, dematerialization leads to the phenomenon that traditional physical products are becoming software. For example, CD or DVDs are being replaced by streaming services. The replacement of traditional event ticket, e-travel ticket service products or hard cash will be the next step, due to the possibility of payment by smartphone. So, (AI) technology will impact human's daily life consumption behaviors in the future. For another example, transportation tools, such as boats and ferries and private vehicles will use sensors and navigating without human input. Taxi and truck drivers will become obsolete, the stock store applies to stock managers and postal carriers of the delivery is distributed by (AI) machine delivery method.

What is the relationship between (AI) and (CRM)?

● Can (AI) technology impact on customer relationship management (CRM) to improve service performance ?

Nowadays , (AI) is a technology almost as old as the computer industry itself, it is similar with the advent of personal assistants function to businesses and personal promotion channel, such as (Amazon's Alexa, Apple's Siri, Google's Assistant) image recognition (face book), personalized recommendations (Netflix , Amazon). Those innovations have been driven by a increase in processing power, lower cost hardware, and the exploding creation and availability of data. It seems, (AI) technology can impact global customer service management method.

How to forecast economic impact modeling to (AI) will affect global economy? Can human forecast business revenue growth and job creation (or destruction) based on (AI) applied to customer relationship management (CRM) activities? In addition to the economic impact on (AI) or (CRM) which can include an estimate of the economic impact attributable to sales forces customer base. What can economic benefits be brought to (CRM) from (AI) technology?

Artificial intelligence(AI) comprises a set of technologies that use natural language processing, machine learning, knowledge graphs, and other tools to answer questions, discover insights and provide recommendations. Computer systems can use (AI) hypothesize and formulate possible answers based on available evidence can be trained through the ingestion of vast amounts of content, and automatically adapt and learn from (AI) self mistakes and failures.

So, any business organizations (customer service departments) can provide efficient and effective customer relationship management of excellent customer service quality if which applied (AI) technology system. The different type of (AI) systems include: (AI) system platforms, machine learning (AI) based data preparation and enrichment tools, machine vision/image recognition, voice speech recognition, text analysis and natural language processing, bots , e.g. face book website and virtual digital assistance solutions, social media pattern analysis , sentiment analysis, advanced numerical analysis (e.g. IOT streaming , machine logs), supporting technologies, knowledge base dialog management, Q&A processing etc. different (AI) technology system customer relationship management (CRM) tools.

(AI) (CRM) of activity can include these categories, such as: corporate marketing, marketing operation, field marketing, customer support, digital commerce, customer analytics, customer influenced product or service design, product or service pricing, finance information, presentation, customer billing, inventory , logistics and fulfilment support, partner management etc. different CRM tools.

(AI) technology of CRM has been carrying on plan different stages to achieve CRM personal assistant tool for businesses. The stages are such as, in the beginning stage of (AI) projects in place, implement now, pilot phase next year in the final stage of (AI) customer relationship management tools are foreseeable future. So, this CRM technology has been improved to plan in different stages every year to prepare to achieve full capacity of CRM service quality for businesses to use in the future.

Hence, how to develop an estimate prediction of the economic impact (AI) technologies could have CRM activities, which depends on gathering macroeconomic information on business revenue and the basic marketing of business revenue and the basic markup of business expenses by major functions (customer support, marketing and sales , production etc.)

An economic impact model that can gather data together and forecast the results how (AI) artificial intelligence technology brings (CRM) customer relationship management benefits to businesses, e.g. surveys investigation includes IT spending by sample countries, GDP and population estimates and forecasts, revenue per employee and ratios of IT spend to GDP. Surveys (questionnaire questions) of forecast results are influenced by (AI) impact can include: results are projected from surveys and rely on estimates are made by respondents on the expected financial improvements in categories of (AI) –assisted customer relationship management activities. The forecast assumes that these estimates are correct; financial estimates are based on estimates of "first year" improvement from full (AI) implementation; forecasts are from planning to implement any artificial intelligence of customer relationship management (CRM) projects, the improvement forecast is of categories of activity , e.g. corporate marketing , digital commerce, and customer analytics. They are not estimates of ROI for the (AI) software. They rely on conservative estimates to which each of these entities might affect company revenue, expenses or productivity. They also rely on estimates of the penetration of software in customer relationship management activities . Net new jobs created are based on the ratio of new revenue to jobs required to support that revenue . They can assume that 50% of the net new revenue will support increases in labor and the rest will go for capital and other operating expenses that may replace jobs lost to automation.

In the future, some of the ways in micro economic benefits to any organizations. (AI) technology is expected to impact CRM activities include: Spending up sales cycles, improving lead generation and qualification solving customer support problems faster (raising service quality), helping companies improve brand campaigns and recognition, lowering costs of support calls when increasing resolution rates, lowering the cost of recruiting employees and partners, increasing revenue from optimized product marketing, optimizing price, distribution logistics and preventing loss through fraud detection. So, micro economic benefits view point, it seems that (AI) CRM technology can raise any companies economic benefits for care term.

Artificial intelligence enables machines or the in-build software to behave like human beings which allows these decisions and act. The advent of (AI) is leading , talking, making decisions and act. The advent of (AI) is leading to new technologies advances and transforming the economic and employment opportunities for humans in a positive way. (AI) related technologies can facilitate our live. For example, industrial robotics, robotic medical assistants, smart games, financial forecasting software, big data analysis, algorithms in health and bioinformatics, pilotless cargo places, drone ambulances and general purpose and workplace robots and others. (Disruptors technologies: Advances that will transform life, business and the global economy).

Artificial intelligence also known as computational intelligence is defined as " the human –like intelligence exhibited by machines or software. It is theorized that intelligence of humans can be described and intelligence machines or software can simulate it. These machines software can be reasonable , learn, perceive and process information, like human mind and thus facilitate human life. They can think and act for us. So, artificial intelligence is an interdisciplinary field of study including computer science, neuroscience, psychology, linguistics and philosophy.

However, (AI) research and developments have economically impacted many industries, such as robotics, telecommunications, computer applications , health, finance, heavy manufacturing, transportation, aviation, e-service and e-commerce, military , music and movie, toys and games entertainment etc. industries.

In fact, many ideas, systems and technologies have been developing in the world of (AI) technology. However, which are net called or considered (AI) products, rather which are mentioned with their specific names, such as smart graphics, machine learning, e-commerce etc. (i.e. this is called (AI) effect).

What is relationship between
(AI) and digital economy

- How can (AI) technology influence digital economy?

Nowadays, (AI) related industrial applications will replace most human power in fields, including call centers, customer services and air cargo transportation. (AI) technologies also help weather forecasting based on repeated rainfall pattern (data) recognition, through robotics (i.e. floor cleaning, moving lawns etc.) transporting people and products with unmanned vehicles, sending space unmanned smart shuttles, developing robotic arms, predicting market values in stock exchanges by internet, making homes safer, helping elderly and disabled using robotic servants etc.

Among the (AI) related technologies , there are a few that significance for the impact on society and especially on digital economy . (AI) is particularly influential in machine learning. Such as robotics, transportation, finance, health and bioinformatics, e-commerce , e-games, big online data gathering and internet-of-things. For example, machine e-learning is based in bioinformatics and robots that can learn new skills for better caregiving in healthcare. What is machine e-learning? Machines can e-learn from e-data gathering, coming up generalizations and making decisions to act in certain ways from internet.

There are important applications , such as e-machine perception, electronic online natural language learning processing, online search engines, online bioinformatics, online brain –computer interface, online game playing, online robot locomotion, online advertising, online computations finances, online health monitoring, online DNA classification and decision making, online in chemistry –cheminformatics . So, online machine learning can positively impact productivity and it can enhance information and analytical system from (AI) online channel.

What is robotics? Robotics is one of the most strongly influenced fields in (AI). For example, heavy manufacturing industries, robots and used and man power is replaced for effectiveness, precision, and accuracy, especially in respective or dangerous tasks, including welding, assembling , picking and placing .

So, robots can acquire new skills or adapt the changing dynamic environment. Also, artificial intelligence can be applied in developing transportation. For example, automated vehicles, driver assistance systems , safety systems, collision avoidance systems and public transportation. Moreover, (AI) technology has proven to produce some of the best tools to predict stock market fluctuations from internet data gathering method. It's predictions are based on ever-evolving predictions algorithms and systems learn new models and make connections between historical data and new data to measure stock market trading more accurate from internet data gathering channel.

In health field, especially in health data processing , analysis, decision making support and medical diagnosis. So, online data can show which patients will need what treatment and what alternative drugs could be used more accurate from (AI) online data gathering method. Bioinformatics is an interdisciplinary field combining statistics, (AI) online technology can help in discovering data patterns and modeling through the application of machine learning, artificial neural networks and genetic algorithms. For example, further (AI) technology development of human genome project of online data sequences.

Online shopping can be facilitated by virtual assistants developed through (AI) technology and these assistants can offer the best advice. (AI) online purchase coming after every product image recommendations and personalization bring important revenue to shopping online sites, like Amazon . Smart computer graphics and games, artificial intelligence is useful in smarter computer, graphics, scene modeling , scene rendering processes in order to create, for example, effective human –robot interactions , online machine learning, online strategic games techniques etc.

online computer related (AI) software.

So, online big data analysis and big data does have a critical need in the world of online intelligence machines and software in our future. In other words, (AI) offers online technology to enable online big data analysis to provide industrial organizations with valuable information for effective decision making in short time. For example, what IBM's Watson achieved: this machine used 200 million of structured and unstructured content with a special technology of hypothesis generation, massive evidence gathering, analysis and scoring from internet channel.

Finally, (AI) online technology another related internet invention (internet of things) (IOT) is the network of machines or objects connected through internet. These connected objects can sense their internal and external environment, communicate with each other, can send critical data and finally can make decisions to act or correct their environment from (AI) online technology. For example, factories can monitor and automatically change production processes, hospitals can monitor and regulate the health conditions of their patients , schools can collect data from facilities and cars can send data to car makers from (AI) online technology.

Partner predicts that (IOT) market will create about trillion amount value by 2020 year. Although machines collect big data from their environment, whether which gain an insight or learn from these online data largely depends on the (AI) online machine learning principals and (AI) online technology. In 2013, Mckinsey estimated that disruptive technologies closely related with potential economic impact in 2025 year between $7.1 to $13.1 trillion amount (automation of knowledge work, advanced robotics, autonomous or near-autonomous vehicles).

What is the relationship between
(AI) and global digital economy development ?

● Could work activities in China be automated
making in the nation with the world's largest automation potential?

Can (AI) technology influence China economy? Could China workers be affected and jobs made up of routine work activities and predictable? Will programmable tasks be particularly impact to China employment market ? When impact on labor market is likely to be gradual at the aggregate level, it can be sudden and dramatic at the level of specific work activities, rending some job obsolete fairly. Overall (AI) technology will raise digital skills when reducing demand for medium incomer inequality for China workers. It seems (AI) technology's effect on productivity could be crucial to China's future economic growth as the population ages are increasing.

In China, some biggest technological companies driving significant investments in research and development. Moreover, China is one of the leading global (AI) technology development county. However, China will need to focus on building its innovation capacity. For example, United States and United Kingdom are currently producing more influential (AI) technological research. However, if China planed to achieve (AI) technology success, it's traditional industries will need to develop technical know-how –to and overcoming implementation costs prepare to develop (AI) . When (AI) technology is introduced into China society, China government needs to raise concerning ethical, legal, technological security etc. business questions. Also, surrounding issues include privacy, discrimination, legal liability and regulation. It aims to encourage overseas investors to choose to invest (AI) technological industry to raise GDP growth and manufacturing industries income growth for long term in China.

If China encouraged overseas (AI) technology investment in its country. It is possible to influence China employment market to be changed. Because (AI) technology will impact to influence China people daily life. Due to (AI) technology is introduced to China society, many rich people will prefer to spend to buy any high (AI) technological products for entertainment or learning or machine man driving etc. daily necessity activities. Then it will raise GDP growth and will raise (AI) manufacturers or related-(AI) technological manufacturers profit. It is beneficial to China because it can become one high knowledgeable and (AI) technological economical society.

But it will bring bad influences to raise unemployment chance for the low skillful labor. In labor economy aspect influence , how (AI) technology can influence China low skillful labor unemployment ratio raising. The raising low skill labor unemployment reason is because China low skillful human labors are argued or are replaced by (AI) technology creating new challenges to introduce to influence China society of simply human manufacturing job nature to be changed to be high (AI) technology manufacturing job nature in any China factories. Moreover, when (AI) technology introduction to China, it will cause other related social challenges in China. The varied (AI) related challenges, including the difficulty of creating safe and reliable hardware for sensing and affecting (transportation and education), the challenges of gaining public trust, a low resource comities and public safety and security, the challenges of overcoming fears or marginalizing humans in China employment and workplace and the risk of diminishing interpersonal trust because the low skillful labors won't believe any China employers will give chance to employ them , due to (AI) technology will replace their skills and man manufacturing of productivity is much less to compare to (AI) technology manufacturing method.

How does (AI) technology influence
the future of employment change?

Are future nature of jobs changed to computerization from (AI) technology? Where are the probability of computing occupations from (AI) technology influence? What is expected impacts of future computing on labor market from (AI) technology influence? John Maynard Keynes's frequently cited prediction of widespread technological unemployment " du to our discovery of means of economic the use of labor outrunning the pace of which we can find new used of labor" (Keynes, 1933, p.3).

In the future, (AI) technology will impact some nature of occupations to change computing. This chance will also influence some countries' economic change. For example, some factory human labors hand routine manufacturing tasks will be changed to computerization of routine manufacturing tasks by (AI) technological machine men hand manufacturing method. it will cause a structured shift in the labor market, with workers reallocating their labor supply from middle-income manufacturing to low-income service occupations.

Arguably, this is because the manual tasks of service occupations are less computerization, as who require a higher degree of flexibility and physical adaptability. So, (AI) technology will influence the human hand labor skillful occupation nature of task cheaper , such as vehicle manufacturing , ship manufacturing, computer manufacturing, steel manufacturing, television, radio etc. home electronic products of heavy machine industry change. Due to (AI) technology machine man will be proper to be used to manufacturing these electronic products when the (AI) technology innovation can develop to the mature stage. Then, any countries manufacturers will choose to use (AI) technology machine man, instead of human hand production.

Supposing the future prices of computing are fallen, seriously, problem solving skills are becoming relatively productive, explaining the substantial employment growth in manufacturing occupations, involving cognitive tasks where skilled labor has a comparative advantage, as well as the increase education needs for (AI) technology computing of machine man subject study.

Prediction of education needs for (AI) technology student numbers will increase, due to manufacturing industry needs many (AI) technology students in future employment market. Another (AI) technology influence if the future (AI) technological innovation, e.g. machine man manufacturing or machine man service industries will both increase demand, then with more sophistic software technologies will be disrupted labor markets by marketing workers redundant.

For publishing industry, what is striking about the case in paper book publishing industry will be unpopular? Due to the electronic book publishing industry will be popular, e.g. Amazon publish . (AI) technology can influence paper book manufacturing method which is replaced by machine man electronic book manufacturing method as well as it will cause the computerization is no longer confined to routine manufacturing tasks. Due to (AI) machine man manufacturing technology will be proper to be used to manufacture any products in short time efficiently and effectively , e.g. electronic book products. In the future, if it is fact to occur this case, such as (AI) technological machine man manufacturing method will be adopted (applied) to manufacture electronic books or any products in possible. (AI) technology will cause many manufacturing workers are unemployed. It is beneficial to employers, who can reduce to spend much wages expenditure to employ manufacturing workers, but it will cause many manufacturing workers loss jobs and reduce income to support whose families lives. It will cause social challenges, e.g. increasing stealing crimes if the manufacturing workers had not other skills to find other jobs to do easily. So, manufacturers need to concern over technological unemployment which will be hardly future phenomenon if who decided to dismiss all manufacturing workers, due to (AI) technology machine men replace to them.

If (AI) technology can be innovated to produce any kinds of machine man to serve any service or manufacturing industries successfully. Then, it will bring these questions: Can future that workers be influenced to be automation employment and productivity by (AI) technology influence? Does it impact to influence the (AI) technology countries' productivity and growth and natural resources development and labor markets and evolution of global financial markets and economic impact of technology and innovation and urbanization etc. issues? How will automation transform the workplace? What will be the implication for employment? What is likely to be its impact both on productivity in the global economy and on employment?

In fact, automatic of activities can enable businesses to improve performance by reducing errors chance and improving quality and speed, and same cases achieving outcomes that go beyond human capabilities. Some economists indicate (AI) technology would give a needed boost to economic growth and prosperity have of the working age population in many countries. Based on the scenario modeling, they estimate automation could raise productivity growth globally by 0.8 to 1.4 % annually. They also indicated that almost half the activities people are almost $1.6 trillion in wages to do in the global economy have the potential to be automated adapting current demonstrates technology, according to their analysis of more than 2,000 work activities across 800 occupations. When less than 5% of all occupations can be automated entirely using demonstrated technology, about 60% of all occupations have at least 30% of worker made activities, that would be automated. More occupation will change to be automated. They also indicated for business performance benefits of automation are relatively clear, but the issues are more complicated by policy making to attract foreign investors. Beyond technical feasibility, the cost of technology, competition labor will include skills and supply and demand dynamics, performance benefits and beyond labor cost savings and social and regulatory acceptance will affect the automation. Their predictions suggest that half of today work activities could be automated by 2055 year, but this could happen 10 to 20 years earlier or latter depending on the various factors in addition to their wider economic condition.

Some scientists suggest (AI) technology is finally starting to deliver real-life business benefits. Computer power is growing significantly , algorithms are becoming more sophisticated and perhaps most important of all, the world is generating vast quantities of the fuel that powers (AI) technology data billions of gigabytes of it every day. Also, online firms are digital natives, such as Google online search service company is investing on (AI) technology. For new though most of the news if coming from the suppliers of (AI) technologies. And many new users are only in the experimental phase. Few products are on the market or are likely to arrive these soon to drive immediate and widespread adoption. As a result, analysts believe (AI) technology's potential will give true economic benefit in the future. (AI) industry will introduce to suppliers and users to raise economic potential of (AI) technology.

In the future, (AI) technology systems can solve business problems. Some scientists categorized those into five technology systems that are key areas of (AI) technology development: robotics and autonomous vehicles, computer vision language virtual agents and machine learning , which is based on algorithms that learn from data without replying on rules-based programming in order to draw conclusions or direct an action.

Such as computer vision and language includes natural language processing, analytics, speech recognition technology, some are about learning from information, such as about machine learning and others are related to acting on information, such as robotics, autonomous vehicles and virtual agents, which are computer programs that can converse with humans. Machine learning and a subfield called deep learning are artificial intelligence applications.

- Can artificial intelligence impact
global economy growth?

Artificial intelligence (AI) is a term first defined in 1956 year. It is a branch of computer science that aims to create intelligent machines that work and react like humans. In contrast today, 60 years later, (AI) is characterized by a number of applications, including computers playing games against humans and understanding human languages, virtual personal assistants, and robotics which involve computers seeing , hearing and reacting to sensory stimuli.

In the future, technologists predict for (AI) technology ranging from (AI) being used as a tool to aid relatively simple processes for robots with human like mental capabilities, who expect (AI) technology can emulate human performance by learning, coming to mind its own conclusions, understanding complex content, engaging in dialog with people, enhancing human cognitive performance or replacing humans in executing both routine and non-routine tasks. In existing industry, (AI) technology is used , such as targeted advertising and virtual used personal assistant as well as the (AI) technology that my exist in the future, such as robots with human vehicle processing capabilities.

The range of (AI) technology's progress in the future will determine the economic impact future of (AI) technology on the global economy with more limited advances and applications (i.e. weak (AI) only) corresponding to more limited economic impacts and more substantial progress, i.e. strong (AI) technology is corresponding to more significant economic impact.

(AI) technology learning that automates analytical model, including predicting cause-and-effect relationship from biological data, identifying new drugs, self-driving cars and protecting against fraud etc. functions. Also (AI) learning can improve natural language processing that allows computers to continue to better analyze, understand and generate language to interface with human using the natural human language, virtual personal assistant, helps users by providing scheduling appointment, reminds organizing personal finance and finding providers of various services, machine vision allows (AI) machine man to identify object, scenes and activities in detect pedestrians and bicyclists. We expect the economic effects of (AI) technology to include both direct GDP growth from sectors that develop or manufacture (AI) technology and indirect GDP growth through increased productivity in existing sectors that employ some from of (AI) technology. If (AI) producing sectors could grow, then it could lead to increase revenues and employment of (AI) technological professionals within these existing firms as well as the potential creation of entirely new economic activities to any countries' societies productivity improvement in existing sectors could be realized through faster and move efficient processes and decision making as well as increased (AI) technological knowledge and access to information available in societies easily.

In the future, if (AI) technology is an increasingly critical component of more products, it will become an integral part of necessary products of many people's lives. The extent of (AI)'s economy effort is also likely to vary from region to region, thought variation may be more dependent on the predominate economic activity of a region and the (AI) ability can influence economic activity, rather then the economic or developmental status of the regions. (AI) technology can move accessibility and can use source development to do international business between one country and another country.

So (AI) technology has the potential to give benefits to different income chooses and to bring significant gains to both developed and developing countries. For agricultural technology, (AI) has the potential to optimize food production around the world by analyzing agricultural regions and identifying what is necessary to improve crop yield. In total, (AI) technology gives greater economic impact to any countries agricultural regions if which implemented (AI) technology to grow crop , fruit etc. food production in the farms.

Investment in (AI) technology is such as capital investment to any countries' public or private enterprises. So, it will have large economic impact to the future . If the (AI) technology is reasonable invested to the different needs aspect by the public or private enterprises in the country. Then, it will have good economic impact to the country in the future. However, when (AI) technology is likely to affect both the productivity and employment components of economic growth in many sectors. Significant public debate has focused on projections of (AI)'s effect on the labor force. However, for instance, some researchers have argued that the rise of (AI) technology and automation will led to significant unemployment as capital is substituted for the low skillful labor. So, they point to the concern that the increasing sophistication of (AI) technology may balance skilled and semi-skilled workers and the reduce the size of the middle class. However, this is not a new argument, due to (AI) technology negatively affecting the labor force and leading to mass unemployment. Because the (AI) technology is the substitution of machinery for human labor. Although, employment in certain industries, has been reduced in the past due to technological advancement. For long term, the labor market has adapted to the introduction of new technology, giving rise to new jobs in new areas. (AI) technology may also be accomplished without a reduction to total employment in the long-term to some Asia countries, such as Hong Kong and Japan. Because Hong Kong and Japan many low skilled labor, e.g. security, cleaner who complaint that employers need them to work long time hours. (abnormal working hours) e.g. one day 12 to 15 working hour per day. Hence, if (AI) machine means invention technology success. Security or cleaning job can be worked from (AI) machine man in some hours every day in order to reduce the long time working hours cleaners or security workers, e.g. one (AI) machine man works 4 hours for cleaning or security job, one day as well as another cleaner or security labor only needs to work 8 hours one day. So total security or cleaning employers can employ 12 hours machine cleaners or security workers and human cleaners or security workers in one day. For long term benefit, Hong Kong or Japan every security or cleaning worker does not need to work 12 hours minimum working hours one day. They won't feel tried and bore and without private with whose families, so who will accept to do these cleaning or security jobs, even they can raise work efficient and performance when who feel happy and health.

So, (AI) technology of machine man invention can raise low skillful labor efficiency and it can help them to avoid abnormal working hours demand in some busy work life countries, such as Hong Kong and Japan. Before, one Japan female labor feel unhappy to work, due to who often needs to work abnormal working hours for her employer and who has less sleeping and without any private time to enjoy her life with her families every day. So this abnormal working hours factor causes her to do commit suicide behavior, then she is die unlucky. So (AI) technology of machine man invention ought avoid abnormal working hours demand for employer in any countries in the future.

The most important occurrence to any employers, some researchers had attempted to do one experiment to find that private research and development , venture capital and public research and development investment all have strong net effect or economic growth with venture capital funding further having the strongest such effect from (AI) technology. The researchers hypothesize the venture capital investment contributes to economic growth through (AI) technology innovation and by the capacity of an economy to use existing (AI) technology knowledge to increase productivity. They predict the impacts of venture capital, business-research and development and public research and development can raise multi factor productivity from (AI) technology introduction.

Can (AI) technology influence the economic development to developing countries? The developing regions of the world contain most of natural resources. If one day, (AI) technology has invent one kind of machine man which can assist any gas or oil workers to seek any new oil/gas natural resource locations easily. I believe that (AI) technology can help these natural resource exploitation countries will gain economic benefit more easily. So, (AI) driven technology can be used to change to create any new opportunities to address poor management or resources and improve human well being, such as Africa Latin America and India can use (AI) technology machine man to seek any oil/gas natural resource countries exploitation activities to attempt to gain much economic benefits.

● Why will (AI) technology grow economic development ?

Nowadays, increases in capital and labor are no longer driving the levels of economic growth, such as (AI) technology. The ability of increase in capital investment and in labor of traditional drivers of production, have no longer to be enjoyed in most developed economies ,e.g. developed country, US, UK . However, artificial intelligence has the potential to overcome the physical limitation of capital and labor to avoid missing out on this opportunity. So, policy makers and business leaders must prepare for and work toward a future with artificial intelligence. They must do with the idea that (AI) is another simply method to enhance productivity method . Rather they must see (AI) as the tool that can transform thinking about how growth is created.

Economists have always thought of new technologies are as driving growth their ability to enhancing. It can replace labor and capital factor of production. So, it brings this question: What is the factor of production (AI) technology characteristics. They key factor is to see (AI) technology as a capital-labor .

(AI) can replicate labor activities at much greater scale and speed, and to even perform some tasks began the capabilities of human. For example, by using virtual assistants , 1000 legal documents can be reviewed in a matter of days instead of taking three people six moths to complete. Some (AI) technology may be one kind of factor of production in the future. For another example, people will work in workplace digitalization environment. So, in the future, working environment and information management are automated. Such as Konica camera sale company will use workplace digitalization. So , (AI) technology can provide workplace digitalization in order to raise productivity efficiency. (AI) technology will be one kind of production which is replaced by workplace digitalization and it will grow any organization productivity efficiently. Then, (AI) technology will assist overall social economy growth , due to productivity is raised and products can be produced in short time to prepare to sell in consumption market. So, time will be shortened to increase GDP growth fast for the development of (AI) technology countries.

● How can (AI) technology impact to global economic and social and psychological changes?

What will be the development of (AI) technology and predictions concerning the future evolution? The computers and robots will develop conscious, intelligent and minds into humans, enhancing psychological and behavioral abilities and allowing for direct communication with (AI) minds. (AI) technology will be impacted human life by (AI) technology information communicative and environmental influence. A " world brain" and " world mind", this psychological system will be enhanced and enriched the capacities of both individual and collective cognition by (AI) technology of service industries.

(AI) technology with influence these human needs of service industries changes, such as , biological science, finance, entertainment, business, biological science, transportation, communication military etc. The personal computer evolution, the internet and the world wide web which exploded on the scene, linking business, homes, schools, social organizations which were a completely unpredicted phenomenon to influence human life. Kurzweil (1999) predicts that by 2029 year, most human communication will be with machines. According to Person, by 2100 year, there will be human machine convergence.

How can (AI) technology influence environmental protection to make benefits to farming economic growth? (AI) technology can be applied to predict how to solve environmental pollution challenge to avoid to damage any crop or vegetable or rice or fruit etc. food growth. Because environmental experts can gather global environmental pollution data from an environmental database to build a perform a systematic analysis from (AI) technology. The first step is this broad analysis can include understanding, statistical and data gathering techniques to obtain the relevant data, the correlation among the variables involved, and a list of possible models. The next step is to select a set of methods and models that cover all kinds of knowledge and functionalities needed for the decision making process. Once the models are selected, they must be fully implemented by means of machine learning , data mining, statistical or numerical technique. After that, those models must be integrated to build the whole EDSS. The EDSS must be tested to check its performance, accuracy, usefulness and reliability, both from the user's and (AI) technology/computer scientist's point of view. If these is any wrong feature in any development stage, such as model's integration, models' implementation, selection of models, database, problem analysis etc. the developers must come back in the update th required components. When the evaluation phase is all right, the EDSS is ready to be applied to the environment. The great contribution of artificial intelligence to EDSS the integration of several methods complementing the classical statistical models/simulation , statistical analysis, linear models, etc. and numerical models (control algorithms, optimization techniques etc.) .

This cooperation makes the resulting systems more reliable and powerful in coping with real world environment systems. Date interpretation has been a principal area of research in (AI) technology since the very beginning. The most demanding problem in the environmental assessment context. Knowledge representation permits the definition of the different types of data that the existing methods adapt to the process. There is also a lot of work to clean, repair and transform the huge available quantities of raw data. Apart from this, the availability of meta-information or background knowledge is required to guide the process. Data mining is multi-disciplinary: It covers expert systems, data based technology, statistics, data visualization and unsupervised machine learning. These techniques operate at the level of data and background information, where numerous and often incompatible new

commensurate pieces of information from disparate sources have to be brought together (K, Fedra, 1994).
So, it seems that in the future, (AI) technology with the increasing maturity in particular those related to knowledge and engineering, new dimensions can be assisted to users in environmental decision making are available. For example, many environmental systems are characterized both by incomplete models and by limited data. Hence, in the future, (AI) technology will be applied to predict climate change to reduce crop or fruit etc. food agriculture challenge by climate change bad influence.

● Will (AI) technology influence digital economy change to manufacturing industry ?

To understand how the manufacturing business must adapt to prosper in the technology, we need to understand how (AI) technology will change us to shape our daily habits to satisfy our expectation of products to how we shop and even the immediate of the entire process. For example, taxi services are in the crosshairs as on demand transportation services like, available of the touch of a smart phone button expand. In fact, Yellow lab, US country , san Francisco city's largest taxi company is filing for bankruptcy as the industry starts to change faster than almost anyone expected. However, at this point, its more than an app that is changing, some our taxi passengers renting taxi transportation to catch consumption behavior.
(AI) technology will influence digital economy for taxi passenger's individual customer experience, offering a growing renting taxi to catch of service and feedback opportunities when any one taxi passenger who chooses to use mobile phone app online tool to prepaid to rent any taxi more easily.

Also in the long term, (AI) technology can influence vehicles drive themselves of behavior. Already, companies like Google and GM are working on projects to bring fleets of autonomous vehicles to cities at the path of a button.
Moreover, this on-demand service model is beginning to appear across a much broader range of markets. For example , Amazon company is investing in its own fleet of trucks, planes and even drone at the same time as it pushes for same-day delivery of products. As some point, vehicles will be autonomous too. So, it seems that (AI) technique will influence any transportations choose to use digital autonomous driving technology in the future . For Amazon company case, it is not stopping of logistics. It is also aiming to automatically manage the supply of consumer home products with its recently launched Amazon replenishment service, Dash. Dash is a digital service that enables that connected derive to automatically order physical products from Amazon when supplies are running low. So, it seems (AI) technology will be applied to logistic function by digital technology method introduction in the future.

Hence autonomous vehicles will optimize industry supply chains and logistics operations through increased efficiency and flexibility. In fact, fully automated and lean supply chains will keep reduce load sizes and inventory by leveraging smart distribution technologies and smaller autonomous vehicles by machine man assistance. If Amazon continues to grow market share for online sales by reducing effort required by the consumer to place an order, when also contributing the almost immediate delivery of products to the doorstep. So, it will further fuel the trend toward on-demand derive. As Amazon company fuels the on-demand economy, consumers will expect immediacy in more parts of the digital economy. On top of speed, consumers increasing expect more personalization options.

So, (AI) technology will influence digital manufacturing, such as Amazon publishing to monitor every aspect of every process in real -time and communicating to self-optimized deep learning robotics, new methods of high volume and high customization will become possible. Then, as products merge into product platforms and even services, manufacturers have the opportunity to provide components and platforms used by smaller players. So, (AI) technology will influence manufacturing industry to choose automated SMI lines, robots installed, automation engineers.

Another future (AI) technology development can be applied to space science aspect, such as Automation engineering space in manufacturing process to achieve digital manufacturing benefits to any businesses in the future. Such as reducing cost, shortening manufacturing time, raising efficiency, shortening delivery products to client individual time. How can artificial intelligence give the need and advanced fast and evaluation methods benefits for space exploration? When US NASA (space exploration organization) achieves any space exploration missions, it will answer this question:

When is it useful to have a machine use (AI) technology to achieve a decision? After all, after millions of years of space exploration and rough 10,000 years of civilization, humans are usually quite good at making decisions in complex uncertain environments. Through, Johns Hoplains University's Applied Physical Lab. Research in (AI) technology enabled systems, which has identified three general use cases for (AI) technology to explore space mission:

First, for some tasks (AI) technology is more cost effectiveness than human. Second, (AI) technology is better suited than humans at solving some, but not all problems. Third, (AI) technology allows NASA organization's space exploration mission to develop machines that ate capable of responding faster than when a human is in the decision loop (D. Scheidt, 2012, A. Castano et. al. 2008).

So, the use of (AI) technology to enable science by observing the pace of rapidly evolving phenomena was demonstrated. It is more effectively coordinating and (AI) technology utilizing to earn economic benefits to use for space exploration mission.

However, (AI) technology also have current risk for space exploration. Today (AI) technology is immature and requires further development to reach its potential. For instance, the (AI) technology algorithms that detected the dust derive could not have identified whether the Martain weather represented a threat to the cover. Also it can not yet use instrument input to determine what, where and how to autonomously make the next space science measurement. An equally important factor limiting (AI)'s deployment is that lacks the methodology and technology to effectively test (AI) technology. So, the challenge will testing (AI) enabled system is how (AI) performance can be measured. It would be NASA organization's difficulty to find (AI) technology to develop to carry on researching any space exploration missions in the future. However, (AI) technology will be a good economic benefit choice for space exploration mission in the future.

- What is artificial intelligence potential benefits and ethical considerations?

The ability of (AI) technology systems to transform vast amounts of complex information into insight has the potential to help solve manufacturing or service challenges for human needs. However, to reap the societal benefits of (AI) systems, humans will need to trust then and make sure that which follow the same ethical principles, moral values, professional codes and social norms that we humans would follow in the same scenario, research and educational efforts as well as carefully designed regulation in order to achieve the most effort of economic benefits goals. For example, international business machines corporation (IBM) is actively engaged both competitors , in global discussions about how to make (AI) ethical and as beneficial as possible for people as social economic benefits. (AI) is usually defined as the " capability of a computer program to perform tasks or reasoning processes " that human usually associate to intelligence in a human being. Often, it has to do with the ability to make a good decision, even when there is uncertainty, too much information to handle. As an example, play chess or complex card games of entertainment activities is believed to need some form of intelligence in a human being, as well as choosing the best medical facilities in a difficult medical case, or creating something new, such as mathematical theorem or even some form of act, or even driving automatic machine man (self driving vehicle) replacing human driving in the middle of a crowded city.

(AI) needs depends on what we consider being intelligence in the behavior of a human being act a certain point in time. If human belief about human intelligence changes and we don't believe any longer that a certain task requires intelligence, then a computer program performing that task is no longer part of (AI), it becomes just another boring computer program. So, it means that (AI) technology will replace some old computer programs, if human can invent new generation of (AI) software for any functions or activities to satisfy human needs.

As IBM, it argues intelligence. This means that we aim to build systems that enhance and scale human expertise and skills rather than replacing them. We therefore focus on practical applications of (AI) capabilities that assist people in performing well-defined tasks of needs by exploiting and wide range of (AI)-based services. We also use the term " cognitive computing" it is mean a comprehensive net of capabilities based on technology. It comprises the fields of machine learning, reasoning and decision technologies, language, speech and vision recognition and processing technologies, high performance and high efficient functions for any industries or individual consumers needs. For example, robotics, which are usually very good at doing what which are supposed to in any environment, much have public shopping center, factory etc. places which need simply services from the robot (machine man), such as cleans the floor of our houses to the robot that can work together with humans in production chains, passing through the warehouse, robots can take care of the tasks of an entire warehouse and the companion robots like Nao, Pepper, Aibo and Giraff, who can entertain use, talk to use and help elderly people to stay connected to their friends, relatives and doctors.

Google company is building automatic machine (self-driving cars) and has acquired more than 10 robotics companies. Facebook had opened whole new research facility only on (AI) research. Apply computer has developed Siri. Microsoft computer company has built a similar personalized assistant. Google has Deep mind, a UK company whose long term aim is to build general (AI) and has already great potential to win game to the world champion

and IBM is investing a huge amount of resources in applying its Watson cognitive computing system to the medical domains to finance and to personalized education. In Europe, IBM is establishing new centers in Munich and Milan focused in the application of cognitive computer capabilities to the internet of things and healthcare respectively.
For example, automatic machine man (self-driving cars) are all about (AI), which used to be able to see what happens in the street (signals ,lanes, other cars, pedestrians, traffic lights, which need to able predict what other cars and pedestrians will do, and who need to be able to cope with unforeseen situations. Since, most car accidents are due to human fault, it is estimated that the adoption of self-driving cars will save about half of the lives that are usually last in car accidents.
IBM Watson company has to understand spoken language, make sense of massive amount to text , respond correctly to questions in many categories, as well as assess its own confidence in responding to such questions. In the future, (AI) technology can own question/answering capabilities that would be very useful, for example, in assisting a doctor when trying to some to the correct diagnosis for a patient and to propose the best therapy .
Intelligent machines can also rely on huge amounts of data to be used to learn how to make better decisions. This data comes from all of us over the years Facebook users have uploaded more than 250 billion pictures and every day who upload about 350 million more. Every second, we submit 40,000 google search queries. So, (AI) technology will be connected through the web from appliances to traffic lights from cars to watches. Other tasks that are very easy for humans are physical and manipulation tasks, such as walking , running, picking up an object to make its shape and location, restricted environment. But (AI) machine man technology still not able to have the general physical and manipulation capabilities even of a 6 year old.
So, it brings this question: Why do (AI) scientists need to concern ethics? Because (AI) technology is complex, information into insight has the potential to reveal long held secrets and help solve some of the world's most difficult problems. (AI) systems can potentially be used to help discover insights to treat disease, predict the whether, and manage the global economy. So, ethic issues is important to and (AI) scientists . If any one new (AI) technology research investigation could success, it will be a secret to and the (AI) scientists can not permit to their loyalty to any competitors to damage the fair (AI) technology products trading market. The country (countries) (AI) technology scientists need to concern ethic issues, who need to keep secrets for their countries economic or/and social benefits. This is moral issues to any countries/country loyalty is whose countries intangible assets. They can not sell (AI) loyalty to any their countries to assist whose economic benefits immorally.

- How can (AI) technology influence to global
health care economy development?

According to (AI) lecturer analysis, when combined key clinical health (AI) application can potentially create $150 billion in annual savings for the US healthcare economy by 2026 year. (AI) technology is re-winning modern conception of healthcare delivery. It enables machines to sense, comprehend, act and learn. So which can perform administrative and clinical healthcare functions (Accenture, 2017).
It will help health care service organizations to reduce health care cost, will improve and raise service quality and

access. So, (AI) health market size will be predicted growth. (AI) applications in health care include robot-assisted surgery, virtual nursing assistant, administrative workflow assistant, fraud detection, error reduction connected machines, clinical trial participant identifier, preliminary diagnosis, automated image diagnosis and cybersecurity.
What kind of benefits (AI) technology can contribute to healthcare service? (AI) technology can deliver what many health care organizations need, such as financial and operational of labor costs, digital expectations from patient consumers how to use (AI) technology to solve interoperability challenges in any healthcare organizations. Also (AI) technology can be applied to wellness an d lifestyle management, diagnostics, delivers financially but also way of organizational and workflow improvement. So, (AI) technology will be continue to become most prevalent and adoption to healthcare organizations , which must need to enhance structure to be position to take full advantages of new (AI) technological capabilities. (AI) technology can change the nature of work and employment is rapidly changing to make the best use of both humans and (AI) talent in healthcare industry in the future. For example, (AI) technology offers a way to fill in gaps and the rising labor shortage in healthcare. According to Accenture analysis, the physicians shortage is increasing. However, (AI) technology will manufacture healthcare machine men to replace physicians in future one day(2017). Hence, (AI) technology will be invented to raise health care service staffs work efficiency and performance in any hospitals or clinics in the future.

In conclusion, (AI) technology will raise efficiency for any service or manufacturing industries in the future, although, it is possible that it will also rise low skillful workers unemployment numbers. But, the most important influence to human technological innovation will be risen and it will influence human life will be changed to be better, e.g. self drive cars, health care physician machine men, machine man cleaners etc. intelligent machine men will be manufactured to serve for our daily life. Furthermore, (AI) technological products will influence countries trading, some low technological development countries manufacturing businessmen can choose to buy any (AI) products to raise whose productivity and efficiency and reducing cost to achieve economic cost saving result. Also, GDP of trading growth income will increase to the (AI) products sale countries. Hence, it will be beneficial to economic development to both developed and developing countries both in the future as well as (AI) scientists time and money spending will be valued to continue to invest (AI) technology development for human life and economy benefits for long term.

In consequent, when (AI) can spend more time to attempt to do human's any tasks every day, then it have possible to raise productivity and efficiency better than human.

Artificial intelligence brings macro and micro economy benefits

How (AI) brings macro and micro economy benefits to impact our future social development ? Artificial Intelligence, as we see it, is a collection of multiple technologies that enable machines to sense, comprehend and act—and learn, either on their own or to augment human activities. Compelling data reveal a discouraging truth about growth today. It is one kind technological manufacturing industry and service industry and product sale business to bring our future economy growth.

There has been a marked decline in the ability of traditional levers of production—capital investment and labor—to propel economic growth. The numbers tell only part of the story. Artificial intelligence (AI) is a new factor of production and has the potential to introduce new sources of growth, changing how work is done and reinforcing the role of people to drive growth in business. Accenture research on the impact of AI in 12 developed economies reveals that AI could double annual economic growth rates in 2035 by changing the nature of work and creating a new relationship between man and machine. The impact of AI technologies on business is projected to increase labor productivity by up to 40 percent and enable people to make more efficient use of their time. Concerning (AI) and economic growth relationship, I shall indicate these questions as below:

1. If A.I. increases automation in the production of goods and services, how will it impact economic growth?
2. Can we reconcile the advent of A.I. with the observed constancy in growth rates andcapitalshareovermostofthe20th century? Should we expect such constancy to persist in the 21st century?
3. Do these answers change when A.I. and automation apply to the production of new ideas?
4. Can A.I. drive massive increases in growth rates, or even a singularity, as some observers predict? Under what conditions, and are these conditions plausible?

In thinking about these questions, we develop two main themes. First, we model A.I. as the latest form in a process of automation that has been ongoing for at least 200 years. From the steam engine to electricity to computer chips,the automation of aspects of production has been a key feature of economic growth since the Industrial Revolution.

Baumol (1967) observed that sectors with rapid productivity growth, such as agriculture and even manufacturing today, often see their share of GDP decline while those sectors with relatively slow productivity growth — perhaps including many services — experience increases. As a consequence, economic growth may be constrained not by what we do well but rather by what is essential and yet hard to improve. We suggest that combining this feature of growth with automation can yield a rich description of the growth process, including consequences for future growth and income distribution. When applied to a model in which A.I. automates the production of goods and services, Baumol's insight generate sufficient conditions under which one canget overall balanced growth witha constant capital share that stays well below 100%, even with nearly complete automation. When applied to a model in which A.I. automates the production of ideas, these same considerationscanpreventexplosivegrowth.

With Artificial Intelligence as the new factor of production, it can drive growth in at least three important ways as below:

On artificial intelligent automation aspect, unlike traditional automation solutions, Artificial Intelligence-powered innovation automates complex physical tasks that require adaptability and agility and AI is capable of self-learning. On labor and capital augmentation aspect, Existing labor and capital can be used much more effectively as Artificial Intelligence enables workers to focus on what they do best—imagine, create and innovate. On innovation diffusion aspect, One of the least-discussed benefits of Artificial Intelligence is its ability to propel innovation as it diffuses through the economy. So, it seems that artificial Intelligence heralds dramatic potential for growth for both the economy and for humans." By acting like a capital-labor hybrid, Artificial Intelligence offers the ability to amplify and transcend the current capacity of capital and labor to propel economic growth. Our research reveals unprecedented opportunities for value creation.

Accenture and frontier Economics indicated that annual growth rates in 2035 of gross value added (a close approximation of GDP), comparing baseline growth in 2035 to an artificial intelligence scenario where AI has been absorbed into the economy as well as percentage increase in labor productivity with AI, compared to expected baseline productivity levels in 2035. Source: Accenture and Frontier Economics.

● How artificial Intelligence impacts on society on micro and macro economic benefits both aspect:

(1) On macro economy benefit aspect

There will be big winners and losers as collaborative technologies, robots and artificial intelligence transform the nature of work. Societies will face further challenges in directing and investing in technologies that benefit humanity instead of destroying it or intruding on basic human rights of privacy and freedom of access to information. I shall indicate these changes how (AI) will impact on our society which aspects daily as below:

What is changing?

1. On computing changing aspect

•Advances in the sheer power of computers will lead to artificial intelligence that becomes progressively smarter.

•Virtual connectivity will enable integration of relevant computing resources to provide users with integrated and seamless services.

•Cloud services will interpret aggregated datasets against patterns to anticipate tasks, activities, and events.

•Developments in cloud services will transition computing from a physical experience to a virtual one available to any user via a simple device operating on ubiquitous networks with seamless connectivity.

•Big Data pattern analysis will take place in the background.

•Big Data will provide context-awareness capabilities.

•Developments in cloud computing will transition computing from a physical experience to a virtual one available to any user via a simple device operating on ubiquitous networks with seamless connectivity.

•Boundaries between applications and services will be blurred to a high degree.

•Every item in will be equipped with a computing and communication core.

2. On surveillance chaning aspect

•Smart sensors, surveillance cameras, and eavesdropping devices integrated with identity recognition systems will allow law enforcement to track and capture or quarantine individuals who might otherwise cause harm to others in society.

•Users will be able to integrate physical world data and the logical world data to draw conclusions.

•To avoid overwhelming users with choices from the infinite combination of vehicle technologies, vehicle templates and capability modules will be evolved within the gaming environments.

•Organizations with mature security operations functions will often share intelligence, techniques, and process with one another.

•Advancements in the business intelligence field will provide tools that will help retailers better understand consumer behavior by examining behavioral patterns and overall trends.
•Predictive analysis and real-time access to artificial intelligence and tasking in the field will be available on modern mobile devices.

Why do they impact on our society ? It will include social and business both aspects as below:

3. On social impact aspect

•Societies will face challenges in realizing technologies that benefit humanity instead of destroying and intruding on the human rights of privacy and freedom of access to information.
•Surging capabilities of robots and artificial intelligence will see a range of current jobs supplanted.
•Professional roles such as doctors, lawyers and accountants could be replaced by artificial intelligence by the year 2025.
•Low-skill workers will reallocate to tasks that are non-susceptible to computerization.
•All the risks will arise out of human activity from certain technological development in this technology, synthetic biology, nano techno and artificial intelligence.

4. On business impact aspect

•There will be big winners and losers as collaborative technologies, robots and artificial intelligence transform the nature of work.
•Data expertise is at least as important and will become exponentially more important.
•The role of a senior manager in a deeply data-driven world is going to shift.
•Information hoarders will slow the pace of their organizations and forsake the power of artificial intelligence while competitors exploit it.
•Judgments about consumers and potential consumers will be made instantaneously.
•Many organisations will put cybersecurity on par with other intelligence and defense priorities.
•Open source information and artificial intelligence collection will provide opportunities for global technological parity.
•In the future, predictive analytics and artificial intelligence could play an even more fundamental role in content creation.

● How Will Artificial Intelligence Affect The Micro and Macro Economy growth ?

Americans today seem to be at odds with themselves when it comes to their feelings on economic growth. People are worried about a future lack of economic growth due to a less productive workforce. Oddly, many of those same people are also worried that robots, automation and artificial intelligence will displace human workers. It's ironic because these two outcomes could actually work together to the benefit of the economy and those of us who invest in it.

Nobel Prize-winning economist Paul Krugman once said, "Productivity isn't everything, but in the long run it is almost everything." What does this mean? While we fixate on the formula for short-term economic growth, which is

C (consumption) + I (investment) + G (government) + NX (net exports), the recipe for long-term potential growth (wealth/living standards) is much simpler: how many people work and how productive or efficient they are.

We've all heard about declining demographics in many countries around the globe. Lower birth rates and aging populations form the fears that we will see less economic growth in the future. In our long-term economic growth formula above, this represents the number of people who work. If we have fewer individuals contributing to our overall economic growth in the future, an increase in individual productivity becomes incredibly important to our well-being.

Let's use a real-life example to put this concept into context. Japan and many countries in Europe have the potential for declining labor forces. There are fewer and fewer humans to produce the levels of output that we currently enjoy. Might robots fill the gap left by fewer humans working, and could they also enhance the output (productivity) of the humans who want to continue working? Indeed, robots in Japan are currently being used to help aging workers remain productive contributors to economic growth. Panasonic, for example, has revealed robotic exoskeletons that help aging humans in a variety of fields lift heavy objects. And this is just one instance in which artificial intelligence is actually contributing to humans' productivity.

● IS THE 'AUTOMATION UNCERTAINTY' DIFFERENT THAN IN THE PAST?

I imagine many people agree with the above analysis yet remain worried about the magnitude of lost jobs due to technological improvements. Data on the subject is mixed, and only time will reveal how many people lose their jobs to technology. However, as with many things in life, people often fixate on only one side of the equation — jobs lost — while ignoring the possibility of new jobs created. I often shape my thoughts by contemplating "what if" extremes. What if I was appointed economic czar and was tasked with providing the best chance that every able-bodied American would have a job? I think this could be accomplished by ridding the U.S. of heavy industrial and farm equipment. In my "what if" scenario I would get rid of all combines, tractors and road bulldozers. By necessity, we would all need to go back to building roads and manually planting and harvesting crops as a way of life. Everyone would have a job, but we'd clearly take huge steps backward when it comes to standard of living. Panasonic, for example, has revealed robotic exoskeletons that help aging humans in a variety of fields lift heavy objects. And this is just one instance in which artificial intelligence is actually contributing to humans' productivity.

I imagine if we were sitting in a room decades ago as farmers, we would rightfully be worried about our future employment. However, as the world evolved, new jobs were created in industries we never would have fathomed would exist. Those who would otherwise have been farmers were now free to innovate and create new industries. While it seems like forever, it was actually just a few years ago that the Apple iPhone was introduced and the personal device/cellphone market as we know it today was created. As it blossomed, the app industry was hatched, and with it, more than a million jobs that didn't previously exist were opened. Today it's an $88 billion industry. While I acknowledge that we will likely need many "app markets" in the future to open new jobs, I'm confident in the process of innovation that envelops the U.S. economy.

● ENVIRONMENT UNCERTAINTY FACTOR THREATENS (AI) DEVELOPMENT

Like any time over the past hundreds of years, the future remains a very uncertain beast. Many jobs will be automated and eliminated. But in their place new jobs will likely be created, and our standard of living will continue increasing from the resulting innovation. This is why we now have TVs, smartphones and computers. It's why we enjoy relatively better living standards than those of the past. For the average investor, continued innovation could mean great opportunity. I don't make light of that fact that much as in the past, the shorter-term costs of job losses will fall disproportionately upon certain segments of the population. But that's no reason to throttle innovations like artificial intelligence. Rather, policy makers and others need to figure out how to care for and retrain displaced workers in the shorter term — this will ultimately position them for intermediate- to longer-term success. Moreover

Moreover, I worry that my job could one day fall prey to artificial intelligence. Perhaps a robot could write a better article. It's an uncomfortable thought at my age that I may have to find new employment in the future, but I intend to deal with that by focusing on what I can control: continuous learning; improving and building my overall skill set; and most importantly, continued saving, investing and planning so I'm prepared for whatever the future may hold. Please remember that all investments carry some level of risk, including the potential loss of principal invested. Returns represent past performance, are not a guarantee of future performance and are not indicative of any specific investment. Diversification and strategic asset allocation do not assure profit or protect against loss. Although stocks have historically outperformed bonds, they also have historically been more volatile. Investors should carefully consider their ability to invest during volatile periods in the market.

(2) On micro economy benefit aspect

● On productive efficient raising to manufacturers benefit aspect: A.I. and Automation of Production micro economic benefit to manufacturers

One way of looking at the last 150 years of economic progress is that it is driven by automation. The industrial revolution used steam and then electricity to automate many production processes. Relays, transistors, and semiconductors continued this trend. Perhaps artificial intelligence is the next phase of this process rather than a discrete break. It may be a natural progression from autopilots, computer-controlled automobile engines, and MRI machines to self-driving cars and A.I. radiology reports. While up until recently, automation has mainly affected routine or low-skilled tasks, it appears that A.I. may increasingly automate non-routine, cognitive tasks performed by high-skilled workers.3 An advantage of this perspective is that it allows us to use historicalexperiencetoinformusaboutthepossiblefutureeffectsof A.I.

Several other important contributions to this rapidly expanding literature should also be noted. Peretto and Seater (2013) explicitly consider a research technology that allows firms to change the exponent in a Cobb-Douglas production function; while they do not emphasize the link to the Zeira model, with hindsight the connections to that approach to automation are interesting. The model of Hemous and Olsen (2016) is closely related to what follows in the next subsection. They focus on CES production instead of Cobb-Douglas, as we do below, but emphasize the implications of their framework for wage inequality between high-skilled and low-skilled workers. Agrawal, McHaleandOettl(2017)incorporate artificial intelligence and the"recombinantgrowth" of Weitzman (1998)into an innovation-base growth model to show how A.I. can speed up growth along atransition path. The next section takes a complementary approach, building on this literature and using the insights of Zeiraand automation to understand the structural change associated with Baumol's cost disease.

On conclusion, artificial intelligent development will bring productive efficiency raising micro economy benefit as well as consumption desire raising on macro economy GDP growth benefit main both aspects to impact our future social development.

Reference

A. Castano et. al. " Automatic detection of dust devils and clouds at Mars" Machine vision and applications, Oct. 2008, vol. 19, no 5-6, pp. 467-482.

Agrawal, Ajay, John McHale, and Alex Oettl, "Artificial Intelligence and Recombinant Growth," 2017. UniversityofTorontomanuscript.

Baumol, William J., "Macroeconomics of Unbalanced Growth: The Anatomy of Urban Crisis," AmericanEconomicReview,June1967,57,415–426.

Accenture, " Why artificial intelligence is the future of growth"(2017) <http://www.accenture.com/us-en/insight-artificial-intelligence-future-growth>.

D. Schedidt , Unmanned Air Vehicle Command And Control, Handbook Of Unmanned Air Vehicles, Springer-Verlag, 2014. Facebook (AI) Research Available at https://research.facebook.com/ai, research at google, machine intelligence available at

http://research.google.com/pubs/machineintellige nce.html; micro soft research-machine learning and artificial intelligence available at http://research.microsoft.com/en-us/research- areas/machine-learning-ai.aspx.

Hemous, David and Morten Olsen, "The Rise of the Machines: Automation, Horizontal InnovationandIncomeInequality,"2016. University of Zurichmanuscript.

K, Fedra , "GIS and environmental modelling" in environmental modelling with GIS, edited by M.F. Goodchild.B.O. Parks and L.T. Steyaert, Oxford University press, pp. 35-50, 1994.

Keynes, J.M. (1933). Economic possibilities for our grandchildren (1930). Essays in persuasion, pp.358-73.

Mckinsey & Company (2013, May). Disruptive technologies: Advices that will transform life, business and the global economy , USA.

Peretto, PietroF.andJohnJ.Seater,"Factor-eliminatingtechnicalchange,"JournalofMonetary Economics,2013,60(4),459–473.

Ray Kurzweil , The age of spiritual machines (1999) is cited numerously through this chapter: Kurzweilai.net http://www.kurzweilai.net

Rich, Elaine & Knight, Kevin, Artificial Intelligence Second Edition, 1991, New York; Mc-Graw-Hill.

Weitzman, Martin L., "Recombinant Growth," Quarterly Journal of Economics, May 1998, 113, 331–360.

Printed by Libri Plureos GmbH in Hamburg,
Germany